ELECTRONIC NIGHTMARE

ELECTRONIC NIGHTMARE

THE NEW COMMUNICATIONS AND FREEDOM

JOHN WICKLEIN

THE VIKING PRESS | NEW YORK

First published in 1981 by The Viking Press
625 Madison Avenue, New York, N.Y. 10022
Published simultaneously in Canada by
Penguin Books Canada Limited

LIBRARY OF CONGRESS CATALOGING IN PUBLICATION DATA
Wicklein, John.
Electronic nightmare.
Includes index
1. Telecommunication—Social aspects.
2. Telecommunication policy.   I.   Title.
HE7631.W53   303.4′83   80-54199
ISBN 0-670-50658-3   AACR2

Portions of this work appeared originally in *The Atlantic Monthly* and *The Progressive*.

Grateful acknowledgment is made to the following for permission to reprint copyrighted material:
Harcourt Brace Jovanovich, Inc., A. M. Heath, and Mrs. Sonia Brownell Orwell: A passage from *1984* by George Orwell.
The New York Times Company: "Where Talking Back to the Teacher is Okay" by John Wicklein, from the January 8, 1979, Education Supplement of *The New York Times* © 1979 by The New York Times Company.

Printed in the United States of America
Set in CRT Primer

TO MYRA JANE, SINE QUĀ NON.

PREFACE

This is a book about clear and present danger. It is a book about the here and now, or very soon to come. When most people hear about the marvels of the new technologies of communication they are apt to say, "Gee, won't that be terrific," and pass it off as some blue-sky thing of the future. Certainly, it doesn't occur to them that the communications revolution is something for them to worry about today.

But it is. Every technique of the communication revolution that I discuss in this book is already in place somewhere in the world. In many cases, the services are fully operational in commercial or government applications. And for almost every blessing these technologies bring, they pose a danger to our individual liberty and our privacy.

What happens in communications affects all of us indirectly and the majority of us directly. It is a commonplace to say we have become an information society. The idea takes on greater meaning when you learn that more than half the people in the developed countries of the world now derive their livelihoods from the gathering and dissemination of information.

In writing this book, I tried to find and describe specific examples of the major developments in communication, to illustrate the point that the blessings and threats are already upon us. I have concentrated on concepts and techniques, rather than the specific pieces of hardware that made them possible.

From studying the developments over the last ten years, and researching and reporting almost full time for two, I have come to feel that the *shape* of things to come is quite clear. How the shape is to be filled out by new equipment is a question the development engineers are answering, and will continually reanswer, as each new discovery makes a specific technique easier and less expensive to use. Knowing the hardware is not nearly so important as knowing the techniques and what they can do for us—and to us.

In a field where so much is happening, I have had to be selective about the techniques and services to discuss. I have based the selection mainly on their importance to the general reader. In some cases, I have excluded or limited discussion of developments that have already come into the public consciousness through serious and popular journals. For example, I have not discussed computer-assisted learning in detail, because it has been exhaustively explored since computers were first applied to teaching in the 1960s, and many sources of information about it are available.

I have tried to present all the main lines of development and a wide variety of specific applications, many of which I think may come as a surprise to the reader. They did to me.

The investigations have led me to some conclusions about social, political, and economic issues raised by the new technologies. I have stated these freely, not in the hope that readers will agree with me completely but in the hope of stirring discussion of serious concerns about which little has been said in the public dialogue. I have suggested some possible answers to these concerns, but mainly I have tried to raise questions to fuel the imminent debate.

In a time of rapid inflation, it seemed possibly misleading to attach specific costs to various techniques that will be essentially the same for years after the book goes to press, although the cost of providing them might be radically different. So, except where I have given illustrations of dramatic drops in prices despite inflation, I have usually used price ratios, such as in "Its cost, affordable now only to middle-class users, is expected with mass production to drop by a factor of one hundred." The point throughout is that, given past reductions in prices of consumer electronic goods, the large majority can expect to have these new information appliances within their financial reach.

In the writing, I have been struggling with a problem faced by authors concerned with sexual equality—the generic use of the masculine pronoun *he* and tne masculine adjective *his* to refer to both men and women. Substituting "their book" when I mean "her book" or "his book" produces a gaucherie. Using "her and his" each time becomes clumsy and sometimes confusing, when it is necessary to refer back to the phrase as an antecedent. I have not used "one" or "one's" because they seem stuffy and cold. I haven't been able to bring myself to coin words such as "s/he" or "hisr"—which might conceivably take hold. In a few instances where clarity of meaning was at stake I have had to revert to "his" for the generic.

So I have not solved the problem, although I think professional grammarians should be giving it priority.

I have tried to use both *she* and *he,* and *her* and *his,* evenhandedly (and sometimes, I hope, surprisingly) when referring to an indefinite or generic instance.

ACKNOWLEDGMENTS

My thinking for the book has been shaped by scores of persons— friends, professional acquaintances, and total strangers—I have talked to over the last several years, many of whom are quoted in the text. It's pleasantly surprising to find how many people are willing to go out of their way to help when you are gathering information for a book, and I thank them all.

It would not have come about without the encouragement of Myra Winchester Wicklein, my wife, who suggested I take time off to write a book on communications. She contributed immeasurably to the content through her close reading and critique of the manuscript and her imaginative and lively discussion of the ideas it should contain. And she went with me to Brazil, an assignment that was not comfortable but which turned out to be an exciting experience for both of us. There, I received a great deal of help in translation and interviews from Dr. Reinhard Brose, then a professor of communication at the Instituto Metodista de Ensino Superior in São Paulo and now a communications official with the Methodist church in West Germany.

Maria Saporta of Atlanta allowed me to read her thesis in progress on urban communications and provided other source material and enthusiastic support. From Frances Goldin, my literary agent, I received excellent professional advice and friendly encouragement.

It has been a pleasure to work with an editor as perceptive about the subject and supportive of the project as A. Richard Barber of The Viking Press. Our early discussions generated interesting ideas for me to follow up, and his suggestions in editing the manuscript led to additions that I think strengthened the book.

Dr. Martin C. Elton and Red Burns of the Alternate Media Center of New York University; Margareta Ingelstam, director of the Everyman's Radio project of Swedish Radio; Dr. Anthony G. Oettinger, chairman of the Program on Information Resources Policy at Harvard University; Lars Ingelstam, director of the Swedish Secretariat for Future Studies; and Michael Rice, director of the Aspen Institute Program on Communications and Society all helped me sort out ideas and provided good leads to other sources.

I benefited from lively discussions of the issues with Ned Schnurman and Barbara Michalak and from research leads they provided.

Toni Hyde did wonders in typing the manuscript from my originals.

I want to express my appreciation to Robert Manning, then editor of *The Atlantic Monthly*, for the concrete encouragement that came from his publishing parts of Chapter II, on the Qube system in Columbus, and Chapter VII, on media censorship in Brazil; to Erwin Knoll for publishing the Swedish Data Inspection Board segment of Chapter VI in *The Progressive*, and to Joseph Michalak for asking me to contribute the piece on two-way college courses offered by Qube to an education supplement of *The New York Times*.

My special thanks to the Kaltenborn Foundation of Palm Beach, Florida, and to Dr. Rolf Kaltenborn, its director, for believing in the worth of the project and for making a grant to help defray the costs of travel.

And finally, to Elizabeth, Arthur, Peter, Joanna, Cass, and Max for letting me know they think I am a good reporter and all those other totally prejudiced things a writer likes to hear from his family.

CONTENTS

crossed a forbidden border. "Hot line" network can connect heads of state anywhere in the world.

The interactive communication network is becoming the new personal information grapevine. Equifax uses satellites to disseminate 50 million dossiers from its computer.

THE SWEDISH DATA INSPECTION BOARD: Every computerized personal data file is licensed, and citizens have the right to correct errors.

DEMAND FOR PROTECTION RISES IN THE UNITED STATES: Public concern over "One Big Data Bank" leads to a privacy study commission and some administration proposals.

FREE FLOW OF INFORMATION VS. RESTRICTIONS: U.S. business and State Department fear privacy statutes will hinder transborder data transmission. The trick is to strike a balance.

Using existing methods of communication, the military government developed suppression to a fine art. Even better tools are at hand.

THE LONG HISTORY OF CENSORSHIP: Since the country was founded, the ruling establishment has restricted freedom of expression.

CARDINAL FIGHTS AGAINST REPRESSION: Dom Paulo Evaristo Arns of São Paulo has been a leader of the Roman Catholic Church's opposition to the regime.

"VLADO" HERZOG: A JOURNALIST DIES: Because his liberal views might influence broadcasts, the news director of São Paulo's public television station is interrogated by the military police. That same day they announce Herzog has "committed suicide."

ARMY HARD-LINERS WANT MORE: Militant faction has been resisting efforts to lift restrictions on the print and electronic press.

MAKING IT EASIER FOR THE AUTHORITARIANS: A scenario on how the new communications technologies could be used to make repression complete.

The new technologies offer benefits, but the dangers may outweigh the blessings.

HOW SHOULD THE SYSTEM BE CONTROLLED?: Is it a "natural monopoly"? Can it be based on satellites alone? Should we hand it to the private corporations?

A NONPROFIT PHONE SYSTEM IN THE UNITED STATES?: Since the

beginning, there has been Bell. Should we think the unthinkable and replace AT&T with a Public Telecommunication Corporation that would set up a national information utility?

DANGER FROM AUTHORITARIAN REGIMES: One danger of a nationalized service is that a dictatorial government could use it exclusively to further its own ends.

CENTRALIZATION OR DECENTRALIZATION?: The new technology could lead us in either direction, depending on the intent of the controlling interests.

IN THE UNITED STATES, THE PRESIDENT MUST TAKE THE LEAD: Only the White House is powerful enough to shape the direction of the new communications to serve the public good.

PRIVACY PROTECTION BOARD NEEDED: A government monitor of personal data banks can reduce intrusion of computers into our lives.

GUARDING AGAINST DEHUMANIZATION: Laws can help, but in the end, it will be we humans ourselves who prevent the new technologies of communication from mechanizing our lives.

SOME CONCLUSIONS: Within the system there appear to be serious threats to our privacy and our individual liberties. How can we prevent these threats from materializing?

ELECTRONIC NIGHTMARE

THE NEW COMMUNICATIONS: PROMISE AND THREAT

All modes of communications we humans have devised since the beginnings of our humanity are coming together now into a single electronic system, driven by computers. Although this new communications system will bring us many benefits, it will also put us in danger of losing our individual liberty.

The focus of the system will be a home communications set (HCS) that looks like a standard television with a keyboard attached. Within it will be a small microprocessor that turns it into a computer terminal as well.

Calling it a "set" seems better to me than a "center" or a "unit" because it has an everyday sound suited to describe an everyday appliance.

I believe it will become as commonplace to turn on the "HCS" as it became to flick on the "TV"—an everyday device that people before World War II thought of as science fiction.

Our HCS will be served by a computerized network that brings thousands of communications pathways into the home. The information and entertainment it provides will arrive over optical fiber "wires" of glass or from a communications satellite sending signals directly to small dish antennas on our rooftops.

Later models will include a small television camera and a microphone, to make possible video telephone calls. The set will give us news in print as well as the usual video form: it can display either text or pictures on its television screen. If we want hard copies of the printed news, it can produce them quickly on an attached printer or photocopy device.

The set will be able to supply hundreds of channels of television. These will be used for standard commercial programming, service programming for special-interest groups, educational programs, or electronic catalogues on "shopping" channels.

The most important feature of the new communications system, from the standpoint of our society, will be its capacity to be two-way, permitting us to respond over the system to what the system is offering us. Through this interaction, we will be able to make store purchases on credit, pay our bills, do our banking, send our mail electronically, or get emergency medical advice from a doctor who can see and hear the patient; we can be "present" in two-way continuing-education classes.

The same controls make it possible for us to ask computerized libraries to present text material on the screen, or printout pages from a reference book. The two-way capability can be used to install a smoke alarm connected to the nearest firehouse, or a burglar alarm connected to the nearest police station.

Business adaptations of the set make possible the exchange of messages and video teleconferences between distant branch offices. They form the basis of what data-processing companies have called the "automated office."

The entire system will be tied together by communications satellites.

All the technology to make the system possible has been developed and tested. Each of its many parts has already been placed in service, in pilot projects or commercial cooperation somewhere in the world. A fully integrated home-communications system will be operational within the lifetime of a great majority of the readers of this book. If this seems a short time for so large a development, consider that within one generation, starting in 1946, three revolutionary technologies came into general use: television, the computer, and the jet airplane. The new "instant transaction" technology is likely to change our lives at least as greatly as any of these. This "revolution" is not coming tomorrow; it is already under way.

Many of the new communications services are now available to the public.

In 1979 the British Post Office (BPO) began commercial operation of Prestel, an information-retrieval service in which users in the home can select, one page at a time, 250,000 pages of textual material for display on a standard television set. All the viewer has to do is attach a small adapter and key pad that connects the television set to a computer through the telephone lines. Since the mid-seventies, the British Broadcasting Corporation and the commercial Independent Television Authority have been broadcasting text services with eight hundred pages of news, sports, weather, travel data, job information, and similar material, all of which are continually updated. In New York, Reuters began using a channel on Manhattan Cable in 1975 to transmit business and financial news in text form to four hundred customers, each of whom could select specific items desired by pressing buttons on a key pad.

By 1980, Warner Amex Cable Communications had signed up thirty thousand customers in Columbus, Ohio, for a two-way interactive television system called Qube. On one of its thirty channels, for example, customers could take part in a meeting being held by their neighborhood association and express their opinions by pushing multiple-choice response buttons on a small key pad that controlled the set. On premium channels, for which they were billed item-by-item, they could choose first-run movies, sports events not available on over-the-air commercial television, and college courses taken for credit.

Home computer terminals tying into specialized data banks are now available to information specialists who pay installation and use charges—or news buffs who want to see wire-service stories as they are being sent out. Terminals tied to commercially run credit-data banks are becoming commonplace for use by stores in making instant checks on the "reliability" of customers. Electronic funds transfer is being offered by a number of banks, allowing customers to withdraw cash or pay bills from walk-up terminals. The U.S. Postal Service began testing electronic facsimile transmission of mail between Washington and London via a communications satellite in 1979. NHK, Japan's public television network, is reaching many homes in the island chain by transmitted signals from their studios in Tokyo to a direct broadcast satellite that relays them to small rooftop antennas.

The electronic merger of communications media was made possible by the discovery that you could marry the computer to the ordinary television set. Its advent has been hastened technologically and financially by three recent breakthroughs: the silicon chip, optical fibers, and the communications satellite.

THE SILICON CHIP was designed by Intel Corp in California in 1971 and refined since then by IBM, Bell Laboratories, and others. It has, for practical communications purposes, made computer storage and retrieval of information unlimited. The technique put together layer on layer of circuits, able to process and store bits of information in a chip about a quarter of a centimeter in thickness and a centimeter square.* Each chip can store as much information as a computer the size of a classroom did in 1960. Because of the incredibly large number of circuits they contain, the chips make it possible to have a fully switched network of home communications sets—so that each set can exchange messages, or video telephone calls, with any other set in the system.

OPTICAL FIBERS were discovered by Bell Laboratories (which earlier discovered the transistor, which led in turn to the silicon chip). Using a drawn glass strand no bigger than a hair, thousands of messages, including computerized data and television pictures, can be transmitted on a light beam from a laser or another light-emitting source. The optical fiber can replace the cumbersome coaxial cable and carry many more television signals and voice circuits. It does this by sending the signal in *digital* form: The sending device, which is a computer, breaks the electronic signal into a stream of bits. Each bit is a pulse of light that reads "on" or "off." Any electronic information—a television picture, a telephone call, textual matter, or computer data—can be converted into these digital bits. The bits are converted back into words and pictures by the silicon-chip microprocessor in a television set adapted for the purpose. A conventional television set receives 92 million of these bits a second to construct its picture. Japanese manufacturers have marketed optical fibers that transmit more than a billion bits a second.

COMMUNICATIONS SATELLITES are space vehicles that orbit the earth in synchronization with its own rotation, so that they appear to remain in a fixed position above a point of the earth's surface. They can receive television, radio, telephone, and data transmissions from a sending station on earth and relay them to a receiving station thousands of miles away. They are capable of replacing telephone landline and underwater-cable transmission across great distances, providing

---

* Eight *bits* form a *byte*—a letter or a number, called an *alphanumeric character*.

the same services at far lower cost. In a broadcast mode, they can transmit television signals from a national station directly to homes, bypassing local, over-the-air stations.

These three developments, used in an integrated system built around computers, make it technically possible to provide hundreds of communications services to the home and office. Because they reduce costs by factors of from ten to a thousand, they can put such services within the financial reach of nearly every person, business, or government agency in the industrialized nations. Projected cost reductions are likely to make these services affordable in most less-developed countries, as well.

The miniaturization of computer memories on silicon chips is largely responsible for the amazing and continuing drop in information-processing costs. In 1972 you could get 1000 bits into a chip costing ten dollars, or a penny a bit. A chip being marketed in the 1980s offers 64,000 bits at 6/1000 of a penny; the 256,000-bit chip produced in prototype reduces the cost of computer data to 1/1000 of a penny a bit.

A technology that can provide all these services could do much to improve the quality of our lives to increase our knowledge, our pleasure, and our well-being. If that is so, why not say, "Fine, I want all of them, right now"? Before we do that, we ought to examine the gifts. With many facets of this new communication technology come potentially dangerous capabilities. These can be used, not to lead us to fuller, freer, more satisfying lives but to restrict our freedom as individuals.

An interactive system which supplies us with most of our information and entertainment programming, delivers our phone messages and our mail, carries out all our financial transactions, and senses movement in our homes can be used to invade our privacy and order our activities. The problem was set out in a report to the White House by the Domestic Council Committee on Privacy:

"Information systems are spreading throughout the public and private sectors of the United States and the world. The question is no longer whether or not we should have [information] networks, but how we could establish them to maximize the effectiveness and efficiency in a manner which will insure their use for public good.

"For many, all of these [technological and developmental] concerns are dwarfed by the questions about the desirability of information systems that involve data about individuals, particularly in light of their potential for political and bureaucratic misuse. How can checks and balances be placed on governmental authority to prevent abuse of such a system?"[1]*

To which might be added a growing feeling among researchers and the public that checks must be placed on *private* and *corporate* use and misuse of such a system, as well. Harold Sackman, in his book *Mass Information Utilities and Social Excellence,* says, "The social stakes are too high to let the information revolution pass as just another economic opportunity to be resolved by the vagaries of the marketplace."[2] Yet the tendency in the United States as the 1980s began *was* to let these developments be decided by the marketplace. No philosophy has been developed on how we should protect ourselves from the unscrupulous use of the new technologies for power or personal enrichment. The Carter administration and many in Congress had decided that services to society that could be expected to accrue from the new communications technologies should neither be regulated nor brought about by government action. The administration set policy that said the government would not subsidize public-service uses of these facilities but would instead subsidize their private development for profit. According to administration spokesmen, the marketplace would meet the public's needs. But the marketplace reckons only in terms of private gain; the public good comes after that.

Not all technical developments mean automatic progress for the human condition, even if they mean profits for the developers. A good case can be made, in retrospect, for rejecting nuclear generation of electrical power. It was developed after World War II because commercial interests saw that peaceful uses of atomic fission could ultimately become profitable, especially if the government subsidized its taming and development. Certainly, the instant and wide-scale acceptance of DDT by the agribusiness to kill crop-destroying insects was a disservice to humans, since the long-term dangers of poisoning the environment had not been considered.

Judging from historical developments beginning with the Industrial Revolution, technological "advances" would seem to be inevitable. But in the past their inevitability has been hastened when commercial or military interests have discovered ways to make them pay off financially or in battlefield advantage. It is they who have pro-

* The superscript figures refer to the Chapter Notes that begin on p. 267.

moted the idea of the "technological imperative." Without intervention by people concerned primarily with human welfare, such technological changes will continue to be pressed upon us when commercial and military managers decide it will be best for their own interests to do so.

We have to make ourselves aware of such technological "advances" and their dangers to freedom *before* they are presented to us as *faits accomplis*. We can become aware, if we choose to be, in the communications area. Technical discoveries and potentialities are usually discussed and checked out for years before they are adopted by the military or by business interests for commercial development. Television was successfully transmitted in a San Francisco apartment in 1927. Its public presentation came at the New York World's Fair in 1939.

The development process has been speeded, but we still have a little time to do with the new technology what we should have done with radio after World War I and with television before Congress adopted the Communications Act of 1934: examine each part of it critically, then work to impose humanitarian constraints on the way each part is used. One problem is that public-interest groups are less well organized and financed than commercial-interest groups to make investigations and take actions in their own interests. So, normally, the profit-oriented groups get the jump on the human-oriented. For example, the time is short if we are to have an impact on regulating or preventing the installation of satellite computer networks that can give any business executive anywhere in the country (tomorrow, the world) instant assessment of our potential as purchasers or our potential as loyal employees.

Other information technologies, the prototypes of which have been built and tested successfully, are further away from full commercial deployment. So much the better—controlling a technology before it is generally installed is far easier than changing it once it is in place. Think of the difficulty, now, of getting the U.S. Congress to pass a law that says citizen-action groups in every local community must have access, one night a week in prime time, to frequencies of the "public" airways that are now licensed to commercial stations. Such a provision would have been reasonably simple to include in the Radio Act of 1927, which set up the assignment and regulation of frequencies.

Intervention of groups representing consumers may cause some delay in the general use of the new communications technologies. But that is better for humankind than to allow commercial interests to develop them as fast as marketing opportunities allow, and then, when the dangers become alarmingly apparent, try to rein them in.

Groups opposed to technology per se argue that, since there are no guarantees that we can impose social controls on the developments, we should turn out backs on all advanced technology and return to the simple life. The trouble with the simple life before technology was that most of the children did not survive, and those who did found they had a life expectancy of about thirty-five years. Some of us can go back to the land and live happily on it—and survive to be seventy or eighty. But for the mass of humanity, that is not a viable possibility. Given the number of people competing for life on this planet, *more* sophisticated methods, not less, are needed to insure reasonable access to its goods—intellectual and spiritual as well as material. Much of the new communications technology could, if properly employed, help us achieve that. The benefits are worth the trouble of fighting for proper controls before the facilities are allowed to be put into general use.

But we must not allow ourselves to be manipulated by chance discoveries that are picked up by commercial interests and developed, not because of an inherent, long-term benefit to people but because they promise a substantial profit for the developer in the short run. Nor should we let government officials, in the name of public service, impose a system on us that makes possible more efficient monitoring of our activities.

THE DANGER OF CONTROL

The biggest threat of a multifaceted, integrated communications system is that a single authority will win control of the whole system *and its contents.* An agency that gained such control, if left to operate it without adequate restraints, could dictate its contents and decide its political, economic, and social applications. It would be far easier to control what is seen, heard, and read on a monolithic electronic communications system than it is today to control content on thousands of radio and television stations and in the diverse outlets of the printed press.

The ending of the film *The President's Analyst,* in which the analyst discovers that the entire world is being run by The Phone Company, is surreal, but the idea is not. If we abdicate control of the system's content to the government, The Phone Company, or anyone else, the system in time will control us.

It is not likely that if they understand what is at stake, the people will roll over and play dead in the face of such threats to our privacy and individual liberty. The tradition of checks and balances, protection of diversity, and regulation of monopoly is strong. But the danger is that because the technology seems complicated, people will leave installation and regulation (or nonregulation) of the new communications to government and business "experts." For all our sakes, this must not be allowed to happen.

At present, in the United States, the federal government and the American Telephone and Telegraph Company are best positioned to win control over such a system. The inherent powers of the government make it a likely candidate to run it. If it did, the Pentagon would be an influential silent partner—the Department of Defense already controls one-third of the electronic spectrum assigned to satellite and microwave communication. AT&T is a formidable contender because it is *there:* its member companies have distribution lines that pass almost every home and business office in the country. It also has a leg up on the new technologies needed to convert its telephone system into an integrated home communications system.

Another likely contender would be a corporate conglomerate, such as Time Inc., with media operations at its core. IBM would be in the running. So would the commercial networks. Justified or not, it is a political and economic fact of life that the people who provide the financing for the new instrument will try to call its tune. That is true whether the financial backers are a government institution or a private organization. In France, where the government finances the television system, it is the party in power that ultimately decides who will be allowed on the air. In Britain, people who pay for television licenses constitute a pressure on the BBC to give them programming they will be willing to pay for. In the United States, the commercial networks and local commercial stations exercise complete control of access to the medium. Often their decisions on what is seen are influenced indirectly or directly by advertisers who support the programming. These same advertisers often are the underwriters of programming in U.S. public television, exerting enormous influence on what will be shown on the public system. Federal administrations and Congress, which provide much of the support for the public system, have often tried to influence its programming.

As in these "traditional" technologies, financing of the evolving system raises policy questions involving basic rights and freedoms. Who will be allowed to put their communications (messages, programs, computer data) into the system? What companies, agencies, citizen groups, and individuals will have access to its facilities? Only those who can pay? Those who cannot pay, as well? Should the communications of social-service agencies be carried free, as a public benefit subsidized by the government?

Who will be able to have the system in their homes? Again, only those who can afford the sets and pay for the service? If almost all public information will in time be carried on the system, would not this make two classes of citizens—the information rich and the information poor?

Clearly, information is power. Control of a unified system by the government would greatly increase its potential for restricting information and determining program content. It could give a future administration power over the electorate little dreamed of by Charles de Gaulle when he used the government-monopoly television system of France to exclude opposition candidates from the air.

Control of both system and content by a private corporation could conceivably lead to its domination, albeit indirect, of the government itself. By shaping and censoring what is seen, read, and heard, a corporation that has a monopoly on the system and its content might be able, in time, to shape the view of the public and of government officials to its vision of what the world is and what it should be.

In 1976 Arthur D. Little Inc. submitted to the White House a report on the future direction of communications.[3] In a scenario, A. D. Little depicted a situation in which AT&T proposes, and Congress agrees, to rewrite the Communications Act to give that corporation a monopoly, beginning in 1991, on distribution of the merged telecommunications media—television, radio, telephone, computer networks, etc. Television and radio stations are taken off the air and transferred to an optical-fiber carrier system, which now carries all telephone, cable, and computer-connected services as well.

The implications of such a development for determining what information gets to the consumer are obvious—it is far easier to control a system in which all information comes into our homes via a single communications set than it is to control what goes out over the air from local television stations, or which comes to us via the diverse outlets of the printed press.

AT&T, in its public statements, has said it *intends* to put content into the system, as well as act as common carrier for all others who want to provide information, entertainment, and other services via the system.

And, after a quarter-century of dogged fighting, AT&T won the concession from the Federal Communications Commission (FCC) that would make this possible. It permitted AT&T to offer data-processing services over its network, removing a prohibition against Bell's expansion into the computer field that was set down in a federal court consent decree in 1956.

COMPUTER-ASSEMBLED DOSSIERS

Anyone who runs a computerized, two-way communication system has a magnificent tool with which to invade our privacy. This, in fact, is the most urgent area of concern in the development of the new communications—including computerized storage and electronic exchange of personal data collected by government agencies, credit rating concerns, personal investigation companies, and private employers.

The reason this is urgent is because here, the invasion is well under way. In the United States, the government keeps 4 billion personal data files in its computers; Equifax Services Inc., the biggest investigations company, keeps 40 million dossiers in its computer in Atlanta, and transmits them across the country by satellite. In Columbus, Warner Amex Cable's computer "sweeps" the Qube two-way interactive television system once to determine which movies subscribers are watching and what political opinions they are expressing via their interactive response buttons.

These computerized "services" make it possible to develop detailed personal profiles on every one of us that could be exchanged electronically between organizations collecting the data. With a computerized data bank tied in to the home communications set, such dossiers could be made available to anyone who wished to pay the service charge.

One of the great dangers to freedom posed by the new communications system lies in this area of computer-assembled dossiers. Since their inception, commercial and government computer data banks have outdistanced efforts by Congress and the public to regulate their use.

Because the home communications system has two-way audio and video capability, plus switching capacity, it would be able to incorporate the present telephone system (or to put it in terms being discussed by AT&T, the phone system could incorporate the new communications). Transmission of private letters by facsimile print-out or for reproduction on the television screen is also envisioned. Electronic surveillance via computer of phone conversations and written communications could then add to the "completeness" of the dossiers being assembled.

THREAT TO PRESS FREEDOM

The question of who will run this system is of major concern in the area of news dissemination. With the electronic merger that is in the offing, it is possible that newspapers, wire services, and television-news organizations will be combined in news operations that generate stories for the HCS, to be printed out as text on the screen or presented as television—filmed, taped, or live. With a unified method of distribution, a system operator would have the capability to impose censorship on transmission of news in any form. If, for example, news selection were placed in the hands of a conglomerate that had manufacturing and service divisions apart from its media functions, the news certainly would be suspect in areas relating to its spheres of interest.

The federal government could attempt to assert its jurisdiction over the merged news facilities through the precedent created by the FCC's Fairness Doctrine. This requires broadcast-news organizations to provide "balanced" reporting of controversial issues in their news broadcasts and documentaries.

Clearly, a First Amendment issue is involved. Newspapers, of course, have no federal rules governing restraints upon their content. If this content is shifted to an electronic-delivery system, they could find themselves under such constraint.

OTHER DEVELOPING PROBLEMS

Control, with its implications for freedom of speech and the press and for invasion of privacy, is one of the prime concerns about the new communications. But many other serious questions should be raised. Here are a few of the broader issues, which will be discussed in the chapters that follow:

- If we absorb information and entertainment, do our jobs, transact our business and engage in personal interchange via the HCS, how will this affect our social relationships? Will we become stay-at-homes, relating mostly to a machine, or will the interactions on the machine lead us into more personal contacts outside the home?

- Will the new communications collect information from the masses and funnel it to the few at the top, tending to centralize government and industry, or will it be a decentralizing force, providing more information to the populace so that more and better decision-making can be done at the local levels?

- Will rich countries and multinational corporations use information extracted from the less-developed countries for national and commercial gain, with no return for the country providing the information? Can the poorer nations *prevent* information from leaving their countries until they can be certain it will not be used to their detriment?

- Will the new technology, *by its very nature,* manipulate us? Will governments and corporations be able to use it to manipulate us, or will we be able to manipulate the new technologies to serve the good of society?

This last concern gets to the heart of the problem that the communication "revolution" presents to society. It is expressed succinctly in the Nora-Minc report, *L'Informatisation de la Société,* commissioned by the president of France, which stirred vehement discussions as the new technologies were beginning to take hold there:

Is it possible to foresee what forms this revolution will take? Pessimists predict the worst: raging unemployment, increased social barriers, emergence of a robotized subproletariat as human skills are devalued by all-powerful "know-alls," increasingly burdensome hierarchical structures, fearsome possibilities of State control over society thanks to computer storage of information. By contrast, the optimists look forward to a society freed from the brutal constraints of productivity by the data-processing miracle, turned toward pleasurable pursuits, convivial, democratic, self-managing. . . .

In short, will the new techniques strengthen the rigid, authoritarian, dominatory aspects of our societies? Or will they, on the contrary, encourage adaptability, freedom, dialogue?[4]

The best way to look for answers to such questions, I thought, would be to investigate parts of the evolving system that are already in place, and report on actions (or inactions) by governments, citizen groups, and corporations that are already influencing social conditions. The growing number of pilot projects and operational installations in North America, Western Europe, and Japan are steps along the way to an integrated electronic system of communications. By choosing existing examples to write about in each of the major areas of the emerging technology, I hope to convey a feeling I developed while reporting them: the threats they contain are today's, not tomorrow's; they will have to be faced now.

Only if we counter the threats by developing informed social and political policies will we be able to reap the benefits of the evolving communications system. Public action is necessary *before* the technologies congeal into a universal, ubiquitous system. By then the essential decisions would have been made, and we would have to live with their consequences.

2 | COLUMBUS DISCOVERS TWO-WAY CABLE

"Go in," says my host. I step through the door into what appears to be a carpeted inner office lighted from above by fluorescent panels. "Take three steps." I do as he tells me. From across the hall, I hear the clatter of a teleprinter springing into action. "The room has sensed your presence—it sent the alarm to our computer," my host informs me. "The computer activated our printer across the hall— but it could have activated one at police headquarters as well."

My host is Miklos Korodi, general manager of Qube, the two-way, interactive cable system that Warner Amex Cable Communications Inc. installed in Columbus, Ohio.

The motion-sensing burglar alarm is one of several home-security services Qube has advertised to its subscribers. "Here, watch this." Korodi holds a piece of burning rope up to a smoke detector in the ceiling. A raucous buzzer alarm sounds in the room, and the computer printer kicks in again. In a live installation, information on the location of the house, flammables inside, and the position of the nearest fire hydrant would be printed out at the firehouse while the alarm was rousing sleepers in the burning home. Qube has also offered a "duress" button to call police in a situation threatening the subscriber's safety and a medical-emergency button to call for an ambulance.

A personal-security medallion is planned as an optional extra: an elderly woman could wear the medallion around her neck and press it should she slip and fall on the ice while putting out the garbage. The alarm, relayed by radio through the "black box" inside the house, would also tell the ambulance crew her medical history—what medication she is taking, any medicines she has to avoid.

The black box, designed by Qube engineers, is a microprocessor about a foot and a half long, six inches wide and four inches deep. It is filled with miniaturized circuits encased in small silicon chips that can duplicate the operation of a room-sized computer of the 1960s.

The Data General computer at Qube's "head end" can query the box continually, asking, in effect, "Is everything all right there?" If it isn't, the mircroprocessor, a compact computer in its own right, can spell out the problem so that the city's emergency forces can respond.

"This is a second-generation black box," Korodi says, showing me the miniaturized circuitry inside. "We're working on a third." Processors down the line, he says, will give the system capability to make decisions about climate conditions in the house, turning the heating plant and air conditioners on and off in a pattern that will conserve energy and save dollars for the consumer. "Of course, the subscriber will have an override button, to get more heat or cooling at any time, if he wants it."

Korodi, an outgoing, enthusiastic man, seems delighted by the things the new two-way cable system can do. So do other Warner staff members; they obviously think they are inventing the wheel for new communications.

To help them make the invention pay off, they have behind them the megadollar financing of the cable company's parent, Warner Communications Inc. This conglomerate, which grew out of and owns Warner Brothers, also owns, among other things, Panavision, Atlantic Records, Warner Brothers Television, Warner Books, and Atari, Inc., makers of video games.

The Warner Amex Cable management in New York thought that the sale of multiple services would make this cable system—at its installation, the most advanced in the country—a commercial success. Qube (a trade name that stands for nothing in particular) is never referred to by its developers as "cable television." They speak of "two-way cable": one line carrying signals from the head end out to the customer, one line relaying his responses back to the head end. Or, better yet, "two-way, *interactive* cable."

There are reasons for that. After all, a burglar *is* interacting with the system when he takes three steps in your home and sets off an alarm. Most of the television services of Qube's multiservice offering are built around its two-way, interactive capability. This permits sub-scribers at home to make decisions about what the system is offering them and then, through the adapter on their standard television sets, tell the computer what those decisions are. On the interactive chan-nels, it allows them to "talk back" to their televisions.

"They like to play the system," says one Warner executive, and, indeed, they are being programmed to do that by Qube's promotional campaign. "Touch the button," says the large, four-color, slick-paper brochure, "and enter the era of two-way participation in the infinite, unfolding, never-ending worlds of Qube."

These worlds include the thirty channels controlled by touch buttons on a key-pad console about the size of a plug-in electronic calculator. Ten channels provide the commercial- and public-television stations, a public-access channel, and a program-guide channel. A second ten supplies "premium" selections—primarily movies that have not yet played on commercial television. Premium Channel 10 supplies something else you don't see on commercial television. For $3.50 a touch, you get soft porno (to use the Qube staff's reference, "hard-R") films with predictable titles such as *Dr. Feelgood* and *Hot Times*. The soft-core channel is fed into the home only if a subscriber specifically orders it. In addition, it and all other Premium channels can be locked by removing a key that, presum-ably, can be kept out of the hands of children. Premiums also include entertainment specials produced or purchased by Qube, self-help courses (such as "Shorthand" and "How to Prepare for College En-trance Examinations"), and local college sports. Unlike Home Box Office, which charges subscribers a fixed fee for each month of pay-television programs, Qube's computer bills viewers for each selection, at prices that range from 75¢ for "Shorthand" to $9.00 (in football-mad Columbus) for a live telecast of an Ohio State football game. This is in addition to the $10.95 Qube customers pay every month for the basic service.

You are not a passive viewer when you push a Premium channel button, because it is going to cost you. The computer is solicitous about your having to make such a decision, and allows you a two-min-ute grace period before it enters your selection into its memory.

Even greater participation is demanded by the system in the third group of ten—the Community channels, where viewers are so-licited to "interact" with their sets. Most of the interaction centers on the "Columbus Alive" channel, which offers programs every weekday, produced out of Qube's studio building on the Olentangy River Road. This "head end," rebuilt from a large-appliance warehouse, has three television studios equipped with color minicams that double as cameras in mobile units on assignments around Columbus. And here is housed the computer at the heart of the interactive system.

A "polling" computer, it gathers billing and response data from subscribers. The computer sweeps all subscribers' homes at six-second intervals, asking: Is the set turned on? What channel has been punched up? What was the last Response Button touched?

The home console has five Response Buttons in addition to the channel-selection buttons. The first two can be used as "Yes-No" buttons; all five can be used to answer multiple-choice questions or punch up number codes to indicate, as one possibility, selection of products displayed on the screen.

One evening I went to the Olentangy studio to watch the staff produce "Columbus Alive," a variation of the original "Today" show on NBC (talk, live remotes, interviews, mini-documentaries). The two co-hosts and their guests were in two-way communication with 30,000 subscribers in Qube's franchise area, which encompassed 104,000 households. The night I saw the show, an attractive, articulate woman was interviewing a priest and a former nun on "What's it like to be a homosexual in Columbus?" She told her audience that it had been estimated there were 80,000 homosexuals in the Columbus "metro" area, which has more than a million people. "Let's find out how many of you know homosexuals," she said. A statement was superimposed on the screen:

I have a friend, relative, or aquaintance who I know is homosexual.

"If you do know a homosexual," said the host, "push Button Number One for Yes; if you do not, press Button Number Two for No. Touch in now."

Within seconds, the computer supplied a result to the studio's character generator, which printed it out on the screen:

YES	65%
NO	35%

The host continued the interview, but interrupted it to throw similar questions to the home audience and get their responses. When the show got slow, I used the key pad to do some channel switching. I punched up the porn channel to find out if it was really there. It really was. On another channel, I found a young, bearded instructor from a local college presenting a three-credit course on basic English composition. Electronically updating the Socratic method, he salted his lecture with Q-and-A segments asking students to use the Response Buttons to answer True or False, or pick the correct answer from five multiple choices flashed on their screens. (In some classes, if an enrolled student got the answer correct, the red Message Light on his key pad lighted up: Instant reward.)

At her home in a Columbus suburb that night, Brenda Hathaway tucked her son, Jamie, in bed and walked down the hall to her television room to attend her "Qube Campus" class in Business Communication.

I talked to her later about the experience. The best thing about this class, Mrs. Hathaway told me, was that she did not have to get a baby-sitter in order to go to college.

Until "Qube Campus," she didn't see how she was going to continue working for her degree. Thirty-one years old, divorced, and with two children to raise, she had already given up the idea of going back to school full-time. Before she was married, she had put in two years in the business administration program at Ohio State University. After the divorce, she enrolled part-time at Franklin University in downtown Columbus.

But attending night classes there while she was working full-time at Toledo Scale Company proved hard to do. "I've gone to class when I had to worry about what to do with the kids, and I tell you it's a hassle," she said.

Then four institutions—OSU, Franklin, Capital University, and Columbus Technical Institute—began presenting college courses for credit by way of Qube. Mrs. Hathaway enrolled in a course in business communication offered by Columbus Tech. "I plan to take as many credits as I can, on Qube, toward my degree," she said. "And eventually I'll go back full-time."

What she found different from conventional television courses was Qube's interactive capability, making it possible for her to answer her instructor's questions by pressing the five Response Buttons on the key pad. The instructor in the business-communication course took attendance by asking those enrolled to "Touch in." The computer told her exactly who was out there.

She asked the class, "Which of these is the best opening sentence for this business letter?" and then showed five choices on the screen for the students to select. Mrs. Hathaway and the other students "Touched-in" their answers, the computer flashed on the screen the percentage of students who had picked each choice. (The instructor could ask an individual student a question, and that response could be displayed, as well.)

"Am I going too fast?" she asked.

Brenda Hathaway, seated on her couch, key pad beside her, punched the Response Button for "No."

Her son Jamie, six years old, and daughter Briana, nine, were usually in bed by eight-thirty, the time the class was offered at its first showing on Tuesday nights. But this night, Briana wanted to stay up to see what went on in her mother's class. This particular session was concerned with the use of verbs.

"Mommie!" said Briana, "you're studying the same thing I'm studying, but you're studying it on television!"

A contribution like that from her daughter can be distracting, Mrs. Hathaway said, but Qube gave her a way around it. "If I happen to miss part of the lesson," she said, "I know I can pick it up when they rerun it later in the week. They're very good about listing it at different times—I've watched this class *very* late at night."

Mrs. Hathaway said the interactive Response Buttons gave her a sense of participating in the class, even though she was sitting in her own home. She got to see her classmates, who numbered about thirty, when she went to the campus for the final exam. The instructor maintained "office hours," by phone, immediately after each class and the day following.

The classes were presented on "open" channels of the cable system. Students got credit by enrolling in the course and paying tuition directly to the individual college.

It would have been simple for the computerized system to channel the course only to those who paid, but the colleges found that open classes, which all subscribers could see, inspired others to enroll. They discovered that the cable courses were also a recruiting device for on-campus courses. And Qube was happy to offer the courses because they attracted subscribers to the system.

Robert Thompson, who handled the courses for Columbus Tech, said his college found that students in two-way classes performed "a little better" than those taking the same course on campus. "Probably we are seeing people who are more highly motivated," he said. "They are older, and they have paid the regular fee—especially for a particular course. In any case, we know now that the system works."

Dr. Vivian Horner, Warner's vice-president for program development, saw two-way cable courses as a method of reaching people who would never go to a campus because they were handicapped, or felt they were "too old," or were just plain embarrassed. "There has to be a group of people who are not thrilled with the idea of sitting in a classroom," she said. "This is ideal for them."

Back at "Columbus Alive" I found a male co-host seated beside a man in a dark gray suit who looked like a bookstore clerk. He was indeed introduced as a representative of Readmor Bookstores in Columbus, and he had come to talk to us about hardcover versus paperback books. After a short exchange with his guest on the merits of each, the host asked the audience a series of interactive questions about its reading habits. The computer reported back the not-surprising information that more people bought paperbacks than hardcovers, and the surprising information that 41 percent said they bought more than ten paperbacks a month. This may reflect the "tilt" of Qube's franchise area: the affluent western side of the city and suburbs, encompassing the Ohio State University campus.

(Three other cable companies had been franchised to cover the rest of the city. Columbus, which has complete jurisdiction over franchising provisions, carved the city into four service areas because it wanted all areas to be wired for cable in a relatively short time. The practice is fairly common in larger cities.)

As the segment was ending, the titles of four books mentioned on the program were posted on the screen, numbered one through four. "If you would like to order one of these books," said the host, "touch the corresponding buttons. The computer will gather your name and address, and Readmor will send you the book."

An interesting thing about this "book interview" was that it was actually a commercial, paid for by Readmor Bookstores. At no time was it identified as such to the audience. When I asked one of the show's producers why it was not, she said it was because they wanted the show "to flow into informal commercials so it won't interrupt the rest of the content." Qube calls these segments "Informercials."

Informercials were also used for test-marketing. Advertisers and market-research firms have long used Columbus, with its 600,000 middle Americans, as Test City, USA. One national magazine asked

Qube viewers to "Touch in" their judgments on five proposed magazine covers, and then published the two at the top. From their willingness to respond, subscribers apparently enjoyed becoming part of the commercial process.

Qube advertisers asked viewers to choose between pilot commercials or rate their "interest level," at ten-second intervals, as they watched situation-comedy pilots. Conceivably, that could lead producers to demand six laughs a minute from their writers.

Computerized two-way systems can make Nielsen and Arbitron ratings obsolete. No "sampling" guesswork—the Qube computer knew, down to the last household, how many sets were tuned to one of its channels. "We can give the advertiser demographics we never had before—how many people in the twenty-thousand- to thirty-thousand-dollar bracket are watching this commercial, that sort of thing," said a marketing executive. He pointed out that the computers could cross-reference answers to opinion questions with income groups, to tell which economic class wanted what.

This, of course, would help advertisers zero in on specific "upscale" audiences for their messages. But it would also permit them to know the interests of a particular section of a city. A ghetto area, for example, could be isolated within the system, and the system operator could find out, through audience-response polling, what products and services might go well if promoted there. One "vertical" channel, set up in effect as a special-interest magazine, could be aimed only at the city subdivision involved, permitting national advertisers of "minority-interest" products to reach a target audience directly. A mom-and-pop business could use a limited-area channel and avoid the cost of having to broadcast their ads across the entire Columbus market—as they would have to do on an over-the-air television station—to reach people in their neighborhood who might patronize their corner store.

A "horizontal" special-interest channel could be beamed to the entire population of the cable system, should two-way market research show a particular area-wide interest in, say, bowling. Fragmentation of content to cater to the needs of parts of the audience, while not possible in mass-audience-approach television, is economically and technologically feasible in a computerized two-way system. It can lead to greater diversity of content than is permitted to appear on general-audience commercial stations.

Nationally, vertical programming to meet the needs of a group with a special interest—an ethnic group that would like to watch Polish folk dancing, for example—can be done by putting together separate elements of this special audience via one channel of a satellite service that goes to a number of local cable systems.

Because the costs would be low, compared to the costs of transmitting a network-television program, it becomes economically feasible to produce programming for audiences of "only" a million people. On U.S. national commercial television, an audience of 30 million is considered necessary for an entertainment service to survive. News documentaries that reach "only" 10 million are tolerated (although less and less) by profit managers because they add prestige to the network's schedule. Why, in the new system, should not "only" 100,000 be a worthwhile group to reach with a message or specialized-entertainment program?

Among the first to see the possibilities this presented were charismatic, conservative Protestant preachers, some of whom have become millionaires by using satellite networks and cable companies to get out their message: "Praise the Lord and send the dollars."

In the Qube system, the computer could charge an order for a book or other merchandise to the subscriber's credit card or to a charge account at a department store, if the subscriber provided the number to be fed into its memory. This was only a step from another service—called Electric Funds Transfer (EFT)—which Warner Amex Cable planned to test at Qube. In this, subscribers could select products and pay for them immediately by transferring funds from their bank accounts to the accounts of businesses that advertised goods and services. Each subscriber would have a confidential Personal Identification Number that he could punch into the system to tell the computer that it was really he, and not an electronic embezzler, who was ordering the money to be transferred.

"This is all possible today," Korodi told me, "but on each service we have to ask: Is it a business? We are addressing ourselves to people's needs, then looking at it to see if it is economically justifiable; then we will market it." After two years of experience with Qube, Warner was convinced that some form of two-way cable was economically viable. The company had put at least $20 million into Qube to find this out. To recoup its investment and begin realizing a profit, Warner began expanding two-way service to others of its 140 cable systems around the country.

Qube II got a go-ahead when the city of Houston granted a two-way franchise to Warner in 1979, with Cincinnati, Dallas and Pittsburgh close behind. Warner, in partnership with American Express, proposed to build a 120-channel system, including Qube, for Brooklyn, Queens, and Staten Island in New York City.

Other companies had experimented with this form of service in a limited way, but by 1980 only Warner had staked a lot of money on the idea that two-way cable might be the wave of the future.

Cable-industry leaders watched Qube closely, on the chance that interactive cable might supply the new element that would eventually lead cable to surpass the penetration of over-the-air commercial television in American homes. By 1980 cable reached into 22 percent, or about 17 million, of the 74 million homes with television sets.

Growth of cable had been steady, but was slow until pay-TV movies and entertainment programs were offered to systems nationally in the mid-seventies. This was done by Home Box Office and Showtime, which distributed their packages to cable systems by domestic satellite. Warner Amex Cable offered its own package of films and shows, called The Movie Channel, via satellite. It also used the satellite to present thirteen hours of children's programs of a nonviolent nature daily to local systems that paid for the service. The programs were an outgrowth of Qube's children's shows and were produced in the Qube studios.

The attractiveness to subscribers of nationally distributed pay-TV shows helped cable grow from 3000 systems serving 5400 communities in 1974 to 4000 systems serving nearly 10,000 communities by 1980.

Annual gross revenues passed the billion-dollar mark in 1977. In cable, profitability grows with economies of scale, as exemplified by the multiple-system operators (MSO's). In 1977 Warner Amex Cable, the fourth largest MSO, reported a return of $15.7 million on gross revenues of $55.7 million in its basic cable operations. Teleprompter Corporation, the largest MSO, earned $19.6 million on a gross of $99.6 million.

Financial analysts looked to cable television as a growth industry, bearing in mind the forecast by Arthur D. Little Company, the research firm, in Cambridge, Massachusetts, that movies seen and paid for in the home would put the majority of movie theaters out of business in the 1980s. Promoting the use of two-way cable television to charge subscribers only for the specific films and shows they watch might make this form of home entertainment big business. It was two-way cable's capability of selective billing for entertainment and consumer services that intrigued cable executives responsible for profit and loss. As one Teleprompter official put it, "We feel definitely that two-way will be here ultimately; it just has to be economically viable."

Supplying only those services that can produce a profit makes sound business sense, but it leaves something to be desired from the standpoint of giving people the services they need, some of which will never turn a profit. A channel whereby a city clinic could conduct a medical diagnosis, with responses, of a person who is housebound is a sure money-loser. So are channels that could be used for two-way communication between city security forces and the people in their homes during a local disaster. Two-way system operators may find that they have to provide some nonprofit services to the community in return for being franchised to make a profit off of the community.

Qube tacitly acknowledged this obligation by offering channel facilities at no cost to the community, for participatory "town meetings" and government hearings. One such meeting was held in Upper Arlington, a prosperous suburb in Qube's franchise area. Using multiple-choice questions, the Upper Arlington Planning Commission asked Qube subscribers to comment on a draft plan for renewing an older part of the city. The computer was programmed to "narrowcast" the hearing to only those subscribers who lived within the suburb. Two previous public meetings on the issue drew a total of about 125 citizens each. The meeting held by two-way, the computer reported, attracted a total of 2000 residents during its two and a half hours. "The point of doing this was to involve the people of the community in their own future," said Patricia Ritter, an Upper Arlington administrator who co-produced the event for the city. In that, she said, the televised hearing was a success.

Among the questions the commission asked was, "Should a building-maintenance code be adopted?" The computer, knowing where each response was coming from, reported that sentiment in favor of such a code ran about 12 percent higher in the older section, which contains a number of apartment houses, than in the newer, single-family areas of town. Residents who Touched-in their responses to the questions knew immediately if they were in the majority or in the minority—results were displayed within seconds after they pressed the buttons. To make subscribers feel free to express their views, the Qube hosts assured them that the computer had been set in a mode that would not identify any answer as coming from an individual home. If it had been set differently, it could have pinpointed the answers supplied by each household and produced a profile of each subscriber's participation for the evening. If the participants had qualms about feeding their opinions into the system, they did not express them. Most, apparently, thought the experiment was an advance in participatory democracy. Asked if they wanted to do it again, 96 percent pressed the Yes button, and within ten seconds the computer, having worked out that percentage, relayed it to the home screens.

In the televised hearing, people could also call the studio on the phone, and be put on air to express their opinions to those present at the studio and those listening at home. Later generations of two-way systems will have video cameras and microphones built into the sets, to permit direct voice and image participation by those at home.

NBC News used the Qube system in 1979 to get an instant reaction of subscribers to a speech by Jimmy Carter in which he outlined his plans to meet the energy shortage. Of seven thousand who pressed the buttons, 39 percent thought his plans were "tough enough," 40 percent thought they were not, and 21 percent were not sure. NBC flashed the numbers across the country as they were produced by the Qube computer.

This kind of test suggested that officeholders might be tempted to get instant reactions from their plugged-in constituencies on issues on which—if they took an unpopular stand—they feared might be disastrous to them politically. Such polling could be done not only locally but nationally as well, by a satellite tying two-way systems together. On an issue in which the people have some background and are reasonably well-informed, the technique can be useful as an indicator of public opinion. But there are inherent dangers, too. On an emotional issue, such as a confrontation with the Soviet Union, a charismatic president might use the national television system to arouse the citizens to support a dramatic but dangerous action and then, by instant polling of the people he has just programmed to react "Ja," conjure up "overwhelming public support" to do what he intended to do in the first place.

As in other parts of the Qube system, the people of Upper Arlington took part enthusiastically in the interactive programming. They had previously been hooked on two-way by being asked to give preferences on products, opinions on political issues, and suggestions for social issues to be discussed on "Columbus Alive." Some had been hooked on the audience-participation game shows presented by Qube. In one program, viewers could direct the show by pressing the Yes or No buttons to tell whether an amateur act should continue. When a majority of those watching pressed No, the talent was dumped in midperformance. Now that kind of power gives you a certain satisfaction. It is fun. Two-way cable is *fun.* Playing the system, subscribers are only vaguely aware that the preferences they state, the products they select, the personal opinions they express can all be stored in the computer's memory and tallied, analyzed, and cross-referenced with the demographic and financial information that is known about them. Several subscribers I interviewed said they were not concerned by this. One young workingwoman told me, "I don't feel that I have any reason to be afraid—I may be naïve, but I don't care if my opinions are recorded." Their attitude seemed to be, Who would *want* that stuff anyway? Who could profit by it?

Someone might.

As the capabilities of the Qube system became known, reporters, city officials, and others in the community considered the possibility that two-way might prove to be a method of invading subscribers' privacy. When I discussed this with Qube executives, they replied, in effect, "Yes, it *could* happen, but it won't happen here."

Vivian Horner of Warner Amex Cable expressed it to me this way: "People don't think of the telephone as an invasion of privacy. Yet each call you make is recorded. When people get as used to two-way cable as to the telephone, they will take it as a matter of fact. If people feel threatened by it, they will drop it—the economics base will keep it honest." A Qube sales executive echoed this idea: "We have a time bomb here. We have to be extremely careful and set up very strict rules. If we abuse them, we're fools."

The Warner Amex Cable management, aware that the issue of privacy would inevitably be raised, drew tight security around the system's polling computer. Access to the computer's records, Warner said, would be restricted to three top-level executives; entrance to the master control room, which houses the computer, would be restricted to those who work there.

At a meeting of the Communication Commission of the National Council of Churches in New York, Dr. Gerry Jordan, Qube's director of educational development, said that on-air talent and moderators of public-affairs programs always warned viewers when the computer was set to retrieve from its memory and print out the names and addresses of subscribers who pushed the response buttons. Qube did not warn subscribers when they pushed buttons to make purchases, on the ground that they obviously realized their names had to be recorded in order to send them or bill them for a product or a service.

When commission members pressed Jordan on what safeguards had been built in to protect the individual's right of privacy, he said, "I think we at Qube are more concerned than the subscribers are. We expected it to be much more of an issue with the public than it has turned out to be." Early on, *The New York Times* put the question to Gustave M. Hauser, president and chairman of Warner Amex Cable. "People who buy the service will simply have to accept that they give up a bit of their privacy for it," he replied. "Beyond that, we'll try to protect their privacy as much as we can."

When I interviewed Hauser at Warner Amex Cable's headquarters in New York, he said he felt the issue of privacy was "a serious one for the whole society." The amount of personal information Qube collects is trivial compared to the total amount computers of the government and business is amassing, he said. "For us, it is a question of responsibility and using the system properly."

Let's assume the good faith—and business sense—of the Warner management, which I do. Could not some future management see it as "good business" to make commercial and political use of the information derived from two-way? Let's build a scenario on that idea.

SCENARIO: THE DOSSIER BUSINESS

THE TIME: 1994, when two-way, interactive cable has spread to hundreds of cities across the country.

THE PLACE: San Serra, a city of 150,000 in southern California.

Colbert Paxton, San Serra's mayor, is running for reelection on a law-and-order campaign. In a comfortable home on a hill overlooking the city, Martha Johnson, Mayor Paxton's opponent, has just pushed a Response Button to order a book, displayed in a department store's information commercial, that advocates abolition of laws restricting sexual activity between consenting adults. She pays for it by punching in the number on her department store charge card. Next, she takes a look at a shopping channel that features personal products for women, and punches in an order for an aerosol spray deodorant.

Martha leaves for a nighttime political rally and Arnold, her husband, takes over the controls of the two-way set. Punching up a public-affairs channel, he finds the cable company quizzing its subscribers on their attitudes toward homosexuals:

Lesbians should be allowed to teach in the public schools:
YES: *Button No. 1*
NO: *Button No. 2*

Without hesitation, Arnold touches No. 2. Then, making sure their two small children are in bed, Arnold settles into a chair and selects a premium film entitled *The Professional Cheerleaders*. Fifteen minutes later, the Message Light on the key pad flashes on, telling Arnold that the cable company or one of its clients has a message for the subscriber. Cursing the interruption, Arnold dials the Message Light number, and is switched by the computer directly to the department store. In a recording, the store's credit manager points out that the Johnsons are in arrears on their credit payments, and says that the book Mrs. Johnson has just ordered cannot be sent until the Johnsons transfer $15.95 directly from their bank account to the store's account. Angry, Arnold punches in the necessary bank funds transfer, using the Johnsons' Personal Identification Number, and goes back to his movie.

At the cable company headquarters, the Information Sales Department, which works around the clock, is compiling data for its confidential clients from information the computer has collected concerning subscribers who have been interacting with their sets. Several clients have indicated interest in the Johnsons' "interactions" and have ordered computer profiles from the system.

Client 1, Mayor Paxton's campaign manager, is delighted to learn that Arnold, whose wife is a feminist and a supporter of legislation to eliminate legal restrictions concerning sex, has expressed an opinion against one of her campaign stands. He chuckles at the quiet use he can make of the fact that Arnold also watched a porno movie while his feminist wife was out. He knows what time Arnold's wife left the house, because the cable company, at the mayor's request, has installed a motion sensor to monitor the Johnsons' doorway from outside the house, relaying information about comings and goings to be checked out by a police surveillance car parked unobtrusively down the darkened street.

Client 2, a publisher of skin magazines, also gets notification of the porno film selection, and sends the Johnsons a sales brochure in a plain manila envelope.

Client 3, a local environmental group trying to decide whether to work for Mrs. Johnson, is disappointed to learn that she would, unthinkingly, order an aerosol product that is dangerous to the ozone layer.

Client 4, a national credit-rating company, gets the information that the department store has rejected Mrs. Johnson's purchase on credit, and notes that information in her dossier for the next customer who purchases credit-rating information on her; it also enters a correction as to the Johnsons' bank balance, which the computer obtained when Arnold paid up for his wife's book.

I could continue the scenario—but is all this *really* possible? It is entirely possible, today, using a two-way cable system no more sophisticated than the pioneering one installed in Columbus.

Yes, but: Would reputable people in government and business do such things? Reputable people in the FBI and the CIA arranged break-ins as a matter of course in search of information to use against political dissidents, which during the Nixon years, could mean Democrats or anyone else who expressed opposition to the regime. Reputable people in the Bell System have cooperated routinely with the Justice Department and the police in setting up wiretaps and turning over records of phone calls of persons those agencies wished to monitor. Reputable people in the state motor-vehicle agencies sell address lists of licensed drivers, updated daily by computer, to entrepreneurs who want to solicit them by phone or mail.

The neatness of getting such information by two-way cable is that it can be done, with no fuss, by a legitimately operated computer. The information-gathering activities I described in the scenario, and the use to which the information was put, are not illegal. Many reputable people are able to justify almost any action—if it is not illegal.

Yes, but: Won't people drop out of a two-way system if they find out that their "interactions" are being monitored? First of all, they do not have to be told they are being monitored: no law requires the cable operator to tell them. But beyond that, people will get used to it. I was angry when I first realized the Motor Vehicle Bureau was selling my name and address to junk mailers, but I did not go down and cancel my driver's license. Once the services provided by two-way become too convenient not to have them, people won't worry about it.

They won't, that is, unless some warning flags are raised by consumer-protection groups and legislators concerned with two-way cable's implications for civil liberties. As the 1980s began, federal, state, and local legislation was nonexistent in this area of concern. All systems were franchised by local municipalities, using guidelines set by the Federal Communications Commission. The guidelines said nothing about restrictions on two-way cable.

In fact, federal regulation of cable was thrown into confusion by a 1979 Supreme Court decision that struck down FCC rules requiring cable systems to provide access for any community groups that wanted to use one of its channels.

In a case initiated by the Midwest Video Corporation, a cable company in Arkansas, the Court said that because cable systems were an adjunct of broadcasting, the FCC could not treat them as common carriers that had to offer service to everyone on a nondiscriminatory basis.

Conceivably, the FCC could make rules in the area of privacy. But, in the move away from regulation that began about the same time as two-way, the FCC was not a likely source of such rules. And in two years of hearings by the House Subcommittee on Communications on bills to revise the Communication Act of 1934, almost no discussion was heard concerning privacy. Few national voices were raised, and, in consequence, Congress for the most part ignored the issue as it related to cable.

The mood of Congress of the 1980s seems to favor less regulation of the new communications, not more. President Jimmy Carter and President Ronald Reagan both gave deregulation their support.

Unless state legislatures act—and they don't seem much concerned—the task of protecting subscribers from invasion of privacy is going to fall on community cable-advisory groups and on council members whose local ordinances set the conditions concerning cable franchises. They have the right to do this because the FCC decided that cable-franchising should be the province of the local jurisdictions, usually municipalities. Thus, a city government may decide to grant a franchise for its entire territory, or, as in Columbus, may divide the area into several sections and grant exclusive or competitive franchises for each. In most states, the local body can approve rates, determine the number of channels to be provided, and decide what those channels will be used for.

A community group that did take action on the privacy issue as two-way was about to be introduced in its area was Citizens for Privacy in Cable TV, in Nashville, Tennessee. It mounted a campaign to inform citizens about the boons and banes of two-way so that protections could be written into the ordinance franchising the system. In a report distributed to the public, the group said:

"The conceivable uses of the two-way system are virtually limitless, and therein lies the problem. It's too easy to counterbalance all of the beneficial services which the system may offer with destructive, evil, or foolish possible uses. In a world of fallible people driven, not by evil intentions but often by folly, shortsightedness, or unwillingness to admit their limitations, the use of the two-way system for evil purposes is a possibility that must be acknowledged and honestly dealt with."

Their prescription for dealing with the problem was an ordinance requiring the cable company to tell potential subscribers what information its computer would collect about them, limiting the collection of information traceable to specific subscribers to that necessary for internal billing and program purposes, imposing security measures to protect confidential information that the company needed to collect, and requiring the erasure of most information about a subscriber held in a data bank, upon the termination of the service to the subscriber.

The Nashville group did not think it was sufficient, as some critics of two-ways systems have suggested, for the cable company to warn users that anything they put into the system could, in effect, be used against them, or that the opinions they expressed by pressing the Response Buttons would become a matter of public record.

Under the heading "Privacy Protection for Subscribers" the group included these clauses:

a. The Cable Television Company is forbidden to give, sell, or otherwise transfer any information about specific subscribers or specific subscribing households to any third party without the express, written consent of such subscriber. Consent may not be obtained through use of the Cable Television System.

b. The Cable Television Company may give, sell, or transfer general information about its entire pool of subscribers or subscribing households to a third party, provided that the information is reduced to a form that does not enable the third party to trace the information provided to specific subscribers, subscribing households, neighborhoods, or any geographic area more narrowly limited than the entire subscriber pool.

The committee report concluded:

The other safeguard against the unnecessary collection or abuse of confidential information about Cable TV subscribers is an informed public. Will people support the enactment of protective legislation? Will *you* tell your television set your most cherished secrets? Or will you approach the new technology with the caution and respect it deserves? Two-way television is not a child's plaything, but the harbinger of a new technological era. Whether it is our Pandora's box or our panacea depends upon our maturity, our circumspection, and our willingness to insist that the purveyors of this new cable-television system and our public officials install the safeguards necessary to protect adequately our precious privacy. This may be our last chance.

In Columbus, Bob Kindred, who publishes *Cable TV Programs,* a guide to what can be found on local cable-television systems in the Midwest, would like to see two-way cable thrive. But he is afraid that sometime in the future people will rebel against two-way cable, unless restraints are placed on how it uses the information that its computer collects. "A number of questions they ask, I don't answer," he said. (A vice-president of a Columbus bank had the same thought: "I won't put anything in there I don't want people to know.") People are going to want protection built in by law, Kindred added, "and this will probably help cable."

When I asked Hauser what he thought about that, he said, "This is a national problem that is being looked into now—there is no particular onus on our business. What we don't need is local regulations in the name of privacy that will inhibit the growth of this business totally, but which may be all wrong. If there is to be regulation, it should be part of a comprehensive scheme of regulation."

Clearly, federal law concerning privacy would be preferable to thousands of varying local laws. But, just as clearly, some law is needed. Otherwise, the privacy of all two-way cable subscribers is potentially for sale.

GOOD TO BE OLD IN READING, PENNSYLVANIA:

About the time the Qube system was establishing its commercial credentials, another pilot project was demonstrating the usefulness of two-way cable in providing public services. This was an experiment involving elderly citizens in Reading, Pennsylvania, a residential city of 88,000 about sixty miles northwest of Philadelphia. The project was developed by the Alternate Media Center of New York University under a grant from the National Science Foundation (NSF).

Privacy was not a particular problem in the Reading system, because the technology was deliberately planned to be very simple, without the benefits (and drawbacks) of the computer so that elderly citizens could run it themselves.

In 1974 NSF asked for proposals for experiments in the delivery of social services via two-way cable. The center, which had spent three years helping to develop one-way cable systems across the country that would promote citizen access, came up with an idea that won NSF support. It proposed linking three neighborhood community centers—a multipurpose center and two housing projects for the elderly—in Reading, to permit older citizens to exchange ideas about mutual problems. The setup also allowed them to contact government and social-welfare officials at remote origination sites such as city hall, the county courthouse, the Social Security office, schools, and other community facilities.

"Technology by itself is an idiot," Red Burns, executive director of the NYU center, told me. "What we wanted to do was set up a system of users who would use the technology in ways that would meet their needs."

Professor Burns, whose hair confirms the nickname she uses, said the designers deliberately set out to use the system as a socializing force. To do this, and stay within the economic restrictions of the grant, the system was designed primarily to bring elderly people together at the three centers, rather than have them interact, as in the Qube system, only through their sets at home. However, to test the possibility of interactive participation by people who were housebound, the center paid the local cable system to adapt the television sets of 117 elderly persons so that they could view the cabled activities and take part by phone. (ATC-Berks County TV Cable Co. provided the cable lines free, but was reimbursed for installing return lines to the centers and for maintenance of the system.) As the experiment progressed, the response from these people was so positive that the cable system decided to carry the service for all of its local subscribers so that they, too, could phone in their comments.

As the final report to the NSF pointed out, most technological innovations are designed to assist the producer, instead of the consumer, of public services:

"Rather than asking how public agencies can use cable television to provide public services, we asked: How can citizens use cable television to obtain public services and provide services for themselves?"

At first, the elderly citizens of Reading showed a desire to "make television"—copy the programs they had seen on commercial television. But then they caught on to the real benefits—to them—of two-way: exchanging ideas and experiences, talking back and forth, and producing simple, interactive segments that gave them the information they needed.

The Alternate Media Center asked them to organize their own local Community Policy Board to decide what kind of programming should be attempted. In the opening stage, the center hired a group of older people with no professional television experience to operate the system. Basically, this consisted of one black-and-white camera and a television monitor at each location, and portable videotape cameras for use at remote points and for interviews in the field. There was a small control room with switching equipment that could cut back and forth, allowing speakers and listeners at each location to be seen and heard by those at the other locations. Almost all the programming was live, with some tape inserts used mainly as discussion-leaders. The system transmitted two hours a day, five days a week.

The content the participants chose included weekly sessions in which they talked about their problems with the mayor, city council members, county commissioners, and representatives of social-service agencies. As they got into it, citizens and the mayor began calling each other by their first names. Evening sessions were scheduled to allow them to take part in city budget hearings and hearings on the allocation of federal community-development funds. Other programs included discussions of local history, cooking lessons, group singing, and poetry reading. More than seventy public and nonprofit agencies were invited to use the system to communicate with older citizens. Members of the community held discussions on the cable system to decide what kinds of programs would be most useful and what should be dropped.

Since many expected to end their lives in nursing homes, the group asked for a series on such homes in the Reading area. The producer used videotape for this one, because the audience wanted to see what the inside of these homes was like. On several occasions, the operator of a home was brought to a center and questioned by elderly participants in the studio, after a tape had been shown on that particular home.

At the request of a citizen who was housebound, a retired volunteer fireman produced "The Changing Face of Reading," on what was happening to the city. One outdoor sequence at night required extensive lighting, and the producer prevailed on his friends in the Fire Department to provide ladders and lights.

To get people to use the system, the Community Policy Board

realized it could not make every program a serious discussion of welfare concerns. So lighter entertainment was presented, usually involving the participants themselves: sing-alongs, reminiscences, quiz shows, and the like. On several occasions the community used peer-group counseling on insomnia, sex, and when to stop driving a car.

People coming to the televised sessions often recognized friends at other centers whom they had not seen for years. Waving and calling out became so prevalent during "serious" discussions with public officials that the system operators decided to include a ten-minute "Party Line" segment at the end of each day's programming so that people could socialize with their neighbors at other centers. Gathering together in the familiar community rooms that were used as studios helped people feel comfortable with the system and lose their early inhibitions concerning the technology, Professor Burns reported.

Programming got under way in January 1976 after eight months of preparation. A year later the Alternate Media Center withdrew, turning the operation over to the Community Policy Board. The project, now operated entirely by elderly citizens, was continued under the name Berks County Community Television. The center had done what it set out to do: establish a two-way interactive system to meet the needs of users, as *they* perceived them, to the point where it had viability to continue on its own.

The costs of equipment, installation, and local personnel to operate the system during the initial period came to $160,000, and were paid for under the NSF grant. The city saw the system's value; local government and local merchants raised enough to cover operating costs of $2000 a week on a continuing basis. In terms of television production, programming was mounted extremely cheaply—an average of $326 an hour. Of course, this did not provide "professional" television, with highly polished production. Rather, the idea was to produce a *service* using television as a community medium.

In developing such a system, older people in Reading liberated themselves from the concept of television as a one-way medium aimed *at* them. They took control and made it two-way communication. In it they found an avenue to influence decision-makers whose decisions affected their lives. It gave them freedom to transcend the boundaries to which many of them felt confined—senior citizens' housing projects.

The Reading operation tilted against the image that is emerging of two-way as a dehumanizing force, with each person sitting alone in front of his HCS, in communication with a computer.

A questionnaire evaluating the experiment at the end of the center's involvement indicated that the citizens' participation in the system led to participation in other social and political activities as well. It led older persons to take an active part in senior citizen clubs and other community-action meetings held apart from the cable. It helped retired persons use skills they had developed over a lifetime and develop new skills as well. The weekly citizen-government teleconferences, for example, were moderated by a seventy-seven-year-old woman who had once been active in local politics.

Participants responded that the programming had reduced isolation and served as a source of human contact. About 25 percent of those who attended the televised sessions and 80 percent of those who took part from their homes identified the interactive cable television system as the major improvement in their lives over the previous year.

In other hands, an entirely different result could have come about: the two-way system could have been used, as public service television has often been used, for the benefit of the professional producers and the interests they represent: the mayor, the council, the school board, the welfare agency that wanted a quick-and-easy way to get their plans and rules understood and accepted by the people they were going to affect. But Reading showed it could be done a different way, with the constituents in charge.

INTERACTIONS IN TAMA NEW TOWN

In the late 1970s, two rival Japanese government agencies conducted experiments that combined two-way elements of Qube and the Reading, Pennsylvania project. The first, at Tama New Town on the outskirts of Tokyo, was made by the Ministry of Posts and Telecommunications; the second, at Higashi-Ikoma in the Nara Prefecture, by the Ministry of Trade and Industry. Both experiments reflected the high interest in electronics by the Japanese government, industry, and public. They were mounted where they were mainly because of each agency's desire to stake out the turf in the new communications area. Officially they were done to test concepts, not as projects that would progress immediately from the pilot stage to operational systems such as Qube or Berks County Community Television.

Plans for Tama New Town were announced in 1971. The Tokyo Metropolitan Government and housing agencies were to construct a large bedroom community of 90,000 homes for 330,000 people. Posts and Telecommunications realized Tama would be ideal for a two-way experiment, since it is much easier to lay a coaxial cable in a city as it is being built than it is to cable an existing city. It coined the term CCIS, for coaxial cable information system, to describe the project, and set up two CCIS research panels. One was to determine the flow of communications among the people and propose ways to enhance this flow. The other studied how to put a local information system into practical use. The panels included representatives of NHK (the public Japan Broadcasting Corporation), commercial broadcasting organizations, newspaper publishing companies, the Nippon Telegraph and Telephone Public Corporation, and the electronics industry. (The Ministry of Trade and Industry had set up a research panel in the same area a few months before.)

From this planning arose a scatter-shot experiment meant to test a number of electronic-communications options. To do that, five hundred households were cabled into a computerized system. As usual in cable systems in Japan and elsewhere, the cable system retransmitted regular television programs of the public and private networks. It offered a number of unusual services, as well.

The most popular was a memo-copy service. A user at home wrote her message on a piece of paper the size of a postcard, and inserted it into the transmitter of her home communications set. Automatically, the message was printed by the facsimile terminal of the neighbor to which it was addressed. (This, of course, amounted to a form of electronic mail service.)

Eighty of the households tested a Broadcast and Response service using a key-pad–response system similar to the one at Qube. In the Tama New Town tryout, it was used primarily for educational purposes. A large number of families with school-age children lived there, and parents were interested in having the system test home-teaching techniques. Students were taught English and arithmetic, and parents could take a course in how to help their children study these subjects. Pupils at home saw the teacher in the studio. They could use the five-button key pad to respond to her questions and the telephone to ask questions of their own.

The idea of using two-way cable for education of children in the home has been around for a long time. Some who promoted it saw the possibility of reducing the costs of school construction, since children could sit in their living rooms, instead of taking up space in classrooms. Others felt a more useful application would be to use the system for students who were housebound, either temporarily because of illness or permanently because of a physical disability. This idea was tried out as early as 1971 in Overland Park, Kansas. A seventeen-year-old student confined to his home after a series of brain-tumor operations was connected by two-way coaxial cable to a classroom four miles away. A camera and microphone attached to his television set let him respond directly to questions; he could also punch in responses via a digital keyboard. Over a six-week period, the student took a course in American history, for which he received credit. Designers of the experiment pointed out that the teacher could conduct a class for several homebound students at once, conserving the time she would otherwise have to spend visiting each individually. Although the technology worked well, the classroom-in-the-home did not take off at that time, largely because few systems had installed the equipment necessary for two-way interchange.

In Tama, the Broadcast and Response mode was used outside of classroom hours for origination of local television programs. A sampling of the titles indicates the community's interests: "Tama TV News," "History and Culture of the Tama Area," "Shopping Information," "Medical Hour," "Japanese Cakemaking for Sixty Years."

Regular public access programs were presented by people in the community. One of them was "Report from Housewives," another, an on-the-spot telecast of the meeting of the PTA at Kita-nagayama Elementary School. About 30 percent of the families monitoring the experiment took part in the community programming. Later evaluation showed this service to be second to the memo-copy function in the community's assessment of usefulness.

Another popular feature was a Flash Information Service, which "flashed" news and emergency information by characters superimposed across the bottom of the regular television picture. The information transmitted alerted residents to local emergencies and breaking news while they were watching other programming.

The ministry found that 50 percent of those who took part in the experiment said that their interest in local matters had been increased because of it. This was considered to be a good percentage because of the truism that commuters often look on their suburban towns as only a place to sleep. "I have become conscious of the solidity of this local community," one man told a researcher. And another said, "I've come to exchange greetings with people I've seen through Tama Television."

The test system set up in 1978 by the Ministry of Trade and Industry at Higashi-Ikoma was more complex than that at Tama. That fact is reflected in its title: Hi-Ovis (Highly Interactive Optical Visual Information System). Optical fibers, rather than coaxial cables, were used to tie the system together, and greater use was made of computers. One hundred fifty-eight homes in an extended neighborhood were "wired" by pairs of glass fibers. The system was programmed from a nearby center with studios and computers. Local program origination included services similar to those in Tama New Town, but added mobile television units to report on developments in the area.

Hi-Ovis tested what was considered the "next step" in interactive television systems: an audio and visual return capability provided by a camera and microphone built into the HCS. This made it possible for people at home to be seen and heard throughout the system when they participated in a discussion of community affairs. They could also indicate their reactions via "conventional" key pads.

Residents could also get information, such as words in a dictionary, from a microfiche file; the computer found the requested fiche and transmitted it to the home screen. Useful information that had to be up-to-the-minute—weather or road conditions, for example—was stored digitally in the computer for transmission on request in Japanese characters on the screen. Audio information was stored digitally and transmitted via the speaker.

The Hi-Ovis experiment had the same social goals as the Tama experiment: testing the usefulness of a local information system in increasing communication, understanding, and cooperation among people in the community. Its evaluations showed that the users felt the system had achieved this result, and that community consciousness had been raised.

Dr. Masahiro Kawahata, managing director of the Visual Information Development Association in Tokyo, reported that Hi-Ovis showed sufficient usefulness to the public to warrant development as an operational medium. "In this," he said, "we can catch a glimpse of what the transition to a new service-oriented society will be like."

ONE-WAY LEADS TO ANOTHER

These uses of two-way had all been predicted in the early 1970s, when a great many people in the United States became cable enthusiasts. Most of them were members of national and local citizen action groups who saw the new medium as a way to increase services for the public and increase opportunities for members of the public to get together, via the electronic system, to solve their own problems.

But commercial cable operators had something different in mind: to make a fast dollar. They were able to do this, in communities where the citizens made no demands on their service other than that of providing clearer pictures for programs transmitted by over-the-air stations. In Upstate New York, for example, some early systems reported 100 percent return on their investment in the first year of operation.

When cable began to develop, the Federal Communications Commission first saw it as its mission to protect the commercial over-the-air broadcasters, whom the commissioners saw as their primary constituency. They did this by forbidding cable companies to import "distant signals" to add to the diversity of programming available to their subscribers. The FCC did not want cable systems to relay programs from stations outside their local viewing areas, because this might "fractionalize" the audiences that local stations were selling to their advertisers. The commission had ignored the needs of cable subscribers in another area, as well: it placed no requirements on the operators for public service. But by the beginning of the 1970s, broadcast-reform groups had achieved sufficient strength to make the FCC pay some attention to consumers.

So, in 1972, the commission adopted new rules that permitted cable systems to import some distant signals. In addition, largely through the efforts of public-interest organizations such as the Office of Communication of the United Church of Christ, led by Dr. Everett C. Parker, the FCC adopted rules requiring new cable systems to provide at least one channel, free of charge for time on the system, to anyone who wanted to use it, on a first-come, first-served basis. It also provided that one channel be set aside for educational use and one for the use of local government. The cable companies were expected to provide production facilities to community producers at nominal rates. Municipalities, into whose hands the commission placed the franchising of systems, could require *more* public access channels than the guidelines called for, but they were not permitted to allow fewer.

(By the time the Supreme Court overturned these federal requirements, most municipalities saw that it was a good thing to write them into the franchises, which they were allowed to do. In any case, many multiple-system operators had found the access channels to be an attractive draw when they were pitching for franchises and selling their services to subscribers.)

Given the access channels, community cable groups sprang up around the country, to try to enlist citizens in cable as a people's medium. But they ran up against unexpected difficulties, one of which was perceptual. People to whom they talked about cable television were likely to say, as did a subscriber in New York City: "What's the big deal? I subscribe to get better reception and to watch the Knicks' games, which I can't get on regular TV." The key word was "watch"—the passive mode that had been inculcated in viewers by commercial broadcasters since the beginning of the medium. "Who needs activists?" was the traditional broadcasters' attitude. "Give the people access to the air and next they'll want to control the station's programming."

At first, citizens thought that community access groups were asking *them* to put on programming similar to that of the commercial stations. And they knew they couldn't do it.

But that was not the message the access groups wanted to convey. They saw cable as a means of social organizing. Instead of a rally on a street corner or a neighborhood meeting in a school auditorium to demand better police protection, the community could be assembled for action via *cable*.[1] Citizens would not usually find such "programs" listed in the TV section of their newspapers. Community groups would have to *organize* the "program" the same way they got together for any civic purposes: posters, ads in local papers or local radio, pamphlets delivered door-to-door. The core of the meeting could have a live audience in the studio or a meeting hall. People at home who could not get out to the live meeting could see it and hear it on cable, and participate in the discussion by telephone call-ins.

A number of such experiments were tried, but the problems they encountered did not lead to continual use of one-way cable for this purpose. In the first place, it was hard to convert people's minds to using an electronic medium to replace meetings that had been conducted over the centuries in conventional meeting halls. Second, most cable operators did not want to be bothered with groups who wanted to use their facilities in this way.

Since they were required to grant access in some form, they usually pointed community groups in the direction of making video-tapes, which they would then place on an open channel, free of charge. Or they would provide a camera and an operator in a small studio, for which they charged minimal rates, and permit an individual or a group to present a live panel show or give a vanity performance for friends who might watch at home.

On occasion they cooperated with government agencies that wanted to hold hearings on the system, or boards of education that conducted experiments, and sometimes continuing classes, over the system. In some areas, health and welfare agencies developed programs counseling residents on subjects such as prenatal care and health care for infants.

One of the places that public access programming took hold was New York City. There, by the mid-seventies, two access channels were programmed regularly by nonprofit talk-show hosts, entertainers who wanted a showcase, and soap-box orators who made tapes for the system. Sometimes tapes were made by "guerrilla television" groups. Usually these were young people interested in social change who mastered simple, portable video equipment and went into neighborhoods to look into problems they thought should gain wider attention. The communication was one-way, and the producers had no way of knowing what effect they were having on their audience. If they had an audience at all.

The need for people to use the media to express themselves and examine the problems in their own local surroundings has been recognized by the government in Sweden. Starting in 1977 local radio was established in twenty-four areas where only the national radio and television service had been available before. Sveriges Radio, the Swedish broadcasting system, was reorganized to include Lokalradio and Utbildningsradio (Educational Radio) to permit area residents to produce their own programs, usually centered on discussion of topical issues and aimed at direct participation of local listeners.

An imaginative experiment by Educational Radio in the town of Gimo could be adapted to the extreme localization that is made possible by the new wired systems. Gimo, a small manufacturing town west of Uppsala, had no local newspaper, and the experiment helped compensate for that lack. The project, called "Everyman's Radio," was directed by Margareta Ingelstam. The idea, she told me in Stockholm, was to encourage townspeople who had never thought of using radio to express their ideas and spread information to come into the studio and make their own presentations. Educational Radio supplied a "barefoot producer" to help them master the simple techniques. The people themselves, not program professionals, determined what went on air.

Ingelstam gave me an example: The question of drinking is an issue in Sweden. One night two young girls turned up to make a tape about a temperance society they belonged to. The grandmother of one of them, who had given them a lift to the studio, sat in while the girls introduced the subject in dull, conventional terms. When they started talking about whether drinking in moderation was a good idea, the grandmother blurted out, "The nicest thing I know is a cup of coffee and a glass of liquor on a Friday evening—and I'm no boozer!"

After that, the "program" turned into a lively and amusing conversation that could happen around a dinner table. It wasn't professional, but it got to some home truths.

Another time the local tenants' movement started a discussion on radio and invited listeners to attend a follow-up at a community hall. A local folk music ensemble played on radio and invited listeners to a music festival the following day. About five hundred people turned up, a record for the local celebration.

Commenting on the experiment in a report to the Council of Europe, Ingelstam suggested that people should get a chance to use the media to shape their own affairs:

"Democracy is based on the idea of man as an actively creative being who should be a part to the decisions affecting him. This means that he needs to participate, not only in the formation of opinion and the specific debate which precede decision-making but also that he needs to become a participant in a living culture, in the social dialogue, and in the whole of the process in which people's ideas, feelings, and experiences can meet together, be made visible, and be developed. I am convinced that the more people who are included in this process, this communication, the broader and deeper democracy will become."

In the late 1970s experiments were begun in Sweden to develop the concept of citizen involvement through the use of cable television.

In 1977 the Center for Non-Broadcast Television, operating out of Automation House in Manhattan, tried to generate interaction of citizens and government officials over the existing one-way cable system there. To do this, they used municipal access Channel L on two cable services—Manhattan Cable TV, with more than 100,000 subscribers on the southern half of the island, and Teleprompter Manhattan Cable Television Corp., with more than 60,000 on the northern half.

Every Wednesday from 7:30 to 11:00 p.m., viewers could tune in Channel L and talk via telephone with decision-makers. The topic of discussion and the phone number were superimposed over the bottom third of the in-studio participants:

> Rate Increase for Con Ed?
> Call 734-9888

A person at home with phone in hand had the unusual experience of looking at and talking to a city commissioner who was impossible to reach on the phone in his office.

Although municipal access channels had been mandated by the city in its franchises, it did not specify who would provide facilities or funds for the channel. Working with the center, Manhattan Cable funded the project as a two-year experiment in "interactive" programming using the telephone as the return mode.

Against this background, there was a resurgence of hope for community involvement with the advent of the simpler and more direct means of interaction provided by two-way cable. Perhaps the capacity to interact *directly* with people in a studio or a meeting hall, either through the key pad's multiple-choice response or, in later and more advanced systems, through keyboard, camera, and microphone return, would "hook" people at home to use the system in all the socially useful ways the cable enthusiasts had seen for it ten years earlier.

The FCC, belatedly recognizing this potential, adopted a rule requiring all new systems to be built with two-way capability; it did not, however, say that the systems had to *implement* this capability.

First reports from Qube indicated a high interest in interactions from subscribers at home. The Reading experiment would seem to point the way to effective interaction among citizen groups and the government and commercial establishments that affect their lives. And evaluation of the Japanese experiments showed that the "Broadcast and Response" mode had a good potential for inducing residents to take a more active role in many areas of community life and social concerns.

DIAGNOSIS ON A CLOSED CIRCUIT

Public access interactions are usually done on open channels, which everyone in the system can see. A more restricted, closed-circuit form could be used for purposes where the users would not want the public looking in. Remote medical diagnosis is an example. An everyday use of this technique began at Logan Airport in Boston in the late 1960s. To test the possibility of diagnosis at a distance, Dr. Kenneth T. Bird of Massachusetts General Hospital got a three-year grant to install a two-way closed-circuit television system between Logan and the hospital in downtown Boston.

A traveler, hit by a sudden pain for which he felt he needed a doctor's diagnosis, could ask for help at the airport's telemedicine station. There, a nurse took basic readings such as blood pressure and temperature, then put him in touch with an internist at Mass General by way of a television screen, a microphone, and two color cameras controlled by the physician.

Speaking directly with the patient, the physician directed the nurse to perform diagnostic tests to help in making a judgment on the nature of the patient's illness. Medical equipment available for the purpose included an electronic stethoscope wired into the system so that the doctor could hear heartbeats, an electrocardiograph whose readings the physician could scan by using the remote camera, an X-ray machine that transmitted its pictures directly to the hospital, and a microscope attachment to a color camera that allowed the physician to examine a slide with samples of blood and urine. Guided by the physical examination and the other tests, the physician could instruct the nurse and the patient on measures they should take, including, if necessary, transporting the patient to the hospital for further care.

Three years' operation of the system showed it to be effective in handling cases that needed early attention from a physician but which did not occur with the regularity that would warrant having a physician at the airport around the clock.

Building on this experience, Dr. Bird developed a two-way program of "teleconsultation" between Mass General and the thousand-bed Veterans Administration hospital in Bedford, Massachusetts. Patients in need of advice from specialists at Mass General were examined in much the same way that air travelers were examined at Logan. Next, the technique was extended to group therapy, with the psychiatrist in Boston and a group leader in Bedford. After several sessions the psychiatrist reported that he could draw patients out faster and in greater depth than he could in person. The patients could see him, and he had the privilege of zooming the camera in on individuals in the group to give him a better sense of the patient's nonverbal reactions. Once, a VA doctor asked that patients be allowed to see a monitor of what the psychiatrist was seeing of the session, but that did not work: The first time the psychiatrist zoomed in, the subject patient said, "That's too close—back off."

"We've uncovered a whole new area of behavior relating to *telepresence*," said Dr. Bird. "I think now that the only reasonable substitute for actual presence is telepresence."

Dr. Bird pointed out that teleconsultation could be extended to great distances by two-way satellite transmission. "If you have a heart attack in Montana," he said, "your specialist in Boston doesn't have to fly out there to see you. He can listen to your heartbeat on an electronic stethoscope." The time saved "could be critical to life or death," he said.

An experiment in satellite telemedicine was, in fact, conducted in Canada by the Federal Department of Health and Welfare and the Department of Communication from 1976 to 1977. This experiment linked a public-service hospital at Moose Factory, near Hudson's Bay, with a nursing station in Kashechewan, a Cree Indian community farther to the north. For specialist consultations, it tied in with the University of Western Ontario Hospital in London, Ontario.

A nurse at the northern station expressed her gratification over the system. Before the satellite transmissions, she said, it often took a month for results of a laboratory test at Moose Factory to reach Kashechewan—with telemedicine, the time was cut to minutes.

It would, of course, be possible to extend remote medical diagnosis to individual homes. All that would be needed is to add a small camera and microphone to the home set, as was done in the Hi-Ovis experiment. The dramatic drop in cost of video cameras puts this well within the realm of economic possibility.

Having your doctor make "house calls" might be a boon. But the two-way visual capability could be used by government welfare and correction agencies in ways that "subscribers" would not be happy with. Welfare clients who now receive visits from caseworkers once a month could be "visited" easily and often by welfare investigators who could pan the camera around the room to see if the client had squandered her monthy allotment on "unnecessary" furnishings. A man paroled on a drug charge could be told, "You don't have to bother to come in here every two weeks—just be in front of your set each morning at nine, so that I can take a look at your arm."

Along less threatening lines, television-news operations could conduct the traditional "man-in-the-street" interview as a "man-or-woman-in-the-home" interview, using the home communications set the way radio news operations use the telephone as a "remote" facility.

What you have, of course, when you tie in visual and audio return with a computerized system, is the capability of providing fully switched videotelephone service, not only between the home and a hospital's telemedicine studio but also between individual subscribers to the system. The subscriber can use his key pad in its video telephone mode to call another subscriber by number and talk with her through the modified television set.

The effect of adding the "new" element of image to the "normal" experience of hearing only the voice of someone with whom you are in electronic contact might prove to be quite satisfying. Many people feel that voice-only phone calls can be misleading—being able to watch a person while she is talking might give a better understanding of her meaning and intention, second only to the indications you get in personal conversation with someone who is physically present. We may be entering the era, as Dr. Bird said, of telepresence.

CROSSING LINES WITH AT&T

At this point, the lines between the cable system and the phone system become blurred. The cable system duplicates the phone system to which Picturephone* or similar device has been added. That potential has set the stage for a continuing battle between AT&T and the operators of cable systems.

In the United States, AT&T was slow to see a threat from cable,

---

* Copyrighted trade name of AT&T's video telephone service.

or even its potential as a source of revenue. Bell companies left the field to small-system operators. Head-to-head conflict arose between them only when cable operators sought the right, for a fee, to attach their cables to Bell utility poles (phone company poles pass the homes of most potential subscribers). To settle growing arguments on rates to be charged, the FCC stepped in to regulate pole attachments when a state did not do so.

As the cable systems spread, AT&T long-range planners discussed whether to try to gain control of the distribution system for cable, if not the content that it carried. Some of its companies were already leasing coaxial lines to cable systems. But at about this time the FCC expressed a concern to preserve diversity of ownership in the cable industry. It adopted an order prohibiting cable system ownership by telephone companies within their local exchange areas, by television stations within the same markets, and by national television networks anywhere in the country.

Later the cable industry and AT&T signed a truce: phone companies were prohibited from providing cable entertainment services, except in low-density rural areas. In return, cable companies agreed not to provide local telephone service. Under the agreement, both were free to provide information retrieval, billing, banking, meter reading, burglar and fire alarm serivces.

With cable revenues passing the billion-dollar mark by the end of the decade, few people believed AT&T would be willing to stay out of the business forever.

The company's president, William M. Ellinghaus, told Congress the Bell System had no interest in getting into conventional cable services. But many of the services cable provides could be provided just as well over a telephone network using optical fiber wires. As the systems come together technically, the phrase "staying out of cable" may become meaningless. When I asked a Bell spokesman if the company might want to take on cable functions, he said, "That's an area we're not interested in right now—but that could change, because the technology is changing so fast it is all becoming very mixed and fuzzy."

In Canada, there was no such truce between the phone company and cable operators. Bell Canada and the Canadian Cable Television Association (CCTA) eyed each other suspiciously. The phone company was wary of cable's potential as a communications common carrier. At a CCTA convention in 1978, the president of the company's long-lines system asked the cable operators, "Will you be customers or competitors of the telephone industry?"[2]

The point had arrived where this was a pertinent question. More than 50 percent of all Canadian households with television had subscribed to cable, and Canada was billing itself as the most "wired nation" on earth. The telephone official made it clear Bell Canada intended to control any plant that integrated all telecommunications services:

"The telephone companies are convinced that they must be the owners of any such plant to be made available on a common-carrier basis to entrepreneurs for various purposes. We believe that it is in the public interest that, if we get to the point where there is one broad-band cable distribution, it ought to be owned by the telephone companies. All manner of entrepreneurs would have access to this facility at equitable rates. This is the philosophy of the common-carrier business."

The Canadian Ministry of Communication gave no indication that it was averse to a telephone company monopoly over communication: in a 1976 agreement with the Province of Manitoba, the federal government allowed the Manitoba Telephone System, a public agency, to own all cable-distribution facilities in the province. Cable companies feared the next step beyond control of facilities would be a step into "their" content. Although they would like to supply some common-carrier services, they did not want to give up their interest in video programming. CCTA described cable as a packager of information and a generator of that "information" as well, whether it be news, educational material, or entertainment. The idea of being a common carrier, with others supplying the programming, did not appeal.

THE END OF A HEALTHY SEPARATION

In the background of the infighting over the emerging two-way system is the recurring question: Who will control its content?

When cable television began in the United States in the early 1950s no one saw a problem over content. Cable was known then as Community Antenna Television—CATV. And in fact, it was just that—a big antenna for a lot of people. It began when a television repairman thought of a way to get a better signal to the homes of his customers in a valley in Pennsylvania. The problem was that their line-of-sight to television stations in Philadelphia was blocked by a mountain, which prevented them from getting a clear picture. The repairman put a master antenna on top of the mountain, ran a coaxial cable down to the houses in the valley, and, *Voilà!* Cable television. His system, and others that followed close on its heels, were not involved with content but with transmitting other companies' content. They were common carriers, in the classic definition. Just as the phone company was in the business of carrying other people's phone messages, the cable companies carried other people's television "messages"—programming. But then a cable television entrepreneur installed a video camera in his "head end," turned it on a clock, and sent the picture out on one of his excess channels. And that changed the whole ball game. The entrepreneur became a *programmer,* concerned not only with the technical quality of the video signal being transmitted over the system but the content transmitted by that signal, as well.

Next, cable operators began "importing" programs from distant cities (a move first blocked, then approved, by the FCC). In Europe, importing programs across national borders seemed to be the only reason for cable. French-speaking people in Belgium wanted programs produced in Paris; German-speaking people in Alsace wanted programs produced by Zweite Deutsche Fernsehen in Mainz.

In the United States, some of the larger systems began originating news and entertainment programs. Usually they programmed one channel, supported by advertising. It was, in effect, a local commercial-televison "station," operating alongside the over-the-air stations that the cable system retransmitted to its customers. With this move, the common-carrier concept died, and the FCC began extending its broadcasting rules concerning programming to *cable* programming. The two-way model installed by Warner Amex Cable in Columbus was gounded firmly on the idea that cable companies were programmers as well as operators of the system. The MSO's were no longer interested in being only *common carriers*—there was more money to be had in providing both the technology *and* the content.

This was a decision arrived at in 1979 by Comsat, the country's largest satellite-communication corporation. Comsat announced it intended to send television programming directly from its satellites to rooftop antennas sold by Sears Roebuck for use in private homes. The service would bypass commercial cable systems as well as the television networks, and put Comsat in direct competition with them for audiences. For a subscription fee Comsat offered to provide several channels of movies and other entertainment programming. "We're not interested in being a common carrier anymore," a Comsat official remarked.

But combining content and transmission under one management's jurisdiction worries many people who are concerned about providing diversity of ideas in addition to diversity of managements. Cable and two-way were touted originally as methods of providing many voices for the public—indeed, the voices of the people themselves—that were not available through conventional-television and radio channels. This was based on the idea of having many program suppliers for the system. If the cable operator is allowed to decide the content of a system in which he has in effect a monopoly service, he is likely to decide in favor of offerings that draw large audiences and, therefore, bring in the most money. Which takes us back to the concept that, at least in the United States, doomed radio and television to least-common-denominator sameness: programming for audience size, as indicated by the ratings. In that system, the consumer is the advertiser (or agency) and the product delivered is an audience—either a mass audience or one that has been tailored to fit the advertiser's sales pitch. This may come as a surprise to viewers who think *they* are the consumers in television.

In 1979 the A. C. Nielsen Company announced it was going to begin a rating service for cable systems. As I have pointed out, *two-way* cable has its own "rating" system built into the computer—the operator of the system *knows* which programs attract the largest number of subscribers, and can use this information to "sell" his subscribers to advertisers on the usual cost-per-thousand basis. Since cable-system operators and multiple-system owners are first and foremost businessmen and women, the content of what they transmit to the American public will normally be limited to "safe," middle-of-the-road entertainment and "safe" public-affairs programming that views the profit-oriented free-enterprise system as the basis for all social considerations.

Many system operators, when promising services to gain a local franchise, say they will provide open channels for diverse points of view. Those who run two-way systems contend that diversity is *built into* their public-affairs programming: subscribers can "talk back" to their television sets. Nevertheless, it is the system operator who decides which producers will be admitted as programmers of his channels, and it is the system operator who controls the public-affairs questions subscribers will be asked.

Henry Geller, the first director of the National Telecommunications and Information Administration, the federal agency charged with developing telecommunications policy, proposed that cable systems be restricted by law to operate as common carriers—with program providers getting on the system on a first-come, first-served basis. Cable operators, he said, should be prohibited from making any program decisions; those who control the technology must be divorced from the messages it conveys. The diversity that this would provide, he said, would make it unnecessary for the government to get into decisions about what content ought to be provided and how "fairness" and "balance" should be handled. The FCC long ago involved itself directly in such matters in over-the-air broadcasting, using as justification the fact that broadcasters must compete for outlets in a limited broadcast spectrum, and, therefore, have to be regulated.

"I'm very strong on this issue," Geller remarked. "If we don't separate the owner from the broadcast, we will have to have regulation. When the structure is right and working for you, then you don't need the government's involvement, and that's desirable."[3]

Separation of technology from content is an extremely important consideration, whether the technology is provided by a local cable operator, a multiple system operator, or a major national carrier such as AT&T or the federal government.

Unfortunately the separation of technology from content has not been the rule in the United States, even though a great deal of lip service has been given to the idea.

The Bell System has insisted it is a common carrier interested only in transmitting other people's messages. This was the argument it used when promoting the "Bell Bill," which would have provided that all cable transmission, data transmission, telephone operations, and television signals be guaranteed to the "dominant carrier" (which of course is AT&T) as a government-protected monopoly. Actually, Bell subsidiaries had been involved in content for many years. Many provide time and weather reporting services. The New York Telephone Company has offered its customers traffic reports, sports scores, stock-market summaries, horoscopes, an advice column, entertainment information, jokes, and children's stories. Content was selected, written, and transmitted by the phone company.[4] Many saw this as the camel's nose under the tent, and I will discuss its implications in the next chapter.

Monitoring of content—your phone calls—is legally sanctioned, indeed *required* in some instances, by the federal government. It is the phone company's responsibility to keep obscenity and threatening calls off its phone system. In addition, AT&T has monitored content of phone conversations to keep prostitutes and bookies from using its system.[5] Suppose the phone company became the operator of the two-way cable system, and brought with it as baggage the past practice of its two-way telephone system. What is to prevent it from becoming the policeman of the system, perhaps out of a misguided sense that, *because* it has been given the awesome responsibility for controlling the system, it has to protect the public from what its managers deem to be "improper" content? Might it not want to intervene, perhaps in response to demands from "decency" groups in the community, to prevent R-rated films from being shown on pay-television channels for which it provided the transmission facilities? And would it not be likely to pull the plug if one of its decency monitors found a wife appearing nude before her husband on a long-distance videophone call? Or if a man were asked by his physician to expose for examination an "indecent" portion of his backside that he had bruised in a fall?

The FCC long ago adopted a rule that said it was the responsibility of the broadcast engineer—the *technician* who was operating the technology that puts the content on the air—to keep obscenity from going out. An engineer knows his license may be lifted if he does not carry out this mandate. This, understandably, makes for the most conservative "editing" mentality imaginable among broadcast engineers.

I found this a particular problem in the early 1970s while managing WRVR, a radio station in New York dedicated at that time to freedom of speech and the First Amendment. The station's chief engineer was a conservative Texan who instilled in his engineers a healthy fear of what would happen to them if they allowed a filthy word to cross their control boards. Most stations, for live call-in programs such as ours, had a seven-second tape delay to make it possible to suppress words the engineer thought might get him into trouble. But the WRVR public-affairs staff and I felt that to censor New York street language used in the context of a hotly debated public issue would be to degrade the principle for which the First Amendment stood. We felt that our own on-air people should not indulge in gratuitous profanity, but that in the heat of discussion, callers in our audience should not be prevented from using words arbitrarily proscribed by the FCC. So we decided we should risk punitive action from the federal government and go live, without bleeps, in our audience-interactive programming. We knew that the technicians' fears were legitimate, so far as the letter of the FCC regulation went. So we took them off the hook by having each public-affairs program producer qualify for a third-class engineer's license. This made the producer technically qualified and eligible to operate the board, and to sign off the radio logs as the engineer of record, during our live public-affairs programming.

What we found was that the tone we set for serious discussion of issues also was the tone adopted by callers. They swore now and again, but the sentiments were heartfelt, and in almost all cases, unobjectionable. No obscenity complaints were filed against the station with the FCC.

WBAI, our neighbor station, was not so fortunate. The FCC, in a *reductio ad absurdum,* had listed seven words as indecent and not to be broadcast at any time of day when children were likely to be listening.

In 1973 WBAI broadcast from a comedy album a selection called "Seven Words That You Can Never Say on Television," in which George Carlin kidded the FCC absurdity that words themselves were indecent, despite the context in which they are used. It started off:

"I was thinking one night about the words you couldn't say on the public, ah, airwaves . . . and it came down to seven, but the list is open to amendment and in fact, has been changed. . . . The original seven words were shit, piss, fuck, cunt, cocksucker, motherfucker, and tits. Those are the ones that will curve your spine, grow hair on your hands, and maybe even bring us, God help us, peace without honor."

The segment was broadcast as part of a serious discussion of the use of contemporary language. On the complaint of one listener the FCC reprimanded WBAI for broadcasting the routine, stating the words were "indecent and prohibited by law." It held out the threat that the station's license could be revoked if it repeated the offense.

On July 3, 1978, the U.S. Supreme Court turned down WBAI's appeal from the ruling. In a narrow 5-to-4 ruling it affirmed the FCC's right to bar the words as "indecent." Writing for the majority, Justice John Paul Stevens said:

"We simply hold that when the commission finds a pig has entered the parlor, the exercise of its regulatory power does not depend on proof that the pig is obscene."[6]

Justice William J. Brennan, Jr., angry, dissented. He accused the majority of "a depressing inability to appreciate that in our land of cultural pluralism, there are many who think, act, and talk differently than members of this Court, and who do not share their fragile sensibilities." The decision, Brennan wrote, "could support the suppression of a great deal of political speech, such as the Nixon [Watergate] tapes and . . . could even provide the basis for imposing sanctions for the broadcast of certain portions of the Bible."

Larry Josephson, station manager at the time, put that thought more bluntly: "The political effect of 'Carlin' is to suppress the natural speech of just about every racial, political, and artistic subculture in America, while establishing the [public] linguistic pieties of the straight, white middle class as the only legal mode of communication on the public airwaves. The effect of 'Carlin' on art is equally devastating; the Order makes it almost impossible to broadcast most modern, and much classical, drama, literature, or poetry."

The "Seven Dirty Words" case was one of a number of decisions by the conservative Burger Court, a legacy of the Nixon years, that restricted freedom of speech and the press in the late 1970s. Its rationale for supporting FCC interference in content went beyond the "spectrum scarcity" reasoning by which previous courts had justified government control of the electronic press as opposed to the printed press. It said radio and television could be subjected to special regulation by a government agency because of the media's "uniquely pervasive presence in the lives of Americans." That thinking could justify intrusion of the FCC into content of any of the new technologies.

The system that is developing will be "uniquely pervasive," in spades. Conceivably, the same justification could be used to ban "indecent" language from a town meeting, such as that in Upper Arlington, if it were conducted via an electronic system. Physical force would probably have to be used to keep you from expressing an idea in a meeting at which you appeared in person. A technician who did not like the "indecent" idea you were expressing could do the same thing by the flick of a switch, and perhaps at a later date be applauded by the Supreme Court for doing it.

Let's suppose this FCC ruling, and similar rulings concerning content in broadcasting, were given as a *mandate* to the system's exclusive carrier to administer. The extension is conceivable, since most or all of the former over-the-air broadcasting would now have been transferred to the wired system. A modern communications carrier would almost certainly not assign one of its technicians to monitor the many disparate elements of the system's content: it would assign one of its computers. Computers have been designed to recognize words spoken in a phone call. One of them, attached to the telephone or videophone network, could provide electronic surveillance to pick out not only "dirty" words but also "dangerous" words, "angry" or "menacing" tones of voice, recording any such "disturbing" words or attitudes so that they could be checked out by the authorities. The capacity of computers to do such monitoring adds a new dimension to the continuing controversy over wiretaps. "Spook" devices now exist for switching on a private telephone from a remote location and amplifying the sound it captures sufficiently for pickup of conversations across a room. The same techniques could switch on the camera and microphone in the HCS, making possible video and audio surveillance of the home without revealing this surveillance to the residents. The capability now existing makes George Orwell seem to have been extremely prescient when he described in 1949 the telescreen's constant monitoring of Winston's presence in his own home in the mythical England of thirty-five years later.[7]

In an authoritarian nation, of course, such monitoring would be legal, and the citizen would have no "legitimate" right to object. Intrusions gain legitimacy, even in a democracy, through the placid acceptance of rules, practices, and customs promulgated not only by government but also by commercial "service" companies. In many states the phone company's installers tell customers that they are "not allowed" to make an installation in which the summoning ring can be switched off on all the phones in the house. Is it possible that you might be told that, once you answer the phone, the camera in your videophone set may not be turned off? You may think that is absurd—under no circumstances would you permit an instrument to perpetrate such an invasion of your privacy. Yet how many times in your life have you been resolute enough *not* to answer the ring of the little bell in your phone that insists you pay attention to its message? Accepting government or industry practices because "That's the way we always do it" is probably more effective than laws in eroding our right to privacy.

Videophones may also present another obnoxious possibility.

Computer-activated calls could present on your screen seemingly "live" people who, as the "personal call" progresses, are revealed to be videotaped salespersons giving automated pitches. Such "junk" calls would be much more obtrusive than junk mail, which you don't have to open.

Representative Les Aspin, a Wisconsin Democrat who said his constituents had complained bitterly about such advertising pitches intruding in their lives through automated dialing, urged FCC action to ban junk calls. "You can tell most junk mail by its cover and chuck it if you choose," he said. "But junk calls bring you on the run from the garden, interrupt your concentration while trying to juggle household accounts, or fall smack in the middle of the family dinner hour."[8]

Aspin urged FCC rules or federal law banning these calls.

The way is being broken for in-house surveillance by seemingly benign "advances" in two-way service. In France, England, Australia, and parts of the United States, two-way systems are being used to read electric, gas, and water meters. Where meters are inside, this makes it unnecessary for a utility employee to enter the house to read the meter, and that is a gain for privacy. But once such sensing devices are installed (the two-way device that senses the motion of a "burglar" in your house is a case in point), the background system has been laid for unauthorized monitoring by government or private investigators.

Without local ordinances or state or federal laws providing effective controls over devices permitted to be installed in homes, coupled with significant penalties for violations, you can have little assurance concerning the microprocessor that the cable system (which could be a government-operated system) has installed in the black box attached to your set. It could be programmed for legitimate two-way communication, or it could be programmed for illegitimate monitoring of your person—voice, image, and motion.

3 | IN VIDEOTEX, THE BRITISH CAME FIRST

In London, John Bull 3d squirms in his chair because of a gnawing fear that Showcase Motors, a highly speculative stock he purchased yesterday, may have plummeted today because the oil skeikdoms have voted once again to double the price of their shakedown product. Bull twists around to his desktop Prestel terminal and taps in the index number for listings of stocks that start with an S. Showcase Motors is down sixteen points; Bull turns off the terminal and, angry, calls his broker to give him what for.

In Birmingham, Jack McKnife, an accomplished dip, sits in his parlor counting out the pounds he finds in a wallet he had just lifted from a businessman on a downtown street. Smiling happily, he turns to the Prestel adapter on his television set and punches up on the screen the "page" on which the Save the Children Fund urges subscribers to "Press a Key to Give 10 P." McKnife presses the key. The computer places a debit of 10 pence on his next phone bill and credits the amount to the Save the Children Fund account.

In Manchester, Gloria Tweet, twenty-one and chewing gum, looks at W. H. Smith Company's listing of records on her new, rented color television set, which has the Prestel adapter built into it. She decides she has to have "Love Me or Kill Me," the latest single by the Yellow Scourge. She punches a key that calls up the Barclaycard page on her set. This invites her to key in her credit-card number, the purchase number of the record, and the purchase price. Immediately, her name and address, pulled out of the Prestel computer, appear on the screen so that she can confirm that this is the address to which she wants the record sent. She pushes a verification button, and the charge is added automatically to her next Barclaycard billing.

In Edinburgh, Barbara MacKenzie is "playing" the Prestel keyboard to find some fun things in the data base. She hits on a cottage-industry poet who offers limericks for 5 pence apiece. On "page" 1906 she finds one that became an instant winner as soon as the Prestel system became generally available to the public:

> *An enormously fat city gent,*
> *Whose excesses no-one could prevent,*
> *Had a torrid affair*
> *With he Swedish au pair,*
> *But, by God, she was never content.*

The characters are fictional, but the services they selected are not. In 1979 the British Post Office became the first organization to begin commercial operation of a two-way, interactive text-on-television service that is spreading around the world. The British system, trade-named Prestel, provided users in businesses and the home with news, useful information, and consumer and business services from banks, stores, universities, computer bureaus, travel agencies, airlines, research firms, wire services, and other organizations. It offered the capability for on-line computing and calculating in the office or the home, and for those who had sets with an electric typewriter attached, the direct exchange of messages between home and business television terminals.

The original basic set displayed the information, in text including letters and numbers, on the screen of a regular color television set that had a small adapter plus a twelve-button keyboard. Graphics, such as a weather map, were displayed in seven colors.

While the Qube two-way concept was an outgrowth of commercial-television ideas, Prestel was a communication technology without a conventional-television overlay. The technical basis of the two is the same: tying the home television set with a computer. Qube used two-way cable to do this; Prestel used the two-way lines of the telephone system.

The sociological conceptions of the two were quite different, however. At Qube, the original idea was to put subscribers (thought of by the cable operators as *viewers*) in touch with people appearing on channels of the cable system. The mind-set promoted by Qube was that you, as an individual, were reacting to your television set, usually in response to performers, advertisers, public-affairs moderators, or public officials in the studio. You the viewer were encouraged to put in "information"—whether that information was a comment on a public issue or your decision to purchase a record you had heard a singer perform. The computer was there, somewhere in the background, facilitating this *exchange* of information. In Prestel, consumers (thought of an information-retrievers) were made to feel they were dealing directly with the computer and its data base without the mediation of "hosts" talking to them from the screens of their set. The information the customer was asked to supply (following instructions in a published directory or given in text form as electronic index pages on the television screen) was, by implication, only incidental to the process of accessing information and services *from* the data bank. So the feel of Prestel was less humanly "interactive" than the feel of Qube. Both had the capability of offering nonbroadcast services, such as fire and burglar alarms, medical-emergency call buttons, and automatic meter readings.

From the start it was recognized as only a matter of time before the two concepts would be welded into a single system combining interaction of subscribers at home with people presenting television programming *and* interaction of those same subscribers with a data base programmed to give them textual information and services via the television screen.

The Prestel system was developed by the British Post Office in 1970 under the name of Viewdata. This served also as the generic name for text displayed on a videoscreen until, by international consensus, the name "videotex" was adopted for this technology.

(The generic name "teletext" is used for a more limited, broadcast version of this technique, which I will describe later. However, the terms are not used with precision, and you sometimes hear videotex called two-way teletext. Especially in the United States, "viewdata" is still used as the generic.)

The idea was to make available a computer data base in which much of the information that people needed in their daily social, economic, political, and cultural lives could be stored and easily accessed from anywhere in the United Kingdom.

The system came about from a quite pragmatic search on the part of the BPO, which runs the telephone system, for ways to increase telephone usage. If people at home could be induced to use their phones to connect themselves with a universeal data base, the BPO reasoned, the payment for the "call" would obviously add to revenues. It was hoped the system would increase usage during the evening hours, when telephone traffic normally drops off. The method devised for achieving both the idealistic and commercial goals was to adapt a standard color set by adding circuits that enabled it to be plugged in automatically to the telephone lines. The adapted set, when activated by a key pad (or, in a business office, by an alphanumeric keyboard similar to a typewriter), would automatically call up the data base.

When you press a button on the Prestel key pad, the adapted set switches from the standard television program you have been watching to an electronic circuit connected to the computer. You then get on your screen the information or services you want by one of two methods:

1. Touching-in the index numbers of specific topics or of specific "Information Providers," such as the London Stock Exchange, listed alphabetically in a published directory similar to the phone book, or

2. Searching electronically through the data base for information that you want.

The Prestel system uses "tree" logic for this search, starting from a broad category that is the trunk and leading through narrower and narrower branches to the twig of information you are looking for. If, for example, you want to know what is playing at your local movie theater, you press a button that displays an alphabetical list of available topics. In this list you find "Entertainment," and press in its code number. This leads to "Media: Cinema, Theatre, Recorded Music." You press "Cinema" and find two categories: "Film reviews" and "What's on?" You press the button for "What's On?" and find displayed on your screen a listing of movie theaters in your area and what is playing at each.

A step beyond this would let you see a diagram of seats available in each house, and, through an interactive ordering page, permit you to pick the seats you want, reserve them, and pay for them by punching in the number of your credit card. Professional computer users prefer more sophisticated logics that permit faster searches of more complex data banks. But developers of Prestel knew that, for residential subscribers, the method of searching out the information had to be extremely simple—-a method they could learn in a few minutes' time. I was able to learn to use Prestel's tree-logic system in five minutes.

(For those who have difficulty even with operating a simple key pad, touch-sensitive videotubes have been devised: read the index number or word you want on the tube, touch it, and the information frame you have indicated appears on the screen. In time, most video-tex systems might offer this mode as an option.)

So that someone in your household (or an intruder) cannot run up a bill for which you do not want to be responsible, you may also enter into the system your own personal password. The Prestel com-puter verifies this each time the key pad initiates a transaction that would entail billing the household according to the identification number built into the set. Prestel planners had in mind the possibility that later models might use a voiceprint for identifying the set user—the purchaser would speak into a microphone built into the set, and his or her unique "print" would be checked against a recorded "print" already stored in the computer. They told me, in fact, that the home terminal would in time most likely be activated by simple voice commands, using words the computer could recognize, to request services or information.*

At the beginning, charges for the services appeared in two bills—one was the monthly phone bill reflecting the cost of "local calls" to the computer; these averaged 3 pence, depending on the time of day. The second was a quarterly statement from Prestel that billed you for the costs of the pages, other than advertising and in-dexes, that had an information fee assigned. (A subscriber was shown in advance on the screen what the cost of the next page of in-formation would be.)

Information providers (IP's) presented information for page fees ranging from a U.S. penny to a dollar. Advertising pages were pre-sented wihout charge.

Other methods of billing were considered as the system devel-oped. Some analysts thought users might be more willing to pay for a

---

* Several Japanese manufacturers are marketing television sets that turn themselves on or off and change channels by voice command. Japanese and American firms have marketed "vocal" electronic translators—pocket calculator-size instruments that pro-nounce the words they translate. Many electronic games, including chess, can "talk back" to their human opponents. A "speaking" microwave oven has been marketed to confirm aloud the instructions the cook punches into its microprocessor, and another has been designed to talk the cook through successive steps of a recipe entered into its memory.

package of information services on a monthly basis than they would be to pay for each item of information that they accessed.

At first, the BPO planned to provide much of the information in the data bank itself, or take the information supplied by commercial sources, edit it into a form usable on the system, and enter it into the Prestel computer. But potential commercial IP's—especially newspaper and magazine publishers—balked at the idea of letting the BPO become the editors of their material. And social critics objected to giving the BPO the power to be gatekeeper, determining what information would be good for the public to have and what would not.

So the BPO backed off and decided Prestel would act strictly as a common carrier in presenting the material. Any information provider who could pay the fee to get into the data base would be permitted to do so. The BPO would exercise no control over the content of the material presented and each IP would be held directly responsible for its accuracy and reliability. The IP's, not the BPO, would be accountable in the courts for any violations of libel or other laws governing publication.

IP's flocked in to try out the new technology. They included publications such as *The Financial Times, The Birmingham Post & Mail, The Economist, The New York Times,* and news agencies such as Reuters, Associated Press, and Dow Jones. They included companies such as the Thomas Cook & Son travel service, Great Universal Stores, Currys, and W. H. Smith, which offered catalogue sales. The Government Meteorological Service presented weather forecasts; the Department of Prices and Consumer Protection gave tips on best buys, and nationalized companies such as British Airways and British Rail offered schedules and travel information. By opening Prestel to all suppliers, the BPO began with the idea that the system would thus offer a wide diversity of information and services: where a gap existed, another IP would come along to fill it.

The initial capacity of the Prestel computer was 250,000 "pages" of information. Each page contained a maximum of 150 words— about the equivalent of two paragraphs in a newspaper. Although Prestel had been promoted by the BPO as an "encyclopedic" medium, IP's soon learned that, because of the wordage limitations, it was not well adapted to detailed articles of information. This disadvantage was expected to correct itself as enhanced print definition made smaller letters legible, permitting many more to be printed on the "page." Some models will also have larger screens.

What the initial limitation did was force people writing for the new medium to condense their ideas into carefully and tightly written items. At the start, this pushed Prestel toward a headline service for news and information, and to directory-style entries (for example, the timetables of trains to Liverpool). The initial stumbling block did not daunt videotex dreamers who saw the system as the coming medium for publishing literature and long works of nonfiction. They were sure that advances in technology would make it possible to fill a screen with sharp, readable text that carried as many words as a page in a standard trade book. They also believed a high-speed facsimile (or teleprinter) printout of whole books would eventually be economical. Technically, this is already feasible. (In a demonstration a prototype machine was able to print out *Gone With the Wind* in two and a half minutes.) The technical capability led system planners to think about a time when published texts—books, journals, and the like—would not reach the public via printing on a press, physical transport to distributors, and, finally, sales through bookstores. This traditional route has become costly and cumbersome. In the new scheme, books would not be printed on a press at all, but would enter the home via the direct expedient of the home communications set. Manuscripts, formatted by computer into electronic pages that when printed out would look like pages of a traditional book, would be entered digitally (that is, broken down into a coded stream of electronic bits) into a computer. The "book" would be stored in the computer's memory until it was called up by someone who wanted to purchase it at home. The facsimile printer on the purchaser's HCS would then print it out and the system would bill him on his quarterly statement. Or the subscriber might "borrow" the book, perhaps in a form restricted to page-by-page reading on the screen. (Authors could be compensated each time their books were borrowed—a practice already common in Swedish libraries.) The borrowing possibility led enthusiasts of two-way systems to envision central libraries—perhaps only one in a state or province in North America or a whole country in Europe—where all computerized books would be stored, ending the need for multiple "hard" copies in a series of local libraries. Books stored digitally in computers would never be "out" of the library when you came to borrow them. And older books would not have to be discarded to make room for new ones on the shelves.

Library reference material might be handled in the same way. If you are a corporate or academic researcher who is delving into the new technologies of communication, it is likely that you accessed *this* book through a computer search of the literature which gave you title and publication information and a summary of the book's contents. In time, you could expect to access the full content, or selected pages, via the system. Pages you wanted to keep could be printed out in facsimile, much the way you now photocopy pages from a book or microfilm at the library.

Roadblocks to development of such a system are more psychological than technical. People like to go to their local libraries, where, rather than the faces of their television sets, they see the faces of other people. They like to browse through the stacks, leaf through the books to see if they want to read them, feel the covers in their hands. ("Will this HCS have a *bindery* attached, I'd like to know? Or am I going to have to put the pages it prints out into a looseleaf binder?") Many people would prefer to read print from paper, rather than from a electronic reading device. That objection is lessened somewhat by the fact that people now accept microfilm readers in libraries and by the point that a hard copy—on untreated paper—could be made available through the facsimile-printer attachment. However, some people do not like to deal with electronic machinery even as simple as a stereo player:

"It's *different* from leafing through a hardbound book—I don't *want* to press a button to see the next page."

"Perhaps," replies the videotex planner, "but it was also different to page through a printed book held in your hands than it was to unroll a parchment scroll spread out on a table. You'll get used to it."

"I'll never get used to it."

The accommodation might be, as in many compromises in a pluralistic world, some of both: books, honest-to-god books, just like the ones we've had since Gutenberg, for high-resolution art reproduction, fine printing and artisan bindings; electronic reproduction, and facsimile printout for mass-market books and research materials. Obviously the transfer of the huge book market to electronic reproduction is not going to come until videotex offers a clear economic advantage to publishers. But, with the high cost of printing and distribution faced by publishers, this day might come faster than bibliophiles would wish. As the transition becomes general ("Not in my lifetime, I hope"), they may find old-fashioned, book-stack libraries and the secondhand bookstores their last refuge. They may feel themselves left behind in the transition from hardcover to softcover to software. And they might feel a sneaking suspicion that those who had control of the electronic libraries were deliberately "losing" from the memory banks books they did not want the public to have. Books have been burned before, but it was hard for the burners to be sure they got all the copies; it would be a lot easier if all the "copies" were in computers in a few central libraries.

A question to be answered in designing commercial operations of videotex was whether it would be looked on as a data base in which subscribers knew in advance what kind of information they would find there or whether the users would want to browse through pages to find something interesting—and whether the subscriber would be willing to pay for the pleasure of such browsing.

Browsing may develop a videotex art, but first users of Prestel preferred to pick and choose from a "menu."

According to one of its larger IP's, Mills & Allen Communications Ltd., videotex is a new mass medium, with many differences. "It has the potential of being the first mass medium to be individually tailored," Mills & Allen managing director Richard Hooper commented after the first few months of Prestel's operation.[1]

"The viewer calls up the pages he or she wants to see when he or she want to see them. . . . Unlike mass print publications, the Prestel viewer does not have to buy the whole package [book, magazine, newspaper] in order to get the single piece of information being sought [cinema times]." The system is individualized in a psychological sense as well, Hooper said—when the viewer calls up Prestel by using the button on the key pad, the computer greets him on the screen by name.

IP's looked at Prestel as a medium over which they had a great deal of control, despite the ability of viewers to select what they wanted to read. To most IP's, this was a publishing or promotional or advertising medium—not the traditional computer information-retrieval system. After all, it was the IP's who were providing the menu. And it was a menu that could be constantly changed to present new bits of intelligence the IP thought the viewer might want to buy.

The ability of the system to update material continually was a great advantage to companies such as news services, which could profit from presenting timely information, as well as to government services, such as the Weather Bureau, which had a responsibility to supply current information to the populace. (The implications of the videotex system for the development of the electronic newspaper will be discussed in the next chapter.) And consider the possibilities for stores that carry on a mail-order business:

In England, Currys, a chain of 480 shops that sell large appliances such as television sets and refrigerators, jumped in with "mail order" pages that described their products in detail. Its "action page" permitted subscribers to press their key pads to indicate which appliances they wanted to purchase and designate the method of payment. The pages could thus replace or supplement the typical mail-order catalogue. When an appliance model changed, Currys did not have to print up a whole new catalogue; it could merely update in the computer the model information on each item as it changed. It could enter any new appliance that came on the market in the same way. The potential of such a system for Sears Roebuck in the United States is obvious.

The Prestel system could also be used for polling citizens on product preferences, as the Qube developers did in Columbus. In Prestel, too, the computer acts as its own "Nielsen" service, telling IP's exactly how many people are calling up their pages. This led many IP's to be guided by the "ratings"—dropping unpopular pages and adding those which they hoped would attract buyers.

In a mail-order catalogue, there is no question in a customer's mind that the information she is reading is a form of advertising. Such was not the case in early applications of advertising to videotex. Although the IP's were not particularly concerned with the problem, it soon became clear that information and advertising, which were considered to be—and *appeared* on the page to be—separate entities in a newspaper, became blurred when presented as pages on an electronic screen. When the Prestel service began commercial operation there was no requirement for an IP to identify advertising as such. So IP's did not do so, even though such identification had become accepted practice in newspapers.

Perhaps the reason is that the concept of advertising on videotex is different from the concept of advertising (at least, in display ads) in newspapers and magazines, and in commercials on television. There the concept is "push" advertising. The advertiser "pushes" information at a large number of readers or viewers, in the hope that some will be attracted to the specific message and buy the product. In videotex, the basic form is "pull" advertising. In this concept, similar to that of classified ads in newspapers, the subscriber is expected to be *looking for* specific information concerning a sale item or service. She or he, then, searches through an indexed listing (the Yellow Pages of the phone book is another example) for the specific data required. For this reason, the "pull" ad must supply narrower and more specific data (often, as in the *Sears Catalogue,* minutely detailed data) in the hope of leading to a sale, rather than sell generically by the persuasive text and seductive pictures of "push" advertising.

In time publishers on videotex who sell information itself, rather than products or services, may become concerned that the credibility of their editorial content might be debased by advertisers who present sales information that may lie or not tell the whole story about the product or service being promoted—especially if the suspect material is being presented to look the same as editorial matter that is not "sponsored."

The British Post Office, having been burned in its original desire to control content on Prestel, deliberately shied away from setting standards for what was being transmitted over its "common carrier" system, saying these were the province of the IP's themselves. The IP's, aware that government regulation of their advertising and promotional conduct was inevitable, got together to draw up their own code of conduct, to forestall more stringent government restrictions. But such industry codes inevitably raise the question: How will they be enforced? The Code of the National Association of Broadcasters in the United States, also adopted to ward off government interference, is voluntary. As such, it is violated at will when commercial radio and television broadcasting companies find it in their interest to do so.

Conceptual problems such as this were inevitable in the new medium. Prestel, a two-way system that asked and collected much the same personal data from subscribers as was being asked by Qube, presented the same threats to privacy posed by two-way cable television. As it advanced into electronic funds transfer, it risked other dangers related to fraudulent manipulation of computerized accounts. The developers were aware of these and similar difficulties, but in the test stages, the problems did not surface. On the theory, "My cabin doesn't leak when it doesn't rain," the BPO was not likely to stop things until specific problems appeared. I was told this by one developer of the system who expressed some social concern about what was happening.

"Prestel is very much 'All systems go,' " he said. "And a lot of things got swept under the rug to achieve that objective." As a result, the BPO plunged ahead into commercial operation despite the danger that the technology would, as usual, outrun the public's preparedness to cope with the societal problems it raised.

Alex Reid, first director of Prestel, was understandably pleased with the inauguration of the system: "We believe that Prestel can become, like the telephone, a universal means of communication, used by all manner of people in all manner of places for all manner of purposes." The Post Office, he said, had adopted a "tidal wave" approach to marketing, stressing its "unusual application in the home and office, in factories, in schools, in libraries, shops, government offices, and public places."

Prestel sets were installed in public places from the start—the lobby of the Piccadilly Hotel, the British Tourist Authority Office, and the post office in Trafalgar Square. By putting in 10 pence, walk-up patrons could find out the chances of sun in the Lake District (10 percent) or the availability of a popular play in the West End.

But although the BPO at first planned to make residential installations a first priority in its marketing plan, it became evident that the initial high costs of terminals would limit home rentals (originally $30 a month) until Prestel became a mass-market operation. So the marketing stress was shifted to business uses. Company managers were used to budgeting funds for acquiring information and services helpful to their operations. The initial cost of a Prestel business terminal (about $3000 in 1980) and the system charges for information were not out of line for funds large concerns allocated for such services.

For business and professional customers, Prestel offered to set up "closed user" groups. Specialized information for these groups could be presented for their exclusive use, much as confidential business newsletters, for a fee, supply information to corporate subscribers. The system permits direct addressing of these information pages to those who pay a premium for it; they have access to material from the bank that is electronically closed off to "regular" subscribers. Prestel is also capable of putting together "closed" groups of terminals for companies that want to exchange information internally, say among branches in different cities.

An ad hoc "closed user" group could be set up in which university researchers concerned with juvenile crime, for example, might exchange ideas, in print, with city law-enforcement officials who have to deal daily with young offenders. Information specialists have known this as "computer conferencing." Groups of scientists connected by remote terminals have used computer conferencing for years to exchange and store ideas about a particular problem.

Home users might sign up for a continuing closed-user-group debate on the reduction of NATO forces in Europe in the face of the Soviet presence there. Individuals could pick up the debate at any point, review opinions already in the computer, and then contribute their ideas. At some point a consensus might be struck, and the gist of it sent on the system as a Prestel message to the foreign secretary.

It is only a step beyond group "conversations" in print to providing a completely switched service between individual subscribers, in business or at home, who have sets with electric-typewriter keyboards. When this adaptation is used, the Prestel system becomes a message-exchange service—in effect, electronic mail. Messages can be exchanged between two "addressees" in real time—or, if an addressee does not "answer" a call in real time, a message can be stored by a sender in the computer, for call-up by the addressee when she returns home. A message light on the home set informs the addressee that a communication is waiting for her. Simple keying on the typewriter "punches up" the message on the screen. Those who wish to pay an additional fee to rent or purchase a printer attachment can push another button and have a hard copy of the message that is then appearing on the screen.

A simpler form of this message service is made available to subscribers who have only the numerical, push-button key pad. "Action" pages containing standard messages can be accessed, and a message picked from the "menu" and entered into the computer for retransmittal to a specific addressee. For example, one message says: "I will arrive at _____ p.m."

By using the number buttons on the key pad, the sender can fill in 3:15 and press the button that sends the completed message on its way. At the other end, the message light can tell the addressee to press the button that will call up the message waiting in the computer for him.

As did the managers of the Qube system, long-range planners of Prestel thought the system would be adapted eventually to provide electronic funds transfer. Citibank in New York and other major banks have electronic banking systems in which a customer walks up to an electronic "teller," punches his or her identification number into a simply operated computer terminal, and then directs the bank to shift funds, say, from his savings account to his checking account. A bank wired into the Prestel system could carry this idea a step further—offering a paperless checking service. With this, a customer at home could pay a bill by transferring a specific amount from his checking account directly into an account of Harrods department store, which is also wired into the system.

The BPO took a go-slow attitude about EFT on Prestel. Ray V. Watkins, a post office administrator concerned with new technologies, pointed out that mistakes—often large ones—were made daily in computer transfer between banks and within banks. Adding customer-billing procedures to the computer mix, he said, might well add to the mistakes.

"I think it will begin to be acceptable when the standard of living is such that a mistake wouldn't matter—when 25 pounds is of so little concern that it isn't worth going through the bank statement to see that it is all right. But you have to remember that, in the U.K., fifty percent of the people don't even have bank accounts."

As to the overall acceptance of Prestel, Watkins feels it will happen, but the question is: How fast? It might suddenly take off, he said. "TV is a technical gimmick people like," he said. "It would give people a positive feeling to add Prestel to their TV sets: 'After all, Bill next door has it, doesn't he?' "

How the Prestel system will develop is a strategic concern of the BPO Long-Range Planning Group in Cambridge. I found that gaining admission to its offices, in a low, modern apartment building on Hills Road between the railroad station and the university campus, was something of a security matter. No sign, just a number, was on the door, which could be opened from the outside only by pressing a combination number onto a key pad attached to the doorframe. A secretary let me in after I had identified myself on the intercom. I talked with John Short, a long-range planner in his thirties, who saw Prestel as a "people's information carrier."

Down the road, he told me, Prestel is very much interested in alarm systems—fire and burglary and emergency. The system could also be used for automated office procedures, including computer record-keeping, invoicing, text-editing of letters, and the like. ("There's where the BPO conflicts with IBM," he said.) With a full typewriter keyboard, the terminal can be made compatible with the telex system of teleprinter-to-teleprinter message transmission, commonly used by businesses in Europe and, less commonly, in the United States. Videotex terminals could be installed in schools so that students could have access to a programmed course—a foreign language, for example—and study it at their own speed. All the ideas of "computer-assisted learning," so popular with educators in the 1960s but which never got off the ground, could have a rebirth with the arrival of videotex.

Short himself had developed an idea for Prestel's future that he offered with enthusiasm, but with some trepidation. Why not let the computer do your newspaper and library "browsing" for you? Each day, the computer searches its memory for items that would interest you. When it finds an item in which you have previously showed an interest—a stock price reaching a particular level, for example—it rings you up and plays out the information. You could, for instance, let the computer know you wanted to be made aware of every new development fed into it on Pre-Columbian archaeology (you might also throw in a request for the day's other headlines), and that you would be relaxed and ready to receive that information at eight o'clock each night. Convenient. You don't have to be home for the early-evening BBC television news, and BBC radio doesn't have to repeat the items over and over again in the hope that you will be out there and catch something you want to know some time during the day.

Or suppose you let the computer take you a step further in abstraction, and ask it to supply you with items and opinions of either a conservative or liberal nature with which to caress your prejudices. That might save you time in browsing through the political journals whose editors, you know from experience, are likely to have selected contents that would interest a person of your predilections.

But here is where the trepidation comes in. Although you have entered your instructions into the computer, it is not the computer that is doing your idea-shopping for you, purely and objectively. It is another human being, making subjective judgments and loading the machine with items that, when you access them later, will appear to meet the criteria you have laid down.

Such a system, Short pointed out, could make more efficient use of the time you have to spare to keep up-to-date on your areas of interest. In an information explosion, no one can keep up with all developments in his or her field. People are going to *ask* for good editing-selection of relevant material from the mass. To the extent that the system succeeded in tuning in to the user's values, he said, it could also become a powerful mechanism for value reinforcement: "Arguably, too powerful." He expressed this concern in a report he made to the BPO management:

"In 1892 *The Electrician* wrote with distaste of the 'modern utopian' for whom life was to consist of sitting in armchairs and pressing a button and who would have 'no ambition, no desires, no individuality, and nothing wise about him.' In the scenario presented here the modern utopian could retain more individuality than he now has. In one way this is an exciting prospect, but as the initiative passes to the machine which shapes the path of the transactions, defines his interests, and meets them, the question one might ask is: Whose individuality is retained?"[2]

Whatever Prestel might come to be, its existing form was ready for export as the 1970s ended. The BPO began marketing Prestel technology and software abroad.

CEEFAX DOES IT OVER THE AIR

Although Prestel drew most of the international attention, another, simpler text-information system—called Ceefax for "see facts"—had beaten it to general availability on television sets in the U.K.

Ceefax evolved from a discovery in 1972 by engineers of the British Broadcasting Corporation that two "spare" lines at the top of the normal television picture* could be used to store digital information that, when converted to a stream of visual dots, would produce a text display on the television screen. In fact, enough "information" could be transmitted over the air in a quarter of a second to fill a screen with twenty-four lines of forty characters each. Thus, a hundred such "pages" could be sent to a home-television receiver, one at a time, in twenty-five seconds. The BBC engineers developed a "frame-grabbing" technique so that viewers could catch a specific page of information as it rotates through their sets.

In this system, which has come to be known as over-the-air videotex,† you don't pick out a page at random from the data bank, as you do in Prestel, which gives you a direct phone connection to the computer. Instead, you must wait until the page you have selected

---

* In Western Europe, the standard television picture has 625 lines. The North American standard is 525 lines. The two "spare" lines at the top are technically referred to as *vertical blanking lines.*

† The older form, "teletext," is also used.

from the index is broadcast in the rotational cycle so that the Ceefax decoder on your set can "grab" it and display it on the screen. The page stays there until you press a button on the key pad to switch to another page or back to a television program. Since the BBC is sending the regular television picture and the text pages on the same channel at the same time, you can see either the picture or the text, depending on which button you push.

The Ceefax index uses a tree logic, similar to Prestel's, to let you find the facts you want. The difference is that the number of pages in an *over-the-air* videotex system is limited by the length of time a user would be willing to wait for the selected page to come by. BBC designers decided that twenty-five seconds—or an average wait of about twelve seconds—was about the limit of the user's patience. This meant that about two hundred pages could be transmitted, a hundred each on BBC 1 and BBC 2.

Since the information BBC normally broadcasts is news, it was decided that Ceefax would specialize in news and useful data such as weather and traffic conditions. The only IP's would be BBC journalists. All of the information would be aimed at everyone, everywhere in the country, just as it was on BBC national television and radio news broadcasts, and not at specialized information-seekers served by the diversified IP's feeding the Prestel system.

Beginning in 1974 Ceefax was provided to BBC viewers as a free add-on covered by the regular color-televison licensing fee. All that was needed was a teletext adapter on the set, which viewers could buy in an appliance store for less than $200. British viewers, however, usually rent their sets, and a set with a Ceefax decoder attached rented in 1980 for about $48 a month. With mass production, these costs, too, were expected to drop.

The Independent Broadcasting Authority (IBA), which supervises commercial broadcasting in Britain, developed a system called Oracle along the line of Ceefax. In content, the IBA took the same general approach as the public BBC. But rather than provide the service free, IBA planned to make a profit through the inclusion of advertising. So a page on Oracle might begin, "Guinness Stout Presents the Rugby Scores."

THE TECHNIQUE SPREADS TO
OTHER COUNTRIES

From these beginnings in Britain, people in telecommunications were not sure what forms of videotex would eventually emerge as commercially and sociologically successful, but they were certain that the medium had a future. By 1980 experiments and pilot projects were under way in Australia, Canada, Finland, France, the German Federal Republic, Hong Kong, Japan, Sweden, Switzerland, and the United States. Many other countries, including some in the Eastern bloc, were planning videotex ventures.

France, as part of its determination to become a technological leader in the new communications, made its telephone-based videotex and broadcast-based videotex mutually compatible. The government promoted the system under the umbrella name Antiope.*

Development of the broadcast-based part was put in the hands of Télédiffusion de France (TDF), the powerful government television monopoly. Phone-based videotex was to be developed by the Ministère des Postes et Télécommunications (the PTT),† which is granted a monopoly over all telecommunications except broadcasting. From the start, it was expected that information would be interchangeable from one mode to the other.

Bernard Marti, one of the theoreticians of the system, gave this example of how this could be done: "The Paris Stock Exchange is open daily from twelve-thirty p.m. to four p.m. While it is open, information on prices, issues, etc., varies quickly, and is of considerable interest to all subscribers simultaneously. It is worth *broadcasting* this information on a short cycle time [currently, a six-second mean waiting time]. Outside opening times, the information is not of interest to everyone at the same time and so is available *via the telephone network* by means of interactive retrieval."[3]

The point of this is that if everyone used the phone connections

---

* The acronym seemed certain to be used more often than the name made up (obviously after the fact) as its base: *Acquisition Numérique et Télévisualisation d'Images Organisées en Pages d'Ecriture*. Antiope does have rather a nice sound, which would be enough for the French, and it provides the added attraction of conjuring up the Queen of the Amazons of Greek mythology.

† In Western Europe, the short form for referring to the government-run telecommunications monopolies is "PTT." It originally stood for "Post, Telephone, and Telegraph."

to call up stock quotations (or, say, to check out a storm warning), the phone connections might become jammed. Everyone, however, could access the "frame-grabbing" broadcast mode at once, with no strain on the system.

France tested out some other capabilities not emphasized in the British trial. One was the incorporation of the Arabic and Cyrillic alphabets in the character generator. Because French manufacturers were developing low-cost facsimile equipment for the general public, Antiope developers planned facsimile as an add-on service of the videotex receiver. This version could not only give hard copies of what was appearing on the screen, but could also receive electronic mail to be reproduced directly by the copier.

The TDF began testing potential services on its Antiope equivalent of Ceefax in 1977, and these included, besides stock market quotations, weather information produced by the meteorological office, and a "magazine" of public information provided by Antenne 2 of the national television network.

The PTT began testing Télétel, the Antiope equivalent of Prestel, in 1980, installing three thousand decoders in residences in Vélizy-Villacoublay, a Paris suburb near Versailles.

One social commentator saw Antiope's two-way communication not only as a technical innovation but as a social breakthrough, as well. "In the past, communications in France have been considered something as dangerous as poison, and so only the state should be allowed to use them," remarked Alain Giraud, who is in charge of communications research for the PTT.

Through the 1960s, France had a poor telephone and telecommunications network: there were only 3 million telephones in a country of 50 million people, ranking it twentieth in the world in phones per inhabitant. The lag, Giraud said, represented a deliberate policy: "It was the French government's idea that communication between people is not good; only one-way communication, from the government to the people, is good. National, state, and local officials agreed that the French people did not need the telephone."

Meanwhile, radio and television, which were one-way and government controlled, were heavily encouraged. Government leaders had looked on the state broadcasting system as a tool to keep themselves in power. They systematically restricted their political opponents' access to the airwaves. General Charles de Gaulle epitomized this attitude when he said of the government broadcasting monopoly during a national election campaign: "They have the press. I have the [TDF] and I intend to keep it."

This attitude, and the public's fear of excessive government control, was one of the issues of the student uprising in 1968. ("A significant date for us," said Giraud.) The people, no longer willing to accept the communications monopoly without question, raised a debate that is likely to continue into the future. It focused at first on the prospects of establishing local cable-television systems as privately run concerns. People in government television opposed the idea of local programming. The Chamber of Deputies killed all local cable projects, reasserting the government monopoly. But that did not end the debate.

Meanwhile, public demand for telephones and telecommunications was growing. Some within the PTT saw this demand, encouraged by equipment manufacturers, as a potential threat to *their* monopoly. But the government realized, finally, that poor telecommunications facilities and service were hurting the potential for increased revenues for the PTT and increased profits for companies which would make the hardware for the new media. The government increased its investment in new technologies to the point where the budget for communications became larger than that for national defense.

In 1978 the Nora-Minc report, the influential French study I mentioned in the first chapter, injected interesting questions into the debate over the changes being brought about by computerized communications. It said that the computerization of society seemed inevitable, and that the state's part in it would be enormous. The authors, whose thinking seemed to be in accord with that of telecommunications leaders in France, recommended that all computerized telecommunications services be placed under a central communications agency that would include the PTT *and* TDF. At the same time, reflecting the contradictions being felt concerning centralization, they said it was also the duty of the state to take full advantage of teleprocessing to bring about a decentralization of decision-making, to maintain a two-way flow of information, and to use the computer revolution to delegate power increasingly to local agencies and "even the individual citizen."

Obviously, one of the computerized technologies that could help bring this about was videotex. Despite government officials' predilection for keeping central control, here was a device that had to be developed if France were to remain technologically competitive with its European neighbors. But, some in government asked, what will be the implications for French society of government entry into computerized communications? To assess these, the PTT moved finally to establish a social research group, headed by Giraud.

(I was struck by the afterthought nature of this move when I found that to get to Giraud's office, I had to walk up steps to an add-on structure on the roof of the PTT's modern-looking telecommunications study center in Issy-les-Moulineaux, just outside the southwestern boundary of Paris.)

When I saw him, Giraud was engaged in setting up a sociological observation of the people affected by the Vélizy experiment—to see whether the local people, the press, and stores would like the service, and what they expected from it.

"It's a substitution problem," he said. "All the information is already being provided by others—the press, banks, stores, etc. Will people accept this in a new form?"

And will the people, in their current skeptical mood about government control, accept information provided to them by a government-operated system, even one that gets its data and service from independent IP's, as in Prestel? Although the French telecommunications agency has said it will act solely as a common carrier for this information, there is no law to keep the government from supplying the information. It could easily be the orchestrator of information, deciding which services and suppliers were needed on the national system, and which were not. In fact, even as it drew up plans for Télétel, the PTT was criticized for turning only to establishment information media such as the stock exchange and the national wire service for input. Reporting on the development, Anthony Smith, a British television producer and media critic, commented, "Antiope may come to preside over a kind of feudal system, in which the right to provide stated categories of information is distributed to named and exclusive organizations; baronies around the feudal court."[4]

Giraud looked on another government experiment as its "Trojan horse" for videotex. In this plan, twenty-five thousand telephone subscribers were being supplied with an electronic phone directory. Each new phone set would have a small black-and-white screen and keyboard terminal. (At the start, the set cost three times the amount of a normal telephone, but when produced in the millions, as planned, this would be substantially reduced.) Subscribers who want a number merely type in the name and address, and the number appears on the screen.

For this experiment the PTT did not have to bother with arranging input from IP's—it had a free hand to supply any directory-related information it wished. Certainly no one would object if the government added time and weather information to directory assistance? Or could they? As I pointed out in the last chapter, time and weather are information services provided to telephone users of the AT&T system. That does not exceed these companies' roles as common carriers. Or does it?

Because people in the French experiment would begin to depend on information supplied by what at the start was essentially a stripped-down version of videotex, the experiment was expected to demonstrate the credibility of videotex in general. Télétel developers believed that its demonstrated success would attract IP's to a fully operational Antiope system. In addition, it would firmly establish a precedent for the PTT to become its own IP—the fact that was the source of Giraud's "Trojan horse" concern.

Sweden, too, was off and running with both broadcast and wired videotex. The Swedes added some interesting variations and expressed some interesting reservations. Sveriges Radio, the radio and television monopoly, provided the broadcast teletext, and Televerket, the telecommunications monopoly, the wired version.

At Televerket's research headquarters in the suburban-looking southeast part of Stockholm, I spoke about videotex with Dr. Bertil Thorngren, a respected social scientist who said he had gone into government service because that was where he felt he could best make contributions to communications for the public interest.

Televerket researchers thought the original Prestel model—communication with a single data base—was too limited to meet the public's communications needs.

"We want a truly interactive communication," Thorngren said. "The system we have in mind basically *contains* Prestel."

The terminal, in the Swedish plan, has an alphanumeric keyboard that can edit and transmit letters and reports, as does the interactive word processor used in offices. It can tie in with high-speed data-transmission networks and the worldwide telex network. It includes graphics and, in later generations, transmission of facsimile. It provided a fully switched service for interchange of messages between individuals.

Televerket also tested "voice teletext": when a subscriber is out, his terminal will answer a voice-circuit call and store the message digitally for reproduction when the subscriber returns and turns on his set.

The Swedish marketing strategy was to offer its system in 1982, first to businesses and professional people, then, based on that experience, devise a simpler variation for residential customers.

Philosophically, the Swedish people and the government are more concerned than are the French to keep the PTT out of videotex content. In Sweden, unlike the United States, Britain, and many other countries, the telephone company (Televerket) does not have the legal responsibility to monitor content, such as obscenity or threatening phone calls.

"In Sweden, if you use the phone to threaten the Prime Minister, officially we don't care—that is the province of the police," said Thorngren. "This is very basic to our system: we are not supposed to intervene. This stems from Televerket's dominating role—we are not supposed to have that much power."

The same is true of the postal system, which is separate here from the phone system; it has no right, for example, to restrict pornography from the mails. This hands-off philosophy has been extended to the new technologies, as well. "I feel it is dangerous to combine content with technology," Thorngren said. "Televerket will *not* put content into videotex."

The outcome is not so clear-cut in Sweden's over-the-air form, Text-TV. This was pioneered by Sveriges Radio, an independent government broadcasting corporation similar in status to the BBC. The rationale by which its tests got off the ground—that of providing captioning for the deaf—guaranteed that some "content" would be supplied inhouse. Starting this way was a political move aimed at gaining acceptance of the larger concept. Nobody could argue with the need for captioning television programs so that citizens who were hard-of-hearing would not be deprived of programming. In 1979 Text-TV began broadcasting regularly to two hundred households in which at least one person was hard-of-hearing. Plans called for captions to be supplied in Finnish for the large Finn minority that has difficulty with Swedish.

In its standard information mode, journalists were in charge, as they were in England. So, besides the captioning, the material they transmitted was news and information similar to that contained on Ceefax. Even during this testing stage, however, discussion was under way as to whether other suppliers of information might be able to use the broadcast-videotex facility, as they would Televerket's phone-based system.

Government planners I spoke to did not want to see the system become a vehicle primarily for companies and organizations that could pay to get on it, as in Prestel. Legislators expressed concern that business or government agencies which put information into the system might—intentionally or unintentionally—be setting the information agenda for the people in an "unbalanced" way. A wealthy political party, for example, might be able to buy up pages in quantities far out of proportion to its representation among the populace. One Liberal Party Member of Parliament suggested that an agency similar to the broadcasting authority might be necessary, directed to set up real two-way communication with the people, with feedback to give them a chance to influence the system's input.

When I talked with Swedes about legislation, I was struck with how solidly the concept of *equity* was entrenched in their minds as the basis for public policy. Everyone must have an equal chance at access to the videotex system, the Swedish planners said, and its development must take place with that in mind.

Japan was faced with a technical problem in videotex that was not faced by Western experimenters. It had to come up with a system that could transmit about 4000 ideographs, not the three dozen numbers and letters used in Western text. This required far greater storage and transmission capacity to form the patterns of the necessary ideographs. The highly advanced Japanese electronics industry solved the problem, drawing on its experience in Large-Scale Integration of circuits and silicon chip technology. By 1980 the Ministry of Post and Telecommunications was able to begin field tests of its system, called Captain (Character and Pattern Telephone Access Information Network). Using an information file of 100,000 pages, it conducted a pilot project with 1000 telephones in Tokyo. Information for the test was supplied without charge by 117 organizations who founded the Cooperative Association for the Provision of Information Materials. They included 20 newspapers, 22 advertising agencies, 25 publishing companies, 10 travel agencies, 10 department stores and the country's public-broadcasting companies.[5] The specific aim of Captain is to provide information of personal interest to the general populace, rather than business data.

Canada built its effort in videotex, called Telidon,* on the work already done in England and France, coming up with a second-generation system that improved on both. Its major advantage was that it could display graphic information, such as a weather map, with greater definition than previous systems. Map contours were curved and smooth, while those on the first European systems were "constructed" of centimeter-size blocks. The Telidon adapter to the television set included a minicomputer that could be used in home calculations. The Canadian Department of Communication, which developed the technology, thought it was important for all videotex terminals in the world to be compatible. For this reason, it pressed other countries to accept its more advanced technology as the international standard.

A one-year field trial of the system was conducted by the Ontario Educational Communications Authority in 1979–80. Schoolchildren used the system to retrieve information from existing data banks and to access computer-assisted learning courses.

U.S. DEVELOPMENT HAMPERED
BY "FREE ENTERPRISE" PHILOSOPHY

I have said nothing about the development of videotex in the United States, which lagged behind the field. The reason the technology moved toward general use in the socially oriented countries of Western Europe and in Canada and Japan faster than it did in the United States was, primarily, that these countries had communications ministries mandated to provide complete telecommunications services to the public at reasonable cost. The United States, on the other hand, adhered to a philosophy that contended the public would be best served by letting commercial organizations develop these technologies when they thought enough demand existed among the public for them to make a profit. But it is often the case that people could benefit from a new technology long before the public perceives its potential and creates a demand for it.

A case in point is captioning of television for the deaf, tried out first in Sweden and later introduced in America. In the United States, it did not come about because the primary providers of television pro-

---

* From the Greek, "at a distance" plus "I perceived."

gramming, the commercial networks, thought they could make a profit on it. It came about because the Public Broadcasting Service thought it was necessary to a large segment of the public, and pushed for a government education grant to develop it. Closed captioning, seen only by those with decoders, began in March 1980 on ABC, NBC, and PBS network programs using decoders that Sears Roebuck had agreed to market. Even then, CBS declined to use it, saying a system they were testing for possible later use was "superior."

Closed captioning was one of the few exceptions in which a U.S. government agency was willing to provide funds to develop a communications service for the public to the operational stage.

So governments that had set up telecommunications-operating agencies to develop these services generally got the jump on the United States, which had not. Because of this difference in philosophy, publicly provided videotex in Britain, France, and Sweden will cost home users less than in the United States, which encourages private companies to add charges for profit on the public services they provide.

In the democracies of Western Europe, there is more willingness for government corporations to compete head-to-head with private companies, even in "business" areas such as automated office applications of videotex. In the United States, the concern of business, like-minded members of Congress and the administration—and most specifically the Federal Communications Commission—has been to keep electronic communications as the preserve of private enterprise.

In England, a Post Office official told me, the government is determined to maintain its monopoly as the provider of Prestel facilities, including automated office services, even where that conflicts with private companies that want to get into the field.

In France, competition with private communications companies and their complete exclusion from transmission functions is an established government policy. This was brought on originally by the fear that the French national business life, and possibly its cultural life, might be dominated by multinational corporations. The scare-company the French mention most is IBM.

Canada has a Department of Communication that is charged with "promoting the development and efficiency of communication, and with helping Canadian communication systems adjust to changing conditions," in the interest of developing a nationwide system that will benefit the citizens. In this role, it conducts research and development independently and sometimes in tandem with telecommunications companies, to develop an integrated system.

Japan, whose policy developed along Western European lines, was pushed toward the U.S. model during the American occupation after World War II. Now the country permits a mix of public and private corporations in its telecommunications system.

In the United States, the Communications Act of 1934 states that the regulatory purpose of the FCC is "to make available, so far as is possible, to all the people of the United States a rapid, efficient nationwide wire and radio communication service with adequate facilities at reasonable charges."

That this worthy idea has not been given priority is attested by two things:

1. A consistent policy at the FCC over most of its life to advance the interests of the telephone company, private broadcasters, and other commercial entrepreneurs against the interests of the consuming public, and

2. The failure of successive administrations and Congresses to consider seriously setting up either a cabinet-level Department of Communications or a government operating agency similar to the PTT's in Europe.

Richard Nixon installed an Office of Telecommunications Policy in the White House, primarily to "encourage" support of his administration among commercial and public television broadcasters. Jimmy Carter moved this office to the Commerce Department, as part of a new National Telecommunications and Information Administration, and charged it with developing a coherent communications policy. But no move was made to set up a cabinet-level department, and thus recognize, as have many advanced industrial countries, the critical importance of information in the lives of the people. Both Carter and the Congresses he dealt with showed instead an inclination to throw communications to the vagaries of the marketplace. Bills were introduced to end the FCC policy-making role and reduce its functions to that of setting technical standards. One result was that, when the videotex technique became known, the country had no communications agency in place to develop it.

Since commercial services such as banks and catalogue sales organizations would be users of a backbone system set up by a government communications agency, the American business community was faced with delayed opportunity regarding videotex. The research department of Kidder Peabody & Co., a New York stock brokerage firm, advised its customers: "In the U.S., there exists an obstacle to the success of a [videotex] service. We believe that countries in which [videotex] is likely to operate successfully and quickly are those in which the communication carrier has a virtual monopoly and is not barred from offering computer services."

Of course, it must be assumed that Kidder Peabody would opt for granting that monopoly to a private carrier such as AT&T, rather than to a government agency.

Because of the U.S. policy, the potential existed for cable companies and multiple-system operators to take the lead in developing text services. Cabletext, a version of videotex or teletext, can be installed fairly easily by cable systems, especially those employing two-way technology such as Qube's. The cable industry, however, allowed other interests, including phone companies, to make the first moves.

Late in the 1970s the British Post Office noted the vacuum in the U.S. market and decided to step into it. Through the Insac Group Inc., the British government's international trading corporation, it offered to license Prestel-type services that could be built to meet American requirements. It granted the General Telephone & Electronics Corporation (GTE), with operating companies in thirty-four states the second-largest phone system, a license to offer videotex to the public. But before GTE could get started, Phone Company No. 1—AT&T—announced it was joining Knight-Ridder Newspapers Inc., the largest newspaper chain in the country, for a 1980 field test in Coral Gables, Florida. AT&T had been developing a videotex system through its Bell Laboratories, waiting for the moment the American climate would support its activity in this area.

Since most of the experiments in the United States in telephone-based videotex, over-the-air videotex, and cable-based teletext grew out of an interest in presenting news in an alternative form, I will discuss them in detail in the next chapter.

PUTTING TWO TWO-WAYS TOGETHER: WHAT ARE THE CONSEQUENCES?

The arrival of interactive videotex and two-way cable along parallel paths moved the new communications technology a giant step toward the fully integrated home communications set. Taken together, these systems had the capacity to provide:

- Textual information on demand.
- Interactive television, including electronic town meetings and two-way education classes.
- An electronic newspaper.
- Electronic funds transfer, including checkless banking and credit-card sales.
- Facsimile reproduction and hard-copy printout.
- Terminal-to-terminal message exchange, including telex.
- Automated office services, including word processing.
- Computer conferencing.
- Computer-assisted learning.
- Home computing facilities.
- Burglar, fire, and medical-emergency alarms.
- Video games.

Add a camera and microphone to the home or office set, and you achieve the capability for video teleconferencing, person-to-person video telephone, and remote medical diagnosis. The Tama New Town and Hi-Ovis experiments together could provide nearly all the services we might expect from an integrated HCS.

One of those services, which I have yet to mention, was a harbinger of the multiple choices in *programming* that will be available to the viewer in the emerging system. Participants in the Hi-Ovis test could request the computer to play for them, individually, movies, reruns of broadcast programs, and locally produced videotapes that had been stored on cassettes at the center. The center's computer reserved a time for playback, since each cassette could be accessed by only one home at a time.

Meanwhile, halfway around the world, Telecable Videotron of Saint-Hubert, Quebec, began offering a variation of this service commercially. It provided eight "on demand" channels by which subscribers could phone up to have programs of their choice sent exclusively to their sets from the Telecable library. The "programs," which included not only sports and entertainment but text material as well, were stored on three thousand videocassettes. Each was fed into one of the channels individually when someone requested it from a program index. The demand at first was heavily for entertainment and sports, rather than for text information and documentaries.

Systems of the future may provide thousands of such programs, stored not on videocassettes but translated into digital information that can be stored in the system's computers. Subscribers would be able to access any selection—rock concert, Shakespearean drama, video game, or a town ordinance in text form—for their individual use. A millisecond later, that same program could start downstream from the central computer to another subscriber who had punched it up independently.

Yes—but haven't I skipped a stage of technology already introduced commercially to meet this demand: videocassettes and videodiscs that can be played at home?

The videocassette, about the size of this book, is played by dropping it into the playback receptacle of a videotape recorder. Attached to the antenna terminals, the recorder plays through a standard television set. Entertainment cassettes, including feature films, can be purchased for use in the home. The video recorder can also tape regular programs being received on the television set. With a small videocamera and microphone attachment, individuals users can record their own "programs" for playback via their machines.

The videodisc is played much as you would a phonograph record. This system, for playback only, is based on prerecorded video-records. Its player, too, connects to the television through the antenna leads.

Video-recorders, more expensive than videodisc players, were produced commercially in the late 1970s by the Matsushita Electronic Industrial Company and the Sony Corporation, both of Japan. RCA, which licensed Matsushita's system, early became the leader in video-recorder sales. Also hoping to take the lead in videodiscs, RCA in 1977 unveiled a video-record player using a grooved disc played with a diamond stylus. The corporation announced it would produce the programming "software"—the discs—as well as the hardware on which to play them. It entered the market in competition with a videodisc system developed jointly by MCA Inc. of Hollywood and N. V. Philips of the Netherlands (Magnavox). The Magnavox model, which costs more, used a low-powered laser to "read" information on a platinum-colored reflective disc. The two systems, obviously, were not compatible.*

What surprised people in the industry was that RCA would promote a technique that was sure to cut into the viewing—and there-

---

* IBM saw business applications for videodisc systems. In 1979 it formed a joint company with MCA to develop and market videodiscs and playback units, mainly for use by industry as sales and training aids. This was the closest the business machines giant had yet come to being in the consumer business.

fore the profits—of its direct subsidiary, the National Broadcasting Company. ABC Inc. added to the surprise by announcing that it was forming ABC Video Enterprises to produce programming for the RCA system and any other manufacturer of videodisc and videotape players. CBS jumped on the bandwagon by negotiating an agreement with RCA to bring out a videodisc system jointly.

Although the presidents of the television networks insisted that nothing would replace commercial broadcasting, the owners of the networks were obviously hedging their bets. Edgar H. Griffiths, president of RCA, predicted that by 1990, between 25 and 40 million videodisc players would be in use in American homes, with annual sales of prerecorded discs at about 250 million copies.

Then again, that might not happen at all. Which is why I seemed to skip a step in describing the emerging situation: The *delivery system* on which videodisc technology is based is likely to be superseded in the coming system. The stand-alone video-playback machine will certainly exist as a major *marketing* step along the way. But the remote-accessing capability I described—the ability of a home viewer to acquire, via the HCS, any program desired from a computerized library—might eventually make the manufacture of videodiscs and record players obsolete. "Software" producers may be making programs (or hit singles) for direct insertion into computers, rather than for duplication on millions of records for sale in record shops. Video games, now being sold in cassettes for play through the television set, could be punched up directly from the computer.

The fact that we could foresee the obsolescence of videodiscs at the moment they were being introduced to the market illustrates the danger, in a field where innovation tumbles over innovation, of not seeing the forest for the trees. The focus should not be on *how* each successive technical development accomplishes a particular communication task but on *what* service the continuously developing state of the art makes possible. The new technologies are the trees; the *new communications* is the forest.

As we pick our way through the forest, what should we look out for? At each step along the way, we risk the snares of control. One appeared as soon as the BPO suggested that *its* employees should be editors of the information on the Prestel system. Although that idea was knocked down by competing institutions that wanted direct access to the public, the BPO still had the power, if it desired, to turn the system off. In Europe, it seemed that control over phone-based videotex would remain with the PTT's. Future control over broadcast videotex appeared likely to be mixed. Most European systems started under the jurisdiction of the government radio and television monopolies. One exception was Oracle in England, operated under the control of commercial broadcasting. In the United States, the question is open, although the betting is that commercial forces will be dominant.

Wherever the control lies, the questions, issues, and battles are likely to be similar. They are the same ones that have existed over the years with regard to guarantees of individual liberty.

Do we have a right to say what we want to say; to read, see, and hear what we want to hear? Do we have the right of access to media to present our ideas; the right to acquire media that present the ideas of others?

In America, "decency" committees, inspired usually by conservative religious and political groups, have sprung up to protect us from reading and seeing material they consider indecent or politically dangerous. These ideas are summed up usually by adjectives such as *pornographic, obscene, blasphemous, socialistic,* and *communistic.* In response, "right to read" groups have been formed, insisting that individuals should have the right to decide for themselves what content they take in, and not be restricted by private groups or government agencies intent on imposing their ideas of decency or political orthodoxy.

A case in point was the decision of the Island Trees, Long Island, school board, following recommendations from a right-wing group called "Parents of New York United," to remove eleven books from the high-school library on the grounds that they were "filthy." The books included *Laughing Boy* by Oliver La Farge, which won a Pulitzer Prize in 1920; *The Fixer* by Bernard Malamud; *Down These Mean Streets* by Piri Thomas; and *Best Short Stories by Negro Writers,* edited by Langston Hughes. Faculty members and high-school students, backed by the New York Civil Liberties Union, filed a class-action suit against the school board on the grounds that the ban violated their First Amendment rights. However, the school board's action was upheld in 1979 by Federal District Court Judge George C. Pratt. "While removing the books from a school library may—indeed in the court's view, *does*—reflect a misguided educational philosophy," he said, "it does not constitute a sharp and direct infringement on any First Amendment rights."

According to the National Coalition Against Censorship, actions by right-wing censorship groups intent on removing offending publications from school and university libraries are becoming more frequent each year. Based in New York, the coalition is composed of more than twenty-five groups including the National Council of Churches, Union of American Hebrew Congregations, National Education Association, American Association of University Professors, and the Newspaper Guild. It disseminates information about censorship attempts, such as this one in Massachusetts:

In Chelsea, a conservative community on the northern boundary of Boston, a parent complained that a poem in a book by adolescents, *Male and Female Under 18,* contained objectionable language and should be removed from the high-school library. The poem, "The City to a Young Girl," expressed in strong language the anger of a fifteen-year-old New York girl toward men who ogled her on the streets. The school committee chairman, publisher of a local weekly, described the poem as filth, and the committee voted to remove the book. The committee also voted to deny tenure to Sonja Coleman, the librarian who had selected it. Coleman, two pupils, two faculty members, and the Chelsea Right to Read Committee brought suit against the school committee in U.S. District Court, charging its actions violated their First Amendment rights.

Judge G. Joseph Tauro agreed that the ban had violated the plaintiffs' constitutional rights. He ordered the book returned to the shelves and prohibited the school committee from taking punitive action against Coleman or the other plaintiffs. The conclusion of his decision in the case was reminiscent of Judge Brennan's dissent in the "Seven Dirty Words" case:

> The board acted on the assumption that language offense to it and some parents had no place in the educational system. With the greatest respect to them, their sensibilities are not the full measure of what is proper education.
> The board claims an absolute right to remove this poem from the shelves of the library. It has no such right. And compelling policy considerations argue against any public authority having such an unreviewable power of censorship. If this work may be removed by a

committee hostile to its language and theme, then the precedent is set for the removal of any other work. The prospect of successive school boards "sanitizing" the school library of views divergent from their own is alarming.

What is at stake here is the right to read and be exposed to controversial thoughts, a valuable right subject to First Amendment protection. The most effective antidote to the poison of mindless orthodoxy is ready access to a broad sweep of ideas. There is no danger in such exposure: the danger is in mind control.

    —Tauro, J.
    —USDC Mass.: *Right to Read Defense Committee of Chelsea* v. *School Committee of Chelsea*, 7/5/78.

Similar instances of censorship in the public schools were running to about three hundred as the 1980s began, according to the American Library Association's Office of Intellectual Freedom.

While right-wing groups have long used pressure to restrict access of the general public to views antithetical to their own in print, films, and broadcasting, their more recent efforts have concentrated on media content accessible to the young. This is probably because, with the exception of some rulings by the Nixon-Burger majority in the Supreme Court, federal judges have upheld the rights of adults to read, see, and hear whatever they please. There is enough doubt, even among liberals, about whether children and adolescents can handle "indecent" words and pictures to give the censors some victories in this area.

But now a whole new medium has arrived to put uncensored printed matter directly into the hands of the young: two-way videotex. This challenge to the monitors of our morals would seem to be almost too great to be ignored. Given the track record of commercial broadcasting in knuckling under to pressure groups, the hope that commercial Information Providers in Europe and Japan and commercial-system operators in the United States will stand up to these pressures is slim.

If recent history is a guide, it is not only hard- and soft-core pornography that will come under attack. Decency groups have campaigned to remove five dictionaries from libraries where they would be accessible to students: The American Heritage, Random House, Doubleday, Webster's New World, and Webster's New Collegiate. The reason? Too many objectionable words. In Texas, the chief state school officer yielded to the pressure and ordered the five removed from the recommended list of the State Textbook Committee. As in many other instances, this campaign "to protect our children" affects adults as well. And that, of course, is the intention.

Two-way television, bringing films and other entertainment to the home on demand, often for payment of a fee, is bound to be another battleground. Movie theaters can limit their patrons to those over sixteen or eighteen, and thus blunt attacks by the private censors. But who is there, other than a parent, to prevent children under sixteen or eighteen from ordering up films that previously had been restricted to adults? Should not society protect these children from seeing adult-theme films over the system? Individuals and organizations that oppose censorship say, No—that is not society's role; it is the parent's or guardian's role to guide children to what they should see, hear, and read. Parents, they contend, are in a better position to judge family mores, or acceptable community standards, than are biased private groups. Or even "unbiased" agencies such as the Code and Rating Administration of the Motion Picture Association of America, which imposes its judgments concerning sex and violence in films on the nation at large.

Some others who value freedom are absolutists about what may be presented, whether to children or adults: It is restriction on information, ideas, and entertainment that is harmful to society, not freedom in presenting it. To such libertarians, even pornography must be permitted, to preserve the principle of freedom of expression. And perhaps to bring about its own defeat: "What is more boring than the second pornographic movie you watched?" is a question asked by many movie patrons in Denmark. There, people flocked to the first pornographic films to be shown openly without restriction. In a few years, pornographic films were past it, and audiences dropped off sharply.

These views are not general, especially in the United States. So the censorship fight, when it begins over two-way, is likely to continue in public and in the courts for years to come.

In Western Europe, which has become accustomed to sexual openness, the censorship argument may well center on political ideas rather than prurient interests. In most Western democracies, books, magazines, and newspapers can offer radical political ideas with impunity. But would it be possible, over a government-controlled two-way system, to advocate overthrow of that government?

On a soapbox in America, revolutionaries may make such a suggestion so long as they don't try to induce immediate, violent action.

(If a soapbox orator shouted, "Let's go down to City Hall and kill the Mayor," a policeman might step in and arrest the speaker.) Would a revolutionary be permitted that much freedom on a two-way video channel she had purchased for the occasion? (The question is virtually untested in commercial television, because the station- and network-owners normally deny access, free or paid, to "their" air to persons who might present radical ideas, left or right.) If a radical were permitted the use of a "soapbox" channel, who would decide where political advocacy ends and inciting violent action begins? Would it be the responsibility of the system operator to pull the switch? Or would a police officer monitor the soapbox channels?

In a government-controlled system, or even on a government-fearing commercial system such as exists in the United States, opponents of the party in power might be restricted from access to the videotex computer. In France, it might be difficult for a commercial-communications concern to get on the Antiope system as an IP if it had suggested repeatedly that the PTT monopoly over telecommunications should be ended.

The ability of a government to monitor interactions on the videotex system makes it possible for a public prosecutor to go on a fishing expedition through your private two-way correspondence and transactions on the system, to see if you are violating any tax laws or have been dealing with known criminals or radicals. Printouts of your textual exchanges might be acceptable as documentary evidence in a court that has become accustomed to the new forms of interpersonal and business transactions.

Either a PTT or a corporate operator could gain affirmative control of content by giving itself the exclusive right to put information into the system. (The BBC has chosen to do that on its Ceefax channels.) Or negative control could be maintained by prescreening any material others may want to add to its input. If such a thing were permitted, the system operator would have a powerful means of setting the agenda for what the public should know, what it could discuss, and, quite plausibly, what it could believe. In a way, American commercial television has, whether by inadvertency or design, established the popular wisdom for the vast majority of people. Television executives say they are merely "holding a mirror up to life." Or they put it another way: "We give the public what it wants." Citizen groups that have studied broadcasting say this is not so: the mirror is actually a one-way beacon that beams out from its surface the views of the commercial and political establishment in support of the status quo. Actually, television gives the people what the commercial establishment *thinks they should have,* to condition them to consume the products, services, and ideas that will guarantee continued profits for their companies and perpetuation of the profit-making system. Little of this "programming" of the American public came about from a diabolical intent of the programmers. What they did, they did with no intention of harming the people, but merely of furthering their own economic self-interest. This process *did* require an attempt to alter the public's abstemious ways, brought on by the Great Depression, to one of eager consumption. ("Why shouldn't you have it—You deserve it," says an ad for a luxury car.) The public was not forced to listen, to watch, to go along with the suggested change. But the seductive powers of the media used were such that the "programming" (produced and induced) worked.

Now the means are at hand to take the programming of the citizens much further. The obvious way this could be done is by controlling *all* the information available to the consumer. It could be done more subtly by enlisting the consumer in his own seduction, by offering him the "browsing" service long-range planner John Short has described. For fun and knowledge, the subscriber could be asked to "fill in" electronic questionnaires that supply clues not only to his intellectual interests but also individual preferences and emotional predilections. The computer could then combine this personal profile with other personal tendencies it has deduced from previous interactive input into the system—purchase of tickets to an antinuclear benefit, a contribution sent to an antiabortion crusade, as examples. Then the computer, acting on instructions from its human programmer, could select from its data base "guidance" items to apply a corrective to the subscriber's mindset.

Here is an example: Citizen A is opposed to nuclear power. She is also against air pollution from the burning of hydrocarbons. From its analysis, the computer "knows" both these facts. It sends her an article placed in an independent electronic magazine, but written by a university hack in the pay of the Edison Electronic Institute, which asserts that nuclear power plants create no pollution from burning hydrocarbons, as oil-fired plants do. What's more, a large increase in electric power output, impossible if dependent on scarce supplies of oil, could increase the use of electrified mass transit, which would further reduce air pollution in the cities. Opposing articles that refute the fallacies in that argument would be hard to come by, because the programmer would have deleted them from the selection of information available to Citizen A. "Guidance" provided by machine on such matters, as well as in emotional areas, could be deliberately tailored to shape the user's ideas and personality.

Overt and disastrous "guidance" could be provided by religious demagogues and other confidence men for gullible subscribers to a combined two-way television and videotext system. Charismatic and often fraudulent preachers and "healers" have become millionaires by using the commercial television and radio networks to con viewers and listeners to send money to their headquarters (usually, it seems, in the Southwest). While working on a story about religious con artists, I visited the headquarters of an extremely successful radio preacher in Tulsa. He proudly showed me a room in which twelve secretaries were dumping listeners' checks out of envelopes, and another in which eight letter-writing machines were signing his name with automatic pens to thank-you notes in which the preacher "personally" asked his benefactors if they couldn't spare a little bit more for his good works. Taking note of future inflation, I think this same preacher would have a good shot at becoming a billionaire if he were able to combine an emotional two-way video appeal with an "action page" on videotex by which, on impulse, his victims would transfer their life savings directly from their bank accounts to his. Radio and television laws, at least in the United States, place no restrictions on the appeal for funds by religious *poseurs* or those making a profit out of ostensibly nonprofit drives to raise funds for charity or to cure a disease.

Some damper on their activities could be imposed by requiring that anyone who makes an appeal for money would *not* be allowed to collect it immediately by electronic funds transfer. Rather, subscribers would be required to ask the fund-raiser to send them a prospectus which would describe the activities the contributions would support and which would have to be filed with a government regulatory agency, as required by the Securities Exchange Commission of those who want to sell stocks and bonds. The prospectus could be serially numbered, and the subscriber required to transmit its registration number when ordering his or her bank to transfer the contribution. Criminal penalties could be provided for fund-raisers who falsely advertised their prospective activities or used the funds in ways other than those specified in the prospectus.

The possibility for more direct embezzlement exists in the emerging system. Computer fraud in the existing electronic banking system is reported to be reaching tens of millions of dollars yearly. The exact amounts are not known because manipulation of funds by computer is usually detected only by accident, and because banks are reluctant to publicize the dangers to their customers. Extending EFT to the home increases the opportunity for sophisticated practitioners of computer fraud to tap into the transactions and divert funds from your account to theirs. Since bank statements would be delivered to you via the system, these, too, could be altered en route to provide a seemingly accurate balance, should you check them to see if the transactions corresponded with your own records.

The way could be cleared for "legal" manipulation of your accounts by government agencies. The convenience of EFT might tempt a court to order the direct transfer of money it decides you owe a creditor from your account to the creditor's. Done in the wink of an eye: no fussy papers to sign, checks to make out, hard cash to be handed over. The Internal Revenue Service, concerned with its inability to get you to pay up quickly on an additional sum it says you owe, might be empowered to attach your bank account electronically, and transfer the funds in question to the U.S. Treasury. *Then* they would be ready to argue with you.

It might be that public outcries could prevent these authorizations. But the technical path to such actions is cleared by the facilities now being installed.

The ease by which money could be transferred (spent) provides still another concern. Buying on credit once meant applying to a bank for a loan. Then it meant department-store charge accounts, which still had the "drag" effect of requiring a credit-seeker to apply for charge cards at individual stores. The process was speeded considerably by universal credit cards, requiring only one application that would cover hundreds of later "loans" by stores, restaurants, and other business establishments. With the application of credit card *numbers* entered through a videotex system (perhaps by inserting your credit card containing its magnetized identification strip directly into a slot in the set), buying on credit takes on the speed of light. Tying product advertising on the system directly to impulse buying through the system is bound to promote consumer debt. High volumes of personal credit transactions are yet another spur to inflation. Even persons in the money-lending business would have to be concerned about the unknown effects on the economy of seemingly un-limited consumer credit tied to a system that facilitates indebtedness to a degree never before thought possible.

This very facility is bound to tempt government officials looking for cheap and painless ways to raise revenue to transfer state lottery and off-track betting operations to the two-way system.

The prospect of betting on a horse race via the HCS, watching the race on a visual channel, then receiving an immediate payoff by EFT of your winnings to your bank account would seem to be an un-beatable inducement to gamble using the system. Although a horse player can tear up losing tickets at the track and throw them away in disgust, he is not likely to smash the key pad after he loses at home. More likely he would immediately use it again, to try to recoup on the next race. Or punch in "his" number for the hourly state lottery drawing. With the powerful attraction this "game" would present, electronic national lotteries would seem only a matter of time.

One potential danger of the new two-way systems is really an in-tensification of a problem that arose in previous modes of communi-cation: only those with money to purchase the service will be allowed access. This restriction could affect both information providers and those who wish to receive the information.

In the United Kingdom, any organization that had the "entrance fee" could get storage space in the Prestel data bank, and thus use the system to sell products or give away "messages" it wished the public to have. But at the start, no provision was made for community groups to have access, free of charge, to get public service messages to subscribers.

Anyone at home could have access to the information in the Prestel data bank if they had the money to buy or rent a television set with an adapter and had the money to pay for the information offered at various fees. (It was also necessary, of course, for them to have the money for a telephone line.)

In the past, money has been the controlling factor in public ac-cess to newspapers, radio, and television, and, to a lesser extent, cable television. "Free" speech has generally been available to those who were able to pay to make their ideas known to people outside their families. You were in a fairly good position to excercise your freedom of speech if you were William Randolph Hearst and could buy a chain of newspapers. Or if you were David Sarnoff and could establish a net-work of radio and television stations. If you had no money you could always write letters to the editor, or ask a public-affairs producer at a radio or television station to schedule a panel discussion in which you might present your views. But if the editor or producer said No, your freedom of speech extended to the distance you could shout from your doorstep.

In the 1960s, about the time cable television became established in the United States and Canada, citizens' groups were forming to try to gain direct access to the electronic media. As I have mentioned, they were unsuccessful in radio and television, and partly successful on cable.

The addition of two-way videotex makes the communications system's potential for community-service purposes greater, and the demand for access is likely to rise as this facility becomes general.

The question will still be: Do individuals and nonprofit community organizations have a *right* to be on the system, and to get information from the system? And if they do, who will fund the cost of providing computer storage and channel time to the individuals and organizations that cannot pay for them? Who will provide a home communications set for those who cannot afford to rent or buy one for their homes or pay the monthly charges for information and services?

The answer to these questions can have a powerful long-term effect on society. If no funding is provided to guarantee that the system will be open to all, it will be a service offered by well-financed corporations and interest groups, plus tax-supported government agencies, to well-off middle- and upper-class constituents. What should be a service benefiting all the people will become a tool and toy of an affluent elite.

4 | BIRTH OF THE ELECTRONIC NEWSPAPER

Computerized two-way systems make possible an electronic newspaper, "edited" by subscribers in their homes. "Electronic newspaper" is probably a misnomer for what is evolving—"electronic news and information service," although not so catchy, is more descriptive. The service will combine all elements of print, television, and radio news through the home communications set. I don't feel that is a dangerous prediction: we can see the system's contours fairly clearly now, from various parts already in operation. Few people believe the newspaper will continue essentially unchanged indefinitely. Economic pressures from the older electronic technologies of radio and television have brought changes in newspaper content over the years; the newer technologies—interactive video sets, computers, and satellites among them—will bring other changes not only in the content but the physical product as well.

When I was a student at the Columbia University Graduate School of Journalism after World War II, the school and *The New York Times* were testing facsimile—"the newspaper of the future." In one of the offices was a bulky machine connected by wire to the Times Building on West Forty-third Street. The dean showed the students that it printed out a newspaper page, "just as it appears in the regular paper," in eight minutes. In the future, facsimile enthusiasts said, every home would have a "fax" machine that would deliver the entire newspaper, page-by-page, overnight, so you could have it waiting for you when you got up in the morning. It didn't happen, and it is not likely to happen, exactly in that form. It is not economical, nor is it necessary to deliver *all* the pages of a newspaper, including those not wanted by a subscriber, to every home, every day. In fact, it is becoming less and less economical to deliver the entire standard newspulp paper physically to newsstands or the home. About 80 percent of the cost of a newspaper goes, not into the collection and processing of its editorial content, as you might think, but into production and distribution of the folded folio of newsprint you are accustomed to pick up and spread out in front of your eyes every day. New systems, all based on computers and electronics, are being found to reduce these costs. Simple economics is pushing newspaper publishers toward their use.

The most sophisticated piece of electronic equipment in the Elizabeth Bureau of the old *Newark Evening News,* where I began as a cub reporter, was the teletype in the corner. Every day, one of the nimbler-fingered reporters sat down and typed into the machine the stories the thirteen reporters in the bureau had written on their mechanical typewriters (there were no electric models) so that they could be copy-edited on the desk in Newark and sent to the composing room, to be set by Linotype machines that produced eight lines of type a minute, cast from molten metal.

I used the telephone as my "remote unit" to phone in stories from the courthouse, a few blocks away, to a rewrite man with a phone receiver precariously clenched between his cheek and his shoulder. When I got a job on the *Times* in the early 1950s as a copy editor, I was surprised to learn that reporters traveling around the country phoned their stories directly into a recording room, where their voice reports were put on small blue plastic discs for later transcription by stenographers.

This sometimes led to goofs uncharacteristic of *The New York Times.* One night a West Coast correspondent rushed from the Academy Awards presentation in Hollywood and phoned the winners to the recording room. Under deadline pressure, they were transcribed in "takes," edited, and set in type in time for the Late City Edition. That edition said that *Two Cats Apiece* had won an Oscar. The actual winner, the wire services teletypes disclosed later, was *To Catch a Thief.* To compound the error, the *New York Post,* which was not noted for its initiative, picked up the story from the *Times* in the morning and informed its afternoon readers that *Two Cats Apiece* had indeed won an Oscar. (That kind of cascading error might be hard to eradicate from a computer's memory.)

On the National Desk of the *Times,* we edited the disc transcriptions by hand with a soft lead pencil (an advance over the storied blue pencil, which was hard to erase) and wrote out heads for the stories on other pieces of copy paper. These were sent up to the composing room by pneumatic tube to be set in type by another machine, or, for the really large sizes, by hand. Most stories the reporters turned in were held until late afternoon, when a host of copy editors arrived to get them ready in time for the first edition deadline at 9:00 p.m.—reworking them, smoothing out the language, checking the facts. Stories that broke after the deadline could be updated during the evening, for the second, or Late City, edition, which closed at 11:30. Then, changes could be made in the Late City hourly until 3:00 a.m. Wire-service copy was flowing into the paper around the clock, but mainly it was collected for the desks to process in the rhythm of these daily deadlines.

Before the copy flow got heavy toward nine o'clock, my compatriots sat around the curved National Desk playing news-type games: "Name the Other Senator," in which the better-known name was given by one editor as a challenge to the others to come up with his lesser-known colleague. We also played "Headlines in History," the rules of which required an editor to reduce to two-line, fourteen-count-maximum "C" head the great events of the past. The clear, all-time winner* was:

MOSES, ON SINAI
GETS 10-PT. PLAN

By 1979, when the *Times* completed its conversion to cold type, national, foreign, and metropolitan copy editors sat at Video-Display Terminals calling up stories that reporters had entered into other VDT's at *their* desks. Editing was no longer done by making marks on paper (A copy-editor friend once said to me, in wonder, "You know, they pay us for making little marks on paper"). It was done by maneuvering a cursor—a bright little "blip"—across the VDT screen to the point where a change was to be made, then typing in the change on an electric keyboard attached to the VDT.

I revisited the *Times* newsroom shortly after the changeover was made. The hardest thing for me to take was that the semicircle of desks—National, Foreign, and City—that defined the heart of the newsroom when I worked there in the 1960s—had disappeared. Na-

* Winning editor: Irvin Horowitz.

tional, foreign, and "metropolitan" copy editors (the old City Editor is dead, replaced by a thoroughly modern Metropolitan Editor) sat in isolation in front of VDT's, in communication with their slot men through other VDT's. (The term "slot man," for the editor who supervised the work of each desk, has no physical basis, as it did when he—and it was always he, never she—sat in the slot of the curved desks.)

It relieved my anxiety about the cold computerization somewhat when an editor friend of mine told me copy editors still played games, but now on the VDT's. In the computer there was a standing chessboard and a running match. One editor specialized in programming moving ships and sea battles. Most of the staff people could call up the "fun and games" index in the directory and watch the performance.

For years, after newsrooms were equipped with electric typewriters, some reporters held out for their own mechanical machines. On my tour of the *Times,* I asked about that when I saw a mechanical typewriter alongside a reporter's VDT. "We have to wean them away," said a *Times*man who had converted to the new. "What do you do with the reporters who won't wean?" I asked. "We slap their fingers and take their machines away," he replied.

From the *Times* newsroom, the editors sent reporters' stories to another electronic device that translated the electronic text into columns of phototype at the rate of a thousand lines a minute. These paper column strips were pasted into page layouts. (In some systems, a display VDT is used to organize these columns into a page layout.) This page was photographed and etched by ultraviolet light on a plastic plate anchored to the cylindrical presses.

And at that point, the point at which huge rotary presses printed the final paper product for trucking through crowded streets of the city to newsstands, to trains for the suburbs, and to planes for faraway cities, the system became an anachronism, stopping the electronic process dead in its tracks.

Doggedly, Sunday after Sunday, four to five pounds of newsprint, including millions of words most subscribers would never read, were hand-delivered to the newspapers' subscribers. Sometimes the deliveries were a day late, or, in distant cities, two or three days late, because of traffic jams, missed train connections, and snowstorms— problems that had been familiar to circulation managers since the rotary press made low-cost papers available to almost everyone.

It is this final product and process of newspapering that is bound in time to give way to electronic delivery of news. The editorial organizations that collect and process the news may still be recognizable, but the product will not be the same.

This will not come about without a fight from traditionalists in newspapers, *The New York Times* among them. "We think print is going to stay," John R. Werner, the *Times*'s director of research and development, told me. "We think the electronic text media will find a niche somewhere between television and newspapers. We think it's a viable niche, but we think it will be a supplemental system."

Newspaper readers may in time be willing to read high-quality facsimile reproductions of newspaper pages, he said. This was one of the possibilities tested out in twenty households during the Tama New Town experiment in Japan, and it had a good reaction from the householders.

Professional evaluators thought it would be most promising in out-of-the-way areas, especially if high-speed transmission could be assured. (Later facsimile tests elsewhere were able to transmit a newspaper page in four seconds.)

The *Times*'s long-range planners concede that, ultimately, they may want to consider facsimile again. But to get people to read news directly from a videoscreen rather than in hard-copy facsimile is going to require them to break a strong reading habit, Werner said. And the *Times* believes that is not going to be viable for a long time to come. "Besides," he remarked, "the accident of reading ads as you read the news is a happy phenomenon which pays the freight."

You are not likely to get the same serendipity with an electronic newspaper, he said, because it will be hard to integrate the ads with individual videotex stories that are called up on the screen. Since the *Times* is one of the largest and most influential newspaper organizations in the world, its opinion carries weight. Even so, the balance appears on the other side, as expressed by the judgments of other heavyweight news organizations that have decided to get in on the ground floor. Among these are the Knight-Ridder Newspapers, the Asahi Newspapers in Japan, and a number of large papers in England. They want to test the possibility that the new system of dissemination will not be supplemental, but dominant.

EARLY STEPS TOWARD
ALL-ELECTRONIC NEWS

The way toward all-electronic news services was paved by several pilot projects that got under way in the late 1970s.

Early forms of text-on-the-screen presentation had made a segment of the American public—those who subscribed to some cable television systems—aware that a television screen could present news and information in alphanumeric (teletext) form, as well as in pictures.

Almost from the beginning of Manhattan Cable Television in New York City, Reuters had provided a teletext news service, called "Newsview," on two channels, one for general news, the other for financial news and sports. The service was an electronic improvement on an earlier practice in which some cable systems focused a television camera on incoming news on a teleprinter of the AP or UPI. By 1980 all three wire services had made news via teletext available to cable companies' satellite receiving stations.

People at home could not punch buttons to call up news stories they wanted—they could merely check the channel from time to time to see if the electronic screens were printing out stories in which they were interested. The service was, in effect, around-the-clock radio news in print form. None of the news agencies saw this medium as a way of supplanting the newspaper. These were mostly headline services, as were radio and television newscasts, and the public was expected to buy a newspaper, as usual, for detailed coverage.

The Mitre Corporation pioneered the first "frame-grabbing" television retrieval system in the United States with an evaluation design study at Reston, Virginia, funded by the National Science Foundation; it lasted from 1971 to 1973. The system, mainly for instruction in the Reston public schools, used a button telephone to connect the user with the Mitre computer. This cycled images at sixty a second, to be "grabbed" by home television sets in a manner similar to the one used by Ceefax on the BBC.

In the mid-seventies, Reuters began marketing its IDR system (for Information Dissemination and Retrieval), a one-way, "frame-grabbing" service. For several dollars a month, subscribers of Manhattan Cable could "grab" news, television program and theater listings, weather and traffic reports, and stock quotations from a computer data bank that was updated continually by Reuters reporters and editors in New York. The system was developed first as a market-reporting service for financial houses, called "The Reuters Monitor." Later it was offered for homes subscribing to cable in the metropolitan area. Next came satellite transmission of the bank's data for accessing by cable systems in the United States and Canada. Viewers at home had to buy an IDR terminal to attach to their television sets. "Reuters would like to see the terminal priced at a hundred dollars," Mike Blair, manager of media services, told me. "We think it's possible—it's just a matter of mass-producing it." A Reuters market survey indicated that 3 percent of cable users would be willing to spend money over the basic cable charge to access news and useful information. The Go signal for home service was given because Reuters believed the potential initial market of 420,000 homes (based on 3 percent of the 14 million cable subscribers in the United States at that time) was economically viable.

Starting in 1980 cable subscribers across the country were able to tune in commercial television news around the clock. The service, carried by satellite, was pioneered by Turner Communications Corp. of Atlanta, which set up a Cable News Network to compete with the conventional network news operations. CNN, owned by Ted Turner, who also owned the Atlanta Braves in baseball and the Atlanta Hawks in basketball, transmitted all-news television outside Atlanta. Turner had laid the groundwork for this operation by declaring his local station, WTCG, a "superstation," and offering its fare of old movies and sports to cable systems via the satellite. Meanwhile, McGraw-Hill Inc. was mining a more specialized information lode. For years it had been known as a publisher of trade magazines, business reports, and Standard & Poor's indexes. From these sources it formed a data base to market information for industry and government by the on-line method. This used telephone lines to connect terminals in the users' offices to McGraw-Hill's central computer. Customers paid large fees to ask the computer for specialized data or developments in their particular fields. By 1980 more than half the corporation's revenues, which were nearing the billion-dollar mark, came from providing information from its data base.

The first attempt to merge television news with a videotex news and information service was made by Station KSL-TV in Salt Lake City in an experiment that began in 1978. KSL, operated by the Mormon-owned Bonneville International Corporation, was the first broadcasting company in the United States to get FCC permission for an over-the-air test of videotex. Its system was almost identical to

Ceefax, and was licensed to the station by the BBC. Testing the setup with a few receiving sets that it moved from place to place, KSL put out a standard Ceefax menu: news heads, weather, stocks, and transportation schedules. Then it fed the UPI national wire's data directly into its computer, with instructions to select stories of particular interest to the region.

KSL's contribution in advancing the medium came in tying the "electronic newsroom" of the television station directly into the system. Stories produced by KSL reporters were processed for video transmission and prepared for the teletext computer, as well. Scripts used by anchor persons were also to be entered, for direct access on the separate teletext channel or for superimposing over the bottom of the regular television news picture as an aid to the hard-of-hearing. As is anyone who has tried to present a complex story on television, KSL television news producers were frustrated by the limits of the medium. Videotex offered a way out. At the end of a capsule report on a story that was likely to take up two columns' space in the next day's newspaper, the anchor could say: "For more details, see Page 222 of your videotex."

The FCC, interested in maintaining its jurisdiction over the new medium, encouraged experiments such as that at KSL so it could eventually set technical standards for the systems. A technically oriented test of broadcast teletext was made about the same time by KMOX-TV, a CBS affiliate in St. Louis. CBS checked out both the Ceefax and Antiope versions, and found both were adaptable to American conditions.

The CBS management, however, decided it should go with the more sophisticated Antiope system, and filed a petition with the FCC to make that the industry standard. To check it out in operation, CBS placed 100 Antiope decoders in the Los Angeles market. It arranged with KNXT, its affiliate there, to supply a "magazine" of local and national news, weather and sports, amusement listings and classified ads. It also contracted with KCET, a public television station in Los Angeles, to supply tests for children, educational material, and cultural listings.

Technical refinements on the basic Ceefax system made it possible for KSL to offer 800 "pages" of information, each one of which could sequence through a number of frames devoted to a single story. KSL trade ads pointed out that the 800 pages could present 100,000 words of information, against 3000 for a newspaper's front page and only 6000 in an entire television newscast.

The designers balked, however, at calling the system a "newspaper of the air." Nor did they consider it a replacement for television news. "It's an entirely *new* form of communication," Gary Robinson, one of the designers, remarked in an interview. "There are too many things teletext can do that other media are not equipped to do. The demand will be for 'new' applications, not for the applications that are being served perfectly well by existing outlets."

The KSL planners felt the approach to broadcast videotex should be different from that to telephone-based videotex. The over-the-air form, limited in its total number of pages, should be the popular medium, to permit people to get short-lived information quickly. The service would be given "free" to everyone, financed by advertising contained on its pages. The telephone-based form, with its almost unlimited storage, should be a specialized medium with a full alphanumeric keyboard making possible a faster and more detailed search for specific pieces of information in its data bank. The system, KSL believed, would be financed by a combination of user fees and advertising. Over the long haul, it was expected that the two forms would be operated in tandem.

The Corporation for Public Broadcasting, which realized the potential of two-way, made a grant to the Alternate Media Center of NYU to conduct consumer evaluations of broadcast teletext in the United States. The experiment was conducted in association with public station WETA in Washington, D.C., beginning in 1980. It used the Telidon system to supply two hundred pages of information to sixty decoders placed in libraries, schools, community centers, and private homes. Using input from *The Washington Post, The Washington Star,* and other information providers, the service offered a range of news and self-help information services. It also tested ways the system could supplement WETA's regular programming—supplying a reading list for PBS science programs, for example. The Alternate Media Center used a meter in the decoders to record the pages selected, and planned to conduct telephone and personal interviews to assess acceptance of the service by the users.

The first test of the phone-based, Prestel-type videotex in the United States was the one conducted by the Knight-Ridder chain and AT&T. Its purpose was to learn the potential impact of the new technology on the chain's main line of business: newspapers.

For the project, Knight-Ridder set up the Viewdata Corporation of America in Miami, using some of the British technology under license. It called its system Viewtron. In 1980 Viewdata selected about 150 families in nearby Coral Gables and rotated thirty modified television sets among their homes. Information providers included the Consumers Union (with material from *Consumer Reports,* devoted to testing and rating products), Eastern Airlines (flight schedules), "Congressional Quarterly" (condensed reports on current issues before Congress), and Bass Tickets (theater and concert bookings). A large array of advertisers signed up for the trial, to test the waters.

"What will happen to affect our newspaper business?" asked Albert J. Gillen, president of Viewdata Corporation of America. The questions he proposed to test were critical to development of the new medium:

"The question is: Does the American consumer perceive this as a real need for himself and his family? If the American perceives it as that, what kind of information does the American consumer feel is of importance to him or her? How much time will the American consumer spend calling up data?

"How will the system be paid for? Will it be paid for like a telephone, by the traditional form of advertising, or be paid for by a combination of both? And how much will it cost to put a business enterprise together? And how much relative to the cost will the American consumer be willing to pay? If there's a vast difference between the two, that will dictate between it being a business or a nonbusiness."

In Ohio, the *Columbus Dispatch* tried to answer some of these questions directly by offering its entire editorial content to subscribers around the country via a computer system called CompuServe. Working from an index, viewers can acquire any article in the paper that day or any article available through the Associated Press. The service, which originally cost $5 an hour, also offers electronic games, display advertising, and classified ads. The paper planned to make available the content of a dozen other newspapers, including *The New York Times, The Washington Post,* and *The Los Angeles Times,* as the system developed.

By 1981 Warner Communications was testing out this service as part of its Qube development. Atari Inc., a Warner subsidiary that makes personal computers, placed a hundred terminals in Qube homes so the users could play Atari video games and retrieve news and consumer information from the CompuServe data bank.

Although the facsimile newspaper proved an interesting feature to viewers in the Tama New Town test of the mid-seventies, first operational steps toward an electronic news service in Japan were taken with the field testing of the phone-based Captain system by the Ministry of Post and Telecommunications in 1980. At that time, twenty newspapers contributed information free of charge for accessing by about one thousand telephone subscribers in the Tokyo area.

Two major newspaper organizations, the Southam Newspaper Group and the *Toronto Star* (Torstar Inc.) joined in 1979 to test out the electronic news service in Canada. They became information providers for a field test of Telidon services mounted in Toronto by the Department of Communication and Bell Canada. In this pilot project, which Bell Canada named "Vista," about 900 television sets modified for Telidon allowed users to choose from 100,000 pages of data. Many of the services available on Prestel were included.

Southam's newspapers in four provinces became involved in subsequent trials, contributing localized news, information, and advertising, to see what interested people in their market areas.

Gerald Haslam, director of videotex services for Southam, said the move was both defensive and entrepreneurial. The defensive part came from a desire to protect each local paper's revenue base on its own turf.

"When you establish a local newspaper in a market," Haslam said, "you stake out a turf for collection of ads which permits you to collect information. You say, 'I am the collector of classified ads in this one market, and I don't want anyone to come along and take that market away from me!'

"The reason someone *doesn't* come along is because others perceived you to have preempted that particular market."

And the Southam papers did not want new information collectors to use the technology to usurp their markets.

Beyond that, Haslam said, the company wanted to promote videotex entrepreneurially as a means of distributing information in a form different from newspapers. It looked on the system as an important medium for selling goods and services.

Southham/Torstar based its service, called Infomart, on subscription fees entitling the subscriber to a given number of pages per month, rather than fees per page as in the original Prestel billing structure. To keep subscription rates attractive, it supplemented them with advertising.

Prestel itself turned out to be a major testing ground for electronic news services. The *Birmingham Post & Mail* went so far as to call its Prestel pages an "electronic newspaper." It drew its revenues from advertising, as in its conventional newspaper format—the bottom quarter of a videotex news page contained an ad for an automobile or another product. The *Post & Mail* offered combination rates, so advertisers could buy space in the paper and on Prestel at the same time.

The East Counties Newspapers stayed extremely local with their news input for Prestel. They, too, were protecting their turf as providers of detailed information about East Anglia.

To UPI must go the credit for the first news organization to glimpse the future of a multifaceted electronic news service, and to act on that vision. By 1980 the wire service had in commercial operation most of the pieces that could later be put together into an integrated video, audio, and videotex system:

• One-way teletext headline summary service sent by satellite to cable systems for programming on their channels. (AP and Reuters were offering this service, as well.)

• NewsTime: Transmission of still pictures with voice-over audio news reports to cable systems. The service was based at the Southern Satellite Systems earth station outside of Atlanta.

• UPI television news service distributing visual segments for television stations to insert into their news broadcasts.

• UPI audio service, hourly distributed news broadcasts for radio stations.

• UPI high-speed national and regional wires, fed directly to computers of newspapers that were editing all copy on VDT's, and to the KSL computer for its Ceefax-style service.

• NewsShare: Delivery of its national and state news reports to home computer terminals from the Telecomputing Corp. of America's computer in McLean, Virginia; news was accessed by typing in requests through the terminal's "typewriter" keyboard. It would then be displayed on the subscriber's VDT or produced in hard copy by an attached printer.

The news agency offered newspapers the opportunity to put local and regional news into the computer for electronic distribution to the home. "Electronic distribution is just another way for newspapers to transfer information to the consumer," said Frank Tremaine, UPI senior vice-president, pointing out that UPI had come to think of itself not just as a "wire service" but as an information wholesaler. "We will provide information for any type of distribution. We might have to reformat it for a new system, but we reformat it in a number of different ways, already."

SCENARIO: "NEWSPAPERS" AFTER A.D. 2000

This, it has been said, is an information society, the information era; the industrial revolution has been succeeded by the information revolution. If this is so, then society, and the individuals and institutions that make it up, must be very much concerned that information be provided in usable and accessible form to everyone who needs it. The new technologies of communications provide an excellent means for supplying not only basic background information, the body of knowledge accumulated by human beings, but also for keeping us abreast of the changing patterns of, and the continual additions to, this information: the substance of what we call *news.*

To help understand what this change will mean to us as consumers of news and information, I want to develop here a picture of what the emerging news services may be like. This is not a forecast of what will be, because there are too many political, economic, and social variables that can knock a long-range prediction into a cocked hat. It is a picture of what *could be,* based on technology that already exists or which could readily be developed as the need increases. I have selected neither "best case" nor "worst case" situations, but operational practices that might reasonably come about. I've chosen a computer as author of the scenario. This particular computer has been programmed by its human mentor to carry out the following instructions:

Synthesize developments in news dissemination over the years with information on the current state of the electronic art in newsgathering and presentation; edit this for the salient points and construct a narrative about news services from a perspective early in the next century. Any projections the computer makes that prove, in time, to be inaccurate are obviously the result of its own error.

Following is a reproduction, in the cold type by which this book has been set, of the computer's printout:

SCENARIO: THE ELECTRONIC NEWS SERVICE

THE TIME: December 31, early in the twenty-first century.
THE PLACE: Washington, D.C.

The AUPI Newscom Unit arrived at the Mall an hour early to set up the control van at a point where the dish antenna on top could get a clear shot at the broadcast satellite.

Video reporters sat at a table in the van talking over their assignments with the unit director. In one corner, a rewrite person was typing an "advance" story into a VDT. The story was that 100,000 people were expected on the Mall by 9:00 p.m. for the start of a First Night Celebration that this year would have a special significance: At 10:00 p.m., President Joanna Hampshire would pull a switch to put on line the first major plant supplying electricity from solar energy to the national public-power grid. Since the plant is a federal project, the private power lobby in Washington has warned off the two remaining commercial television networks from covering the event live. Public television couldn't get station clearances for live coverage, either. So live, beginning-to-end coverage of the event was left to AUPI Newscom, feeding television signals by satellite to the cable systems and to individual homes that had installed the small, rooftop receiving dishes. Other news-gathering organizations were supplying coverage for the various electronic media as well. But only the AUPI had coordinated all available forms of news presentation into an integrated service.

Mingling in the crowd, one Newscom reporter with a walkie-talkie ad-libbed "color" items into the voice-recognition computer in the van. That computer translated his words into text for the Newscom editor's VDT; she corrected the words that the computer had "misheard," and then retransmitted them in their corrected print form.

A staffer using a hand-held electronic camera with a small antenna attached sent pictures from the crowd to the van so that the director could intercut close-ups with the crowd shots from the fixed camera positions.

Balancing a portable electronic typewriter on the edge of the speakers' platform, a reporter assigned to write the lead story aimed the tiny directional dish on her portable toward the control van so it, too, could be relayed to the satellite.

The unit director at the Mall was responsible for dovetailing video and print coverage of this particular event. To do this, she had to be concerned with how best to tell the story in picture terms as well as print. But she did not face the problem of a commercial television news producer who is forced to go for the attractive pictures and can pay little attention to elements of the story that cannot be told live or on video-tape. The Newscom unit director has it both ways; she can send "moving pictures," but she can also supply all the print that is needed to explain and interpret the story in detail, because both pictures and print are coming to the home viewer on the same set.

The television anchor person in the van, apprised by the unit director about print stories that were being transmitted at the same time, informed people at home that they could see an index of additional stories on solar energy by typing in the word "Solar" on their keyboards. She also suggested that the viewers might want to refer later to a documentary on solar energy that had been videotaped a year before and stored in the AUPI central computer for accessing by individual subscribers any time they wished to see it.

(In Newton, Elizabeth Hershey typed a note into her set telling it to remind her, later that night, about the solar documentary. Then she ran off to get her ten-year-old daughter, whom she had heard dawdling about an hour after her bedtime, to go to bed.)

In the Newscom headquarters in Atlanta, a producer repackaged part of the First Night video coverage into short segments that went into Newscom's twenty-four-hour satellite television news service. Video stories from this service are also stored digitally in the computers until they are superseded. That way, a viewer at home who misses the live transmission, or is interested in only one particular story from the newscasts, can key up specific video reports at his or her convenience.

Newscom's around-the-clock audio service offers the same capability, in car radios as well as in the home.

(In Montauk, Ned Ballou, listening to the live event as he is driving his car to a New Year's Eve party, says the command, "Audiotex—solar" and the radio switches automatically to an announcer, on tape, who reads him a background story on solar energy. On the Upper West Side, Jean, in her kitchen preparing hors d'oeuvres, says "Audiotex—nuclear" and hears a story, read to her while she is working, about how the antinuclear forces had won the long fight to switch to solar energy.)

Exactly at 10:00 p.m., the president pulled a switch and the people around the world saw a glowing white "ball" drop down a gas panel strip from the top of the Washington Monument until it "hit" a shining red "button" at the bottom. A cheer went up as the crowd, watching a huge video screen, saw the lights of Tucson, two thousand miles away, flicker for a quarter second as the old nuclear power station cut out and the solar station came on the line.

Although Newscom presents the most extensive combination of video and print in its national electronic news service, many other news-gathering organizations, local, national, and international, feed news and information into the country's two-way electronic communications system.

Almost all homes are now tied into the system by optical fiber "wires," which replaced coaxial cables in the eighties and nineties. Videotex in the United States and Canada is based almost exclusively on cable and telephone connections to the computers, although in some remote areas that can't be wired it is supplied by an over-the-air satellite service to home antennas. In the United States, most national news and information services are transmitted on a common-carrier basis by *Pubsat III*, operated by the U.S. Postal and Telecommunication Service, to earth stations in each city and rural area to be served. At the earth stations, private cable companies or public cable agencies pick up the signals for distribution over their systems, which are also restricted by law to common-carrier service. (Some big cable organizations had developed videotex and program-origination services before the federal law was passed forbidding cable operators and AT&T from engaging in program production. After that, they spun off their programming efforts into production companies that became Information and Entertainment Providers for the systems.) Local phone companies, also rigidly restricted to common-carrier service, pick up the signals for telephone-based videotex systems.

Since national news is provided by satellite-users such as Newscom, most city and suburban news organizations (which have grown out of the former local newspapers) report only local and regional developments.

The availability to residential subscribers of a wealth of information has made it imperative that local news services provide better coverage of their communities than the former local newspapers on which they were built. To attract subscribers, this coverage is all they have. But people are always interested in what is happening to their neighbors and their town, so the demand for a good, purely local electronic news service is high.

Alternative publications that seek a local or regional audience, or even national attention, have an easier time of it today. In the print-distribution days, many of the large, conservative distributors could refuse to handle alternative papers, even though the distributor held a monopoly over a particular delivery area. But the U.S. Postal and Telecommunication Service and the local electronic carriers are not allowed to bar users who pay the basic rates to get on the system.

Because costs of production and distribution have been reduced drastically, many local news operations are able to support themselves on the proceeds from subscriptions. For many newspapers, this move was forced by the fact that merchandisers, especially those that sold through "pull" advertising, were able to reach customers directly via shopping channels on the system, rather than through the papers' advertising columns. It is surprising how many people will punch up even the display ads, if they are offered "free," that they formerly chanced to see as they paged through their newspapers. Social scientists who have queried viewers about this phenomenon find they were first attracted by the superior seven-color capability and fine definition offered by the interactive systems toward the end of the century.

Classified advertising, of course, was siphoned off by entrepreneurs who realized they could make money offering this service alone, not packaged together with news. People eagerly sought out this service, also "free" on their sets. And, as with display ads, studies have shown that they like to read through classifieds even if they are not immediately in the market for what they see offered.

By the time the papers reacted to the threat—cued obviously by the fact that their own classified sections were getting thinner and thinner—it was too late for them to preempt the field. Many tried to catch up by selling, at first, a joint print and videotex package to classified advertisers, and later shifting all their editorial and advertising content to the two-way system.

The subscription-supported descendants of the newspapers are in stiff competition, as they were in the paper-distribution era, with "shoppers"—local advertising operations that offer neighborhood news and information for "free" distribution.

Most former newspaper operations now look upon themselves as information suppliers, rather than strictly as news publishers. Since the cable and phone companies may not act as information sources but only as information storers and transmitters, many organizations that have made the transition from newspapers to electronic news services operate "umbrella" services on the system. For a fee, they process announcements that local governments, community groups, and businesses want to put directly into the computer. Their m ánstay, however, is still their own hourly coverage of news in their areas. Many former papers find they can still carry advertising on the same pages as their news, because advertisers want to identify with the credibility and popularity of the "paper" (people persist in calling them "papers") rather than chance presenting their ads directly by buying pages on the system themselves.

For electronic papers, taking advertising in their news pages has become something of a two-edged sword nicking away at their credibility: readers don't make the separation on the tube that they did on printed newspaper pages between editorial content and ads. Many of them believe that the news on the page is "sponsored" by the advertiser and thus, perhaps influenced by the advertiser.

(Many municipalities support public-information services, in which announcements from welfare, health and safety agencies, educational institutions, and other nonprofit community services can be accessed by citizens without charge. These are sometimes entered into the system directly, sometimes though "umbrella" organizations.)

The news services provide "action pages" through which subscribers can buy products directly from their advertisers.

Personal news and information can be entered into the news services' pages by subscribers who want to spread some word about themselves. The news may be restricted to a specific list of friends and neighbors whose HCS "addresses" the subscriber has given to the news service. Or, if it is news the subscriber would like everyone to know, it can be entered on the news service's Open Pages for anyone who wants to scan them, or called up by anyone who punches in the subscriber's name and HCS number, to see what's new with him. For instance, Mr. and Mrs. Max Benjamin recently announced the birth of a daughter by typing in the facts to the personal page of *The St. Petersburg Times*. By punching in an instruction code, they brought the arrival to the attention of everyone who had listed *their* names as friends about whom they wanted to know the latest news. The couple could inform others of a personal emergency by activating the "Flash News" service in the sets of friends and relatives. The computer superimposes "Flash Alert" in bright orange over a portion of the video screens at any time the sets are in use.

The News Service sends out public Flash Alerts ("Hurricane Warning!") accompanied by an index number that tells the viewer where to get details of the warning. If the homeowner desires, an alarm bell will sound, calling him to the set when a Flash Alert, either personal or public, has been transmitted.

A club can use the News Service to list the name of the next meeting's speaker for members who call up the club's private news page.

In the United States, the ever-growing chains of local news operations are able to offer a combination of national and local information services to their subscribers. Knight-Ridder-Gannett, for example, presents essentially a Prestel-type videotex service, with many news and information providers. The service is sold locally by chain members whose major draw is their local news coverage. Bonneville, the satellite network owned by the Mormon Church, offers a combined video and teletext news service using reports from the newsrooms of its various local television stations, all of which now have their programs transmitted to viewers on the cable.

The arrival of two-way electronic systems gave *The Wall Street Jour-*

nal the opportunity to become the first national, and then worldwide, "newspaper." In the latter part of the last century, it was printing editions not only in New York but also in three other cities, from photo-offset plates transmitted by satellite. Now it offers a complete business and general news service via satellite videotex, across the country and overseas. *The Christian Science Monitor* has become a worldwide publisher of news in the same way.

The Washington Post has combined with its sister Post-Newsweek stations in providing a television and videotex news service to cable systems around the country, integrating the former newspaper and broadcast news staffs into a single news-gathering organization.

Papers, such as the *Post,* that have switched to videotex, no longer distribute hard copies. All the content they previously presented on paper is in the computer. "Back copies" (actually, "Back stories" is more appropriate) can be accessed as easily as their hour-by-hour offerings.

Most newspaper morgues—library files of all stories previously printed in the paper—had been computerized by the end of the century. Reporters and editors had by then become used to "looking up" a story or a fact in a reference work in the computerized library, rather than leafing through clips in the files or thumbing through a reference work that might be out-of-date by as much as a year. News-clipping files and reference materials are now on line for subscribers to access, as well.

People at home who want hard copies of stories or pictures that appear on their screens press the facsimile key, and a sharp copy emerges from the photoprinter slot in seconds.

The copy is printed out, not on paper, but on a thin sheet of cheap, reusable plastic, which the reader can keep or reinsert into the set to be erased and overprinted with another story. The unwillingness of subscribers to lug home heavy stacks of 8½-by-11-inch, one-time newsprint sheets for their facsimile printers was a conceptual problem local news organizations had to solve before substituting electronic delivery for physical delivery of the paper. The breakthrough to electrostatically erasable plastic sheets (called in the industry a "synthetic substrate") provided the solution.

Of the major national newspapers, only a few, including *The New York Times,* still print complete editions on newsprint for subscriptions and distribution to newsstands. The *Times* publishes a national edition at plants around the country with photocopied plates supplied by satellite and a facsimile edition at various foreign capitals. After tests on the Prestel system in England and the Telidon system in Canada, it decided to enter the videotex field, but only as a supplement to its printed product. It has simplified the computerized information-retrieval service it began providing to other papers and businesses in the 1970s, and is now marketing it to the public through the electronic system.

The New York *Daily News,* conscious that many of its readers still do not have an HCS, is still producing papers (manufactured now by vegetable fibers, rather than scarce wood pulp) to be sold on newsstands. The papers are not printed at a central plant and trucked to the stands, however. They are turned out by ink-jet printers in each of the large major newsstands in the city, and sped to smaller stands by the three-wheeled, electric-powered mini-vans you see darting in and out of traffic on Manhattan streets.

Computerized transmission to the big stands makes it possible for the *Daily News* to localize news and play stories according to the individual interests of individual neighborhoods. News of Israel, played heavily in the Williamsburg section of Brooklyn, is downplayed along Atlantic Avenue in Brooklyn, with its heavy Arab population. In East Harlem, a Spanish-language version of the paper is spewed out of the ink-jet printers for the 2 million Puerto Ricans living there.

It is surprising, but it is in the fully wired and electronified cities that print-on-paper still finds a place. Some neighborhood papers are delivered door-to-door without charge to people in poorer sections who don't have HCS's or don't use the sets for anything other than entertainment.

Newspaper-based organizations that entered the two-way field found they could no longer produce "editions" that were updated once or twice a day. People are no longer satisfied to read news that is a few hours old. So, considerable competition exists to get videotex news into the system first. The fever for immediacy reminds you of the way sensational papers competed for readers at the end of the nineteenth century. Those papers sent eight editions, usually with scare headlines, to the newsstands every day. And between the "regular" editions, newsboys ran through the streets crying "Extra" to hawk news of a startling event such as the sinking of the *Maine.* Now the bell on the set proclaims the "Extra," and people complain that the editors are tempted to ring it too often.

People want to flick on the set when they wake up and find headline summaries of stories that were not fixed in print at eleven the night before. They want the videotex stories on matters that interest them to be available immediately, and up-to-the-minute. So the pressure is on print-based news providers to get breaking stories into the system as fast as the radio and television news operations did in the 1980s. Some of the print-based services try to attract subscribers by presenting interesting sidebars and pictures along with the breaking stories, or by detailed background information on the issues at hand. But unless they can be first or very close on breaking stories, readers turn to other services.

In dealing with this plethora of possibilities, there are as many styles of accessing news as there are subscribers. Each subscriber becomes his or her own content editor. This was true to a limited extent when paper was predominant, and television news was separate from print news. The reader selected from a large array of newspapers and magazines the ones likely to give the news, information, opinion, and entertainment that interested him most. In New York, one reader might buy the *Times, The New York Review of Books, Tennis* magazine, and *Newsweek;* another, the *Daily News* and *The Sporting News.* On commercial television, the choice of a favorite news program was dictated more by a liking for a particular "anchor" person than by special interests or educational background.

Today the HCS with its alphanumeric keyboard allows you to become your own editor in an even more selective way. As a news-service subscriber you find your own pattern for getting what you want.

For example, Peter Anthony of La Jolla has asked for a "First Page" (actually a headline summary) to be ready for him on the tube, each morning at eight. Using the index number attached to each story summary, he reads each story he wants to know about immediately on the videotex channel. He knows he can come back to the others later, since they will be waiting for him in the computer.

He went to bed too early to see the finish of an extra-inning game of the San Diego Padres, so he instructed the set to print out the play-by-play account for him to read in the morning. (It could have held a rerun of the game for him to watch, if he had had the time.) Since Peter had previously told the News Service he wanted to know when gold reached $1500 an ounce on the Zurich market, and this is the day, that information is flashed at the bottom of the news-summary page. The News Service also alerts him to a new book by a feminist author because he has asked to be kept informed of any developments in the women's movement. Over breakfast, he watches the author on a monitor in the dining area, because the News Service, knowing of his interest, has cued up for his special attention an interview done with her the day before.

As he leaves for work, he asks the Service to give him another summary at 6:00 p.m., when he next expects to check the set, and to assemble stories in his areas of special interest that break during the day. The computer keeps track of the time he last accessed the Service, and drops from his menu the stories it has already presented to him.

Although the "First Page" summaries still suggest what stories the

editor thinks is important, as the Front Page did in newsprint days, subscribers now have a better chance to decide that for themselves. That is
because the News Service includes in its data bank stories that, solely
because of space limitations, would have been "spiked" on the old
paper-and-print journals. They are available through an additional
index that supplements the summary index that represents the News
Service's judgment of what is the best news and information available
at any particular moment.

The whole arrangement gives the reader a greater sense of participating in "his" or "her" newspaper than was possible before. Most services
have a feedback line to their newsrooms which prints out complaints
and comments from subscribers at home. Those who have requested a
personalized news package take a proprietary interest in what they are
receiving, often complaining immediately and directly if the stories they
are getting are inaccurate or do not answer the questions a reader expects to have answered by the reporter.

Editors report the most frequent feedback goes like this: "There's a
mistake today on my Sports Page A3542. I'm sure Mrozek's batting average can't be as low as .225. Will you check it out and send me a correction?"

Editors find this feedback channel useful. Granted, they do get some
crank complaints, but that is a cross editors have had to bear since they
first put out broadsheets on flatbed presses. What they find good about
it is that readers concerned with a specific area often have special
knowledge that enables them to catch errors a general copy editor
might miss, or to suggest coverage that the editors or reporters might
not have known about on their own.

Persons about whom a story has appeared on the system have a
chance to request a correction, or if the editor insists that the News
Service version is correct, have their rebuttals entered into the data
base and indexed in a follow-up to the story being questioned.

All editors know it is humanly impossible to avoid mistakes, but in
the old paper-print days, it seemed to some to be a stigma to admit their
errors. Only a few of the best papers ran regular correction boxes. Now
it is considered both responsible and responsive to carry corrections
pages, and flag major ones on the index pages for a reader who might
otherwise continue to have a mistaken fact cached away in his brain's
storage cells.

Readers are pleased by the fact that they can talk back to the editors.
They like it that they can count on getting their letters to the editor
published: in the old days, lack of space limited the letters to a few
edited versions the "Letters Editor" chose to print. Each News Service
today has a "Letters" category in its menu. Letters are indexed according to subject matter, and entered in full in the computers. The services

find this is an attractive feature drawing attention to their output. People like to read what other "ordinary" people have to say about items in the news. Lively exchanges develop between them, much in the style of the correspondents who once brightened the letters column of the old *Times* of London.

With news offered via videotex, video picture, and facsimile, the combinations available to subscribers are very large. People in the middle classes have had successive models of the set for a number of years, and can manipulate its capabilities with ease.

But it has been harder for the former newspapers to get their working-class readers into the system, because many of them do not feel that they need the extra information. Home sets are not much more expensive than the cheaper color-television sets that even the poor manage to afford. But obviously, there are many at the poverty level who can't pay the extra money. Some government social agencies are now supplying the cheap, mass-produced model of the HCS—the one with the small, ten-digit key pad—to welfare clients. The theory is that the information system is as necessary to their well-being as the telephone, which is universally provided without charge for those living below the poverty level. The problem, they find, is to motivate them to call up news and information that will be beneficial to them, rather than be satisfied with the sloppily edited content of the shoppers delivered free to their doors.

In England, the Social Democrats began a campaign at the turn of the century to get a set into every home in the country. The British Post Office provided local, two-way connections free, as part of the National Service. Almost everyone can afford to rent a set, and those who can't are entitled to receive a government subsidy to cover the cost of the rental.

Reuters, *The Financial Times,* and *The Guardian* have become major providers of national news for Prestel, with local news entering the system from the former newspaper publishers in cities such as Birmingham. The BBC has fully integrated its Ceefax system into BBC News, and is providing a combined text-and-television news service, over the air, to all parts of the country.

In France, an angry fight developed early between the PTT and Télédiffusion de France over control of the national news and information system, and the contest has not been decided yet. Télétel, the PTT's phone-based system, uses Agence France Presse as its chief supplier of national and international news, but it provides much information and news input of its own. Separation of content from technology does not exist. TDF sends its Antiope news service to set-owners by direct-broadcast satellite. All news on the service is provided by TDF, and content is closely monitored (some say controlled) by the French government. *Le Monde,* with the help of a government subsidy, is providing a French-only videotex edition to systems throughout France, North Africa, and the Republic of Quebec, renting channels on the Franco-German communication satellites. After some political difficulties, *The International Herald Tribune,* published in Paris, has been permitted to use the French PTT facilities to transmit an English-language videotex service throughout Western Europe.

Japan's videotex news services are also split. Asahi Newspapers, working with Nippon Telecommunications Public Corporation, is using the Captain system to provide a full news and information service, including facsimile printout of stories, to all homes that have the telephone-HCS combination. NHK is using its direct broadcast satellites to transmit a Ceefax-style "updater" news service to homes on every one of its islands, from Okinawa to Hokkaido.

On the North American continent, Canada led the way in setting up a backbone transmission system for news and information. It was based on Telidon, which set a world standard by becoming the first videotex to present "still pictures" in full color. National videotex services are provided by ST Electronic News and CBC News. Their output is transmitted by Telesat Canada, now a government common carrier, to the earth stations of all cable systems and by direct-broadcast satellite to private homes in remote localities.

Through the use of subsidies, Sweden was the first country to achieve 100 percent saturation of home communication sets. In Stockholm, *Dagens Nyheter* ("Daily News") and the Swedish Central News Agency have joined with Televerket in providing a service in Swedish and English for the Scandinavian countries and systems overseas that contract for channels on the Nordsat system.

The Soviet Union has a videotex news service supplied from Moscow to the entire country by Tass. It uses direct-broadcast satellites and a combination of telephone and over-the-air transmission. Brazil has installed a similar service, originated and controlled from Brasilia. China's service, controlled by the central government, is available to people in community centers in all the larger municipalities.

Many of the developing countries in Africa and Asia have installed videotex news services as government entities. Domestically, they supply information to government agencies and businesses. Some countries that exclude Western- and Eastern-bloc correspondents make these services available to foreign electronic news agencies as a means of getting approved information into the international information market.

The United States, which got a late start in videotex, has now pretty well caught up. It ranks behind only Sweden, Britain, and Canada in the number of sets in use per capita.

CONCLUSION

It is interesting, in looking backward, that as late as the 1980s, most newspaper editors and publishers were *not* persuaded that any major change in distribution of their news product was in store. Television network officials blithely assumed that their fixed-time news programs, featuring performers on a set cuing video snippets of "actualities" of the day, would continue in public favor forever.

This, of course, turned out to be a monumental lack of foresight. Today, in the beginning years of the third millennium, we have integrated, multifaceted electronic news services that provide news and information in forms and detail only hazily envisioned by the public as little as thirty years ago.

Objectively, this system has provided a number of improvements in the general availability and delivery of news and information. Its rapid development has obviously presented problems to society, as well.

This computer, which recognizes its limited status as a servant, not a savant, cannot go beyond its instructions (to synthesize these developments) by critiquing them, as well.

END OF RUN

THE SCENARIO AND THE REALITIES

Despite my computer's disclaimer, I think it has made one prognostication that borders on a value judgment: it has suggested that, by the early years of the next century, a common-carrier system, open to all IP's, had been set up with the expansion of the U.S. Postal Service into a Postal and Telecommunications Service. I think the more likely outcome is that AT&T will gain control of the system, as forecast in the Arthur D. Little study. And by its executives' own account, the phone company will not be satisfied to restrict its activities to providing a common-carrier service. When I asked the AT&T executive in charge of long-range planning if the company planned to develop a data base of information to feed into its own videotex systems, he said Bell companies already had begun to build such data bases, and could expand on them indefinitely. "Our planning aim is to have full access to the [videotex] market and to see if we can market this information," he said.[1]

It is conceivable that, in successive attempts to push through Congress a "Bell Bill" for total control of telecommunications, AT&T will one day get, not two hundred senators and representatives to sponsor it, but a clear majority. And that bill may permit the phone company, in the name of operating efficiency as a "regulated" monopoly, to provide any kind of cable, satellite, and data transmission services it wants. This could well include editorial responsibility for its own news and information videotex services for transmission to subscribers via local phone companies across the country.

The FCC opened the way for this to come about, de facto, when, on April 7, 1980, it authorized AT&T to enter the data-processing business.

The choice by my computer of the Postal Service as a preferred alternative makes clear a point I want to emphasize about computers: their output reflects the subjective selections *and* the predilections of their human programmers.

It *does* seem to me that the public would have more effective control over its information system if the backbone transmission network were run by a public corporation whose mandate is to keep its hands off content. The planning and decision-making processes of private corporations are traditionally kept secret, while those of the Postal Service, in theory at least, are not, and eventually must be aired. In any event, the ability of the people and their elected representatives to call the Postal Service to account is greater than that of the people to call to account the world's largest private corporation with an annual budget and revenues greater than most countries of the world. The temptation of such a powerful entity to influence, to interfere with, or subtly or openly to try to control the content of the nation's news and information lifeline over which it had been given exclusive jurisdiction would be very great indeed.

To state a concern about monopoly or market-dominance control of the integrated telecommunications system it is not necessary to impute motives to executives of AT&T (or some multinational conglomerate) other than their evidenced desire to maximize profits. In the American system, that is what their stockholders and their board of directors expect, and that is what they are paid for. It is hard to imagine a Bell executive yearning secretly for more power and perquisites than he already has. It is *not* hard to imagine him doing many things to achieve favorable public opinion and a favorable political climate that would guarantee the corporation's profit goals in perpetuity. And these efforts might not necessarily be in the public's best interest, insofar as an electronic news and information service was concerned.

In the early 1920s AT&T was making a profit from controlling both system and content in a communications network. It owned and operated twenty-three radio stations, anchored by WEAF (later WNBC) in New York. When RCA decided to assemble a network in competition, expecting to use AT&T telephone lines to link the stations together, Bell threatened to deny it the use of its system. So RCA and AT&T struck a deal: in return for allowing RCA to get into the radio-network business, AT&T received a promise from RCA that it would not compete in supplying transmission lines for networks. the deal established a virtual monopoly for AT&T in this area.[2]

The first cracks in the arrangement did not appear until the late 1970s, when Congress provided money for the Public Broadcasting Service to link its stations by satellite, at a rate far cheaper than was being charged by AT&T for landline transmission.

Strong competitors, IBM among them, have also begun to challenge the AT&T monopoly, and the FCC has approved competition in some facets of AT&T's business operations. If it is forced to compete, AT&T will insist that it be allowed to compete in all areas—including those involved with content, such as cable and videotex. In fact, the phone company set the stage for videotex competition with a trial of an "Electronic Information Service" based on the innocuous-sounding idea, also being tested in France, that telephone-directory information could be transmitted electronically to the home, rather than delivered physically in bulky telephone books or provided by information operators. In conjunction with the New York Telephone Company, AT&T began testing the service by supplying customers in the Albany area with a terminal that included a telephone set, a visual display screen, and a typewriter-like keyboard. Customers could type in requests for numbers and other information normally provided in the White Pages (general phone listings) and Yellow Pages (classified business listings) in any local directory of the ten-thousand-square-mile area covered by the 518 Area Code. The terminal permitted customers to enter an unlimited amount of personal phone numbers, then push a single automatic dialing button when they wished to dial one of those numbers.

But in addition to that, a company spokesman told me, customers could *also* ask for and get weather, time, and sports scores; a daily horoscope, a daily thought from Dr. Joyce Brothers—supplied by phone company "editors."

"We are looking for customer reactions—what additional kinds of information customers might want if the service were made generally available. We will try to decide the cost-effective way to charge for information in this service—by the piece or on a monthly service-charge basis." (Telephone directory information traditionally has been "free," included in the base charge for monthly service.)

In Albany, AT&T was involving itself directly in content, as opposed to its collaboration with Knight-Ridder in Coral Gables, where it was mainly interested in testing the technology it had developed for videotex. GTE, second only to AT&T in operating phone companies, intended also to get involved in content when it became the commercial partner of Prestel to set up videotex information systems in the United States. When they were announced, not a murmur of public concern was heard about the camel's-nose implications of those moves.*

However, newspaper publishers themselves raised objections when AT&T took its next step—testing a home information service that included classified, catalogue, and display advertising. The company, through a local operating arm, Southwestern Bell Telephone, got permission from the Texas Public Utilities Commission to place free computer terminals, wired to regular phone lines, in 680 homes and 60 businesses in Austin to test such a service beginning in June 1981. Texas publishers immediately charged that the test gave AT&T and "unfair advantage" in developing services directly competitive with newspapers. *Editor and Publisher,* the bible of the newspaper industry, picked up the challenge in an editorial:

"AT&T intends to establish squatters rights in [the electronic information] area. . . . It is a move that the newspaper business must fight at the federal and state levels with every weapon at its command."

DOMINATION OF THE NEWS AND INFORMATION SERVICE

With its Albany experiment, the phone company arrived at the door of the electronic news and information service. In trying to enter, it was bumping into media conglomerates that had also been staking out the premises. One of the biggest problems in offering a news and specialized information service is building up the data base. In this, AT&T had to start from scratch. Conglomerates that have been acquiring media properties over the years have the information already in hand, waiting only to be formatted for the computerized services.

* I have already mentioned Alain Giraud's criticism of the French PTT's version of phone directory-videotex.

Even if, as in the Scenario, the United States were to achieve a nationwide common-carrier service, with entrance guaranteed without restriction to all news and information providers *excluding* the phone company and the government, it might still be possible for a single private corporation to dominate what we see and hear on that system. Media conglomerates that proliferated with the information explosion of the sixties and seventies would seem to be tailor-made for a multifaceted electronic news and information service. Perhaps some of them *were* tailor-made.

Some come easily to mind: RCA, CBS, and ABC, for example. Others, such as McGraw-Hill Inc. and The Times-Mirror Corp,* could emerge as dark horses.

And then, there is the biggest of them all: Time Inc. A headline in *The New York Times* proclaims: "Time Inc. Gets Bigger and Richer as It Moves Into Other Fields."[3] As it rolled toward the 1980s with revenues closing on $2 billion a year, Time Inc. acquired *The Washington Star,* American Television and Communications Corp. (ATC, a company second only to Teleprompter in cable operations), and the Book-of-the-Month Club. It planned to distribute videocassettes using the BOMC formula. Time already had large-circulation national magazines in the news and information field: *Time, Fortune, People, Sports Illustrated, Money,* and the reborn *Life.* It was involved in book publishing through its ownership of Little, Brown & Company and Time-Life Books. It owned twenty-one weekly papers in the Chicago area and a computerized data-marketing business.

Time Inc. had a television station and was looking for others. Its Time-Life Films syndicated television shows. It acquired David Susskind's Talent Associates to develop projects for the three commercial networks.

In 1975 Time made the decision that revivified the entire cable-television industry: it put its Home Box Office, which offered first-run movies for pay cable, on the RCA *Satcom I* satellite. This began the satellite era in national distribution of television programs (which led in turn to Comsat's plan to use satellites to broadcast television programming directly to rooftop antennas on private homes). By 1980, 1700 cable systems with 4 million subscribers—two-thirds of the pay-

---

* Times-Mirror, the corporation that publishes *The Los Angeles Times* and *Newsday,* blossomed into a conglomerate of newsprint, book publishing, information services, magazine publishing, cable communications, and directory printing. It has the data base to become its own Prestel.

television market—were HBO affiliates. That same year, the Time Video Group began another satellite-distributed network, "BBC in America." This offered popular British programs via cable television, supported by commercials. "Our competitors," said a Time Video executive, "are ABC, CBS, and NBC. . . . We're another program service, another option for the viewer."[4] Time Video had now become the largest contributor to the corporation's profits.

Is there an area of the new media that Time forgot? The ATC Corporation would be the most likely entry point of the Time conglomerate into an electronic news service. When I asked an ATC representative if it planned to get into electronic print, she replied that it did not, but that might change. "We are," she said, "following videotex developments in the industry, as we do all innovative programming that can offer additional services for our subscribers."

Although Time Inc. would seem to be positioned in the forefront of those conglomerates that might dominate an integrated system, similar cross-ownerships put the other media giants very much in the running. The race for domination will not be decided overnight. With luck, and some enlightened public policy, it may never be decided.

Public policy in the media, as reflected in the actions of the FCC, was inspired by a new popular wisdom: You can "guarantee diversity" through competition in the marketplace. The FCC forbade the phone company and the networks from engaging in cable operations. It forbade one person or corporation from owning a television station and a cable system in the same viewing area. Newspapers were forbidden to own a television station in their primary circulation areas. But accommodations, changes, and "special" exceptions were made in areas where the financial stakes were high. During the Carter administration, "Free enterprise!" became the rallying cry of the commission. Solicitousness for the radio and television business, where the stakes were highest, continued to be first priority. Under the guidance of its chairman, Charles D. Ferris, it attempted to take onerous restrictions off the business by proposing the immediate deregulation of radio and easing regulation of television.

In a show of being responsive to the public's ideas on these and other matters, the FCC went on the road with "workshops" in various cities. Ferris denied the workshops were forums for the commission to advocate decontrol. The one in Boston, which I attended, certainly appeared to be that, however. Every answer Ferris gave to questions from the audience indicated that commercial concerns were FCC concerns, and that commercial concerns—the "marketplace"—would solve all problems concerning radio and television in the public interest. When he was asked by a reporter from WGBH, the public television station in Boston, why the FCC wanted to drop a requirement, pushed through years earlier by public-interest groups led by Dr. Everett C. Parker of the United Church of Christ, that stations formally ascertain the public concerns and social problems of their areas and produce programs to meet these concerns, he replied: "Broadcasters will be motivated by profit to go out and find out what the audience wants, therefore they will have the incentive to meet these needs."

The only public-interest research I saw initiated by broadcasters was to pay an audience rating service to tell them, after the fact, how big were "the numbers" for specific programs. They found that public-affairs programs, on which they spent almost no money to make them interesting, predictably drew small audiences; the marketplace remedy for this was not to do better public-affairs programs that would interest more people. The remedy, since they were "money losers," was to cut them back to a minimum and put them in what is known in the trade as the Sunday-morning public-affairs ghetto. Even the FCC admitted deregulation would mean an end to public-affairs programming.

Manipulation of the marketplace by a large corporation, if permitted by the government, could put it in a dominant position in popular communications. A case in point was the attempt of International Telephone and Telegraph in 1967 to take over the American Broadcasting Company.

The FCC, adhering to its tradition of protecting the interests of broadcasters against the interests of consumers, approved the merger. Nicholas Johnson, a commissioner dedicated to reform in broadcasting, did not. Johnson dissented because he felt IT&T would be in a strong position to influence ABC News in areas in which it had a financial interest. These interests were substantial: IT&T owned communications businesses in the United States and forty other countries.

"Chile, Peru, Brazil, or India might someday wish to nationalize the telephone companies which ITT now owns in whole or part," Johnson wrote in his dissent. "It has happened to ITT in the past and could easily happen again. ABC news and public-affairs personnel will have to comment on the affair at length. If one admits the possibility that such nationalization could be put in a favorable light, the potential for conflict with ITT's economic interests is obvious."[5]

ITT had been notorious for its willingness to use influence with congressional representatives, government agencies, political parties, and national administrations to gain a favorable climate for its commercial operations. It used improper pressure on news reporters and publishers to slant stories in its favor. Johnson asked if it were conceivable that, while trying to pressure other television and print media, its officers would keep their hands off ABC's coverage of its affairs.

Cued by dissents from Johnson and two other commissioners, Kennethh A. Cox and Robert T. Bartley, the Justice Department appealed the commission's decision to the federal courts. Because of the mounting opposition, ABC and ITT canceled the merger plan.

Commenting after the fact, Johnson said: "I ponder what the consequences might have been if ITT's apparent cynicism to journalistic integrity had actually been able to harness the enormous social and propaganda powers of a national television network to the service of a politically sensitive corporate conglomerate."

There is little likelihood that any multimedia conglomerate that gained domination of the system would not try to influence its content and restrict access to those who have more or less the same world view. Restrictions would not usually take the form of direct censorship or flat refusal of time on the system. (Although both happen in television, where stations point out that they have been given legal responsibility for what goes on the air.) As any reporter knows, pressures from management are more subtle. Usually, media corporations, including many newspaper enterprises, do not impose their views by telling a reporter or news producer "You can't say that." Their views, which journalists come to know intuitively, are imposed by the carrot of advancement for those who conform and the stick of firing or ostracism for those who don't. On good newspapers, reporters and editors can publish some stories that don't conform, so long as they have the facts to back them up. (But not on all good newspapers: on some, reporters run up against "policy" stories that must be cleared by management and sacred cows who by common knowledge within the newsroom must not be touched.) On corrupt newspapers and in most television operations, they haven't a chance, and most of them don't try.

Self-censorship, rather than orders from the top, is by far the most common restriction on honest news production. Reporters, editors, and news producers often precondition their minds to filter out stories or program ideas that will get them into trouble. This accounts for the fact that, of all the areas of current concern, activities of corporate establishments are subjected to the least amount of scrutiny by investigative reporters.

What is badly needed, to guarantee that noncorporate, nonestablishment points of views are included in the public's electronic information systems, is the formation of a nonprofit, "public interest" news organization on the model of Ralph Nader's consumer-interest research organizations in Washington. Its content could be carried side by side with news produced by the profit-making news services, which would still provide the public with its major budget of news and information. To be viable, the service would have to pay its own way from subscriptions, in competition with other established services. A national news-gathering and transmitting agency of this kind, associated with local public-interest news services, would have to be guaranteed access to the system, under common-carrier rules provided by law. Otherwise it could be muscled out by commercial competitors that want to preserve the domain for themselves.

In the Scenario, AP and UPI have apparently been combined into a news service called AUPI, using the name "Newscom" for its integrated media operation. Another projection could have had Time Inc. buying out UPI, using its HBO satellite operations and ATC Corporation cable network to preempt the field with an integrated news service including videotex. In this Scenario, AP, a cooperative owned by newspapers and broadcasting enterprises, might survive as a text-only service for the remaining one-way media. With the public reeducated to want news and information instantly in print as well as video forms, the nation could well turn to the integrated service for all its news and information. Because it operates many local cable systems, Time Inc. could have a leg up on controlling local news, as well as national. I see Time as a likely power in the new media, but you could replace its name in this Scenario with a half dozen other conglomerates that could also master the system.

From this vantage, we can't be certain what the shape of a combined news organization would be. It would appear that an organization that can put together a service that combines real-time and taped video news with videotex, via satellite, with local video and videotex may have established the base model for electronic news services to come.

GOVERNMENT INTERFERENCE
IN THE SYSTEM

The threat of overriding government interference exists no matter who runs the backbone system—AT&T, a corporate conglomerate, or a public telecommunications corporation. One danger is that the Fairness Doctrine, a concept devised by the FCC, first applied to television and then to cable, might be extended to print. As defined by the FCC, the Fairness Doctrine imposes a twofold requirement on broadcasters and cable operators:[6]

1. They are expected to devote a reasonable amount of time to the coverage and discussion of controversial issues of public importance, and

2. Coverage of these issues must be fair in that a reasonable opportunity is afforded to presentation of contrasting points of view.

The right to reply to a personal attack broadcast by the programmer and the right of a candidate to rebut the station's endorsement of an opponent are corollaries of this doctrine.

Obviously these are laudable principles to be followed in the handling of news and public affairs. But the fact that they are imposed by government raises a First Amendment issue. Newspapers, of course, have no federal rules governing restraints upon their content. As I have mentioned, the justification most often given for content regulations such as the Fairness Doctrine, Personal Attack Rule, and Equal Time Rule in broadcast news has been that since the electronic spectrum was limited the FCC could make rules concerning how a broacasting station was to exercise its franchise and use a portion of that spectrum. This has often put the FCC in direct conflict with the First Amendment.

The commission itself does not acknowledge this conflict. It has asserted that the Fairness Doctrine upholds the principle of free speech by requiring that persons on different sides of a controversy by given a chance to be heard on a medium limited by technical restrictions. Broadcasters, on the other hand, have always seen the doctrine as a limit of their constitutional freedom. With the arrival of cable, they argued that scarcity of outlets posed by the limitations of the radio spectrum had disappeared, and that practically everyone could have access to the electronic medium.

After a long inquiry on the effects of the Fairness Doctrine, the FCC in 1974 issued a report in which it emphatically reaffirmed the doctrine, and stated that adherence to it constituted a licensee's principal obligation. It held that, at that time, despite the development of new technology, a scarcity of broadcasting frequencies still existed. This fact, it said, "impels governmental promotion of a system insuring that the public will be informed of the important issues which confront it and the competing viewpoints on those issues." The commission continued:

"The commission disagrees with arguments that the Fairness Doctrine inhibits and restricts broadcasting journalism. In the commission's view, even absent the Fairness Doctrine, broadcasters who fail to present controversial issues—because certain views are offensive, coverage is too expensive, etc.—would be violating their duty as public trustees."

Civil libertarians are torn between what they see as restrictions on free speech and the need for broadcasters to open their programming to discussion of controversial issues and a wide range of views. They are certain that the broadcasters, if left to their own devices, would steer away from a controversy and far-out points of view. Broadcasters do this because they know that advertisers don't want to be associated with controversial programming, because of fear of government pressure, and fear of displeasing a good part of the mass audiences they want to maintain.

Using the Fairness Doctrine and similar FCC regulations, Dr. Parker has fought effectively for years to gain access to television, radio, and cable for minorities and those whose views are controversial. In a talk on media ethics, he argued the Fairness Doctrine issue this way:

> The First Amendment was devised to protect the right of the people to speak freely and to circulate their ideas widely; so they might debate issues and ferret out the truth, and thus govern themselves wisely.
>
> The framers of the First Amendment did not contemplate a monopoly on the effective means of circulating information and ideas—especially such a monopoly as exists through television networks, our chief purveyors of information, entertainment, and taste-setting standards. Nor did the framers mean to establish a self-appointed class of individuals called journalists who can take on the role of sole arbiters of what is true and worthwhile for the people to know.
>
> Our society is increasingly dependent upon electronic media to disseminate ideas and to provide a forum for the debate of issues. Free

speech requires access to the forum where speech can be heard. Therefore, a diversity of persons must have access to the electronic media. A journalist has an important role to seek out and expose subject matter. But having done this, the journalist cannot insist that his or her exposition is the last word. It is the beginning, not the end of the democratic process of debate and problem solving.

Unfortunately, there are some broadcasters who think that their decisions should be final and irreversible. They claim an immunity from review and criticism that would have embarrassed a James I.[7]

Anthony Oettinger, director of the Program on Information Technologies and Public Policy at Harvard University, would agree with Dr. Parker on the obligation of a limited media to allow all sides to be heard. But, in a talk to newspaper executives, he said that the new technologies were changing the picture:

> The Fairness Doctrine on television . . . may have had a rationale back in 1934 or even 1959, but doesn't make terribly much sense in an era where cable television can bring into the electronic media the kind of First Amendment protection that you in the newspaper business take as a matter of right, and are accorded largely because the printing press is not the same kind of monopoly that the scarce electromagnetic spectrum is.
>
> The fiction that newspapers are distinct from television and cable television, is just that—a fiction. If rights, First Amendment rights, either of publishers or broadcasters or of the public, are abrogated in the broadcast medium . . . they will sooner or later disappear in the print media. At the moment, the print media are still one of the strongest bastions of the First Amendment, but they may not last much longer.[8]

The Fairness Doctrine or other regulations of content, in Professor Oettinger's view, is an opening wedge for government attempts to regulate print when print is disseminated by an electronic system. In the long haul, he said, the First Amendment must be made to apply equally to all forms of the media.

Using the argument that spectrum space limitations no longer had meaning, Representative Lionel Van Deerlin of California and others in Congress introduced in 1979 legislation that would deregulate radio and cable immediately and lead to the eventual deregulation of television (H.R. 33333, "The Communications Act of 1979"; not adopted).

When the FCC also moved to deregulate radio, some of the commissioners contended that, with more than 8400 radio stations in the country, there was sufficient diversity for various views to get an airing.

Opponents of these moves pointed out that no station permitted people with something to say to walk into the station and have their messages put on air (as they were permitted to do on cable systems that had public access channels). A voice on a cable channel, they pointed, out, did not have the same clout as a broadcaster's voice on a television station. And the established television and radio stations were likely to continue to dominate the electronic media for some years to come. As long as access to the main channels of electronic communications is restricted, they contended, government regulation guaranteeing some diversity of viewpoints is a practical necessity.

I agree that most traditional broadcasters would not allow voices of dissent. The existence of the Fairness Doctrine, in many instances, has pressured broadcast executives into allowing discussion of controversial issues. I think fewer commercial stations would present news and almost none would present public-affairs programming if the Fairness Doctrine and other FCC regulations promoting public service were dropped. So the public has benefited to some extent from these policy guidelines (although not always from the FCC's interpretation of its rules in specific cases).

But letting the government make rules about content has had some adverse effects as well. Broadcasters have often used the Fairness Doctrine as a reason *not* to broadcast controversial material, such as investigative reports developed by their own staffs. In the 1960s, while running the day-to-day news operation at WABC-TV in New York, I had to fight off arguments by the management that certain controversial subjects should not be reported. Usually the "reason" given was the Fairness Doctrine, as in: "We really shouldn't get involved in that—it could lead to a Fairness Doctrine hassle, and we don't need that."

In fact, the FCC itself has seldom pressed the "affirmative obligation" to devote a reasonable amount of time to controversial public issues. No station's license has been taken away from it for ignoring that mandate. The commission has been far more prone to act on complaints that individual programs were not "balanced." The mere forwarding of a single citizen's complaint from the FCC has been enough to scare off some stations from doing further programming in that particular area.

Although the Fairness Doctrine has been interpreted by the FCC to mean that "balance" had to be struck over a period of time, it has been willing, on occasion, to order a broadcaster to "balance" one program it has aired with another giving equal weight to "the other side."

It did that in the case of an NBC network news documentary called "Pensions: The Broken Promise." Much of the program reported on specific pension programs that had failed, with losses to employees who had thought they were protected. Accuracy in Media, a right-wing organization in Washington that monitors broadcasting, filed a Fairness Doctrine complaint charging the program was a one-sided attack on the entire private pension system. The FCC agreed; it ruled that further programming would be needed to achieve "balance."[9]

The U.S. Court of Appeals for the District of Columbia reversed the commission by a vote of 2 to 1. Judge Harold Leventhal, who wrote the majority opinion, said NBC had acted reasonably, within the bounds of investigative reporting. A broadcast journalist, he said, does not have to balance off an exposé "solely because the facts he presents jar the viewer and cause him to think and ask questions as to how widespread the abuses may be."

The order by the FCC, the judge said, substituted a government agency's judgment for that of the broadcast journalist. "Investigative reporting," he said, "has a distinctive role of uncovering and exposing abuses. It would be undermined if a government agency were free to review the editorial judgments involved in the selection of theme and materials, [or] to overrule the licensees' judgments as to what is presented."[10]

In that case, the FCC seemed to be demanding that there be one-for-one "balance": a program criticizing private pension systems must be balanced with a program praising them. If that idea were upheld, a government agency could conceivably order a station to broadcast laudatory statements about an institution that the reporter knew to be untrue.

Congress, as a matter of fact, permitted the FCC to do this in the case of public television stations. A 1967 law governing public broadcasting required "strict adherence to objectivity and balance *in all programs.*" (Emphasis added.) For good measure, it forbade public broadcasting stations from editorializing.

Certainly, any newspaper in the United States would be outraged if a federal agency ruled that an investigative story was not "objective" and ordered the paper to balance it with another story "on the other side." Philosophers have foundered on trying to define "objectivity"; surely newspapers would not permit government to define it for them. And papers would never sit still for a law that said they could not print editorials. They would instantly challenge all such acts as abridgments of their constitutional right to be free of government regulation.

A better idea would be to require that, in radio and television, where spectrum allocations are limited, say 15 percent of prime-time evening programming each week (a total of about three hours) be devoted to public-affairs programming, including documentaries. And that another 5 percent of prime time be provided as "open time" on local stations for community groups to present information in the public interest, on a first-come, first-served basis.

I know that proposing that public-affairs programs be presented in "costly" prime sales periods is heresy. But commercial broadcasters often joke among themselves that being given a television license is being given a license to steal: perhaps only the oil companies have a higher return on investment; returns on stations owned and operated by the three commercial networks range from 25 to 75 percent, once you clear away the tricky bookkeeping the network corporations impose on them to make their returns appear smaller.

Since what the stations are "stealing" is a public resource, it would seem equitable that they be required to return some of the proceeds in the form of public-service programming. All would have the same obligation, and so the burden would be shared: in time, broadcasters might come to feel they could live with making only a 20 to 70 percent return.

With public service time requirements, as an alternative to regulation of content, you eliminate government controls over the *editorial* matter the programs present, yet guarantee time on the air for access programming and information programming that is not shaped solely to meet the stations' primary concern to make a dollar.

The FCC, however, is unlikely to make any rule that would cause stations to give up a dollar in the name of public interest. Instead it has pressed on with the Fairness Doctrine (which the station entrepreneurs have shown they can live with) and extended it to the channels on which cable systems originate programs. When I asked an FCC official whether the Fairness Doctrine and the Equal Time rule would be applied to teletext transmitted on a cable system, he told me there had been "no commission answer to that." But Richard E. Wiley, former chairman of the FCC, told newspaper publishers at a convention in Atlanta that the commission could, indeed, regulate content of text on the cable, thus imposing these same provisions on print for the first time.

Although broadcasters have become accustomed to government restrictions on content since the 1920s, newspaper publishers have not. Publishers and editors would be extremely unlikely to transfer their operations from print to videotex if the government insisted on extending broadcast rules to this new print medium, as it did to cable when that medium arrived. (The FCC has also asserted jurisdiction over the *leasing* of cable channels—the most likely entry route into electronic distribution for newspapers in the United States.)

Editors, apparently, think the government *will* insist. In a study on the reaction to videotex of 258 managing editors of U.S. newspapers, 58 percent said they thought government regulation of news content was inevitable. The survey, published by the Indiana Center for New Communication, showed that although all of the editors opposed regulation of the print press, 25 percent said they thought that telecommunications, including cable, should be regulated.

For Bruce M. Owen, a Stanford University economist, government regulation of content is a present danger:

> One can imagine a process by which the material which is most controversial, violent, subversive, and prurient is gradually concentrated in old-fashioned, unregulated mechanical print media; electronic technology, regulated as it seems likely to be, would then increasingly assume a greater role in the information process.
>
> At first it would be intermediate transmission, then computer storage, then other stages would follow. As this happens, what is eventually transmitted will have been subject to electronic regulation at one or more stages of the process in increasing degree, with the effect of sanitizing the material involved. Controversial material that would not gain access to this process either because of direct regulation or because licensees exert caution so as not to endanger profitable licenses would be relegated to old-fashioned mechanical means—obsolescent presses and physical transportation modes. Eventually it will be possible to stamp out such material entirely.[11]

Newspapers have fought hard to protect freedom of the press under the First Amendment. This freedom came under increasing attack in the 1970s in attempts by government officials and judges to impose prior restraints on what may be published.

The most notorious instance was the attempt by the Nixon administration in 1971 to keep *The New York Times* and *The Washington Post* from publishing the Pentagon Papers, an analysis of the Vietnam war that had been produced (and classified) by the Department of Defense. On June 30 the Supreme Court overturned a restraining order obtained by the Nixon administration that had blocked publication for seventeen days. The Court ruled that the papers had the right under the First Amendment to publish the documents without prior restraint.

(The Pentagon Papers were given to CBS at the same time they were given to the *Times*. CBS management, fearful of retaliation from the Nixon administration, sat on them.)

Over the years judges have from time to time tried to ban press coverage of activities in their courtrooms. These assaults on press freedom and the right of the public to know what goes on in the courts have been opposed vigorously by the press. But until the advent of electronically transmitted print, neither the Congress nor the executive branch had proposed that the publications of the print media be regulated. Once cable, over which the FCC had claimed jurisdiction, began presenting news and information in text form, the specter of government regulation was raised.

Because of their concern for freedom of the press, newspapers in Japan insisted that regulation regarding broadcast programming not be applied to transmission of facsimile by cable. (Japanese broadcast law is similar to U.S. law in that it uses spectrum scarcity to justify government provisions concerning broadcast content.) As a consequence, facsimile was specifically excluded from regulation when the Cable Television Broadcast Law was passed in 1973. That law, incidentally, made it obligatory for a cable system to grant access to other programmers on any channels the system licensee did not intend to use.

The Japanese publishers pointed out that further legislation would be necessary to prohibit interference in news content by government communications agencies that provided the facilities for the telephone-based Captain system.[12]

Press freedom was also at issue in West Germany, where a fight developed in the late 1970s between the broadcasters and the newspapers for control over screened text. The broadcasters, who wanted to operate over-the-air video-text and the Bundespost (the West German PTT), which controlled the telephone-based setup, called the system *Bildschirmtext* (television screen newspaper). The German Newspaper Publishers Association declared that press was press, regardless of whether it was printed on paper or on a cathode-ray tube. If videotex were defined as broacasting or cable-casting, then it could be directly regulated by the Länder (states), whose governing parties had shown more and more willingness to interfere with programming of the existing holders of the public broadcasting monopolies, ARD and ZDF.* Therefore, the press argued, videotex must be operated by the newspapers. However, in an apparent compromise, the publishers' association agreed to participate in a field test with the Bundespost. The Bundespost indicated it would be willing to accept an independent authority that administered the input of information providers but kept its hands off content. Meantime the broadcasters went ahead with plans to mount their own Ceefax-style system.[13]

In the United States, disputes over interference with press freedom often end up in the courts. In a precedent-setting case, the Supreme Court in 1972 struck down a Florida law that gave a candidate the right to free space in a newspaper to reply to an editorial attack during a political campaign.[14] A state legislator, Pat L. Tornillo, Jr., had demanded that *The Miami Herald* grant him space, after the *Herald* had printed editorials criticizing his record. The *Herald* refused, pointing out that the First Amendment said that Congress and, by extension, the states, "shall make no law . . . abridging the freedom of speech, or of the Press." The Supreme Court ruled that a law ordering a paper to print a candidate's reply did just that.

The courts, however, have upheld the FCC's Political Editorial Rule, which grants to candidates exactly what, according to the Supreme Court, is denied them in the case of newspapers: the right to reply, using the station's facilities, to an editorial attack by the station's management.

The courts have also upheld the Equal Time Rule—often confused in the public's mind with the Fairness Doctrine. The rule does not state, as is often assumed by people who file complaints, that a station must give "equal time" to opposing points of view. What the

---

* ARD = Allgemeine Rundfunkanstalt Deutschland; ZDF = Zweite Deutsche Fernsehen.

rule does say is that, if a station, outside of its regular news programming, grants air time, free or for a fee, to one political candidate, it must afford an opposing candidate "equal time" on air in a comparable time period, for his own presentation.

Would the federal agency monitor an electronic news service to make sure the number of feature stories it did on a Republican or Democratic presidential candidate was exactly equal to the number it wrote on the Vegetarian Party's candidate?

As I have noted, the French public has seen past administrations use the government radio and television networks to promote their own candidates and *restrict* access of opposition candidates to the medium. If broadcast videotex remains the exclusive domain of the TDF, the potential is strong for extending this partisan practice to print. People concerned about telephone-based videotex have expressed the fear that not only political information but all information put into the system by the country's newspapers and press services might become subject to the editorial scrutiny of the PTT.

In Europe, the possibility exists that electronic news services will be licensed by the PTT's or other government agencies charged with supervising videotex.

The idea of licensing the press was anathema to the drafters of the American Constitution, who had recent memories of suppression through government licensing and other restrictions such as the Stamp Act. *Publick Occurrences,* the first Colonial newspaper—issued in Boston on September 25, 1690—was promptly suppressed by the British governor. He forbade any further printing "without license first obtained from those that are or shall be appointed by the Government to grant the same."[15]

Similar licensing continued until 1730. After that, the Colonial press was kept in line by prosecution for Seditious Libel, another concept soon disavowed by American legislators.

Licensing of broadcasters came about in the United States on a technicality. To avoid chaos in the radio spectrum, with stations interfering willy-nilly with each other's signals, Congress in 1927 granted the Federal Radio Commission the authority to issue licenses to broadcasters to use a designated frequency. The commission, having only so much of the spectrum to use for this purpose, set a limit on the number of stations that could have licenses, and drafted conditions applicants would have to meet to qualify for them. It seemed a natural extension of the "limited spectrum" rationale to establish rules (the Fairness Doctrine was one of them) that broadcasters would have to observe to *continue* to use the nation's airways as a "public trust."

A similar head-on attempt to license newspapers to the new technology would meet such vehement opposition as to make it highly doubtful that the FCC or a successor agency would try it. Still, licensing of IP's on videotex systems in Europe might set a precedent for government officials in the United States to try to follow. More likely, licensing of the American press would be indirect. A federal agency now sets rules for the phone system and for cable operations, the two most likely means of videotex news dissemination. It has claimed jurisdiction over Post Office transmission of electronic messages and electronic mail. If its practice in broadcast operations is a precedent for its practice in the computerized videotex system, we can expect to see rule-making regarding content. At some future date, news organizations might find themselves obliged to delete "indecent" words from their stories because of rules not imposed directly on them, but on AT&T, the cable systems, or a Post and Telecommunications Service that has been set up to provide the technical facilities over which their news is transmitted. Liberal administrations in the future would be likely to oppose such restrictions, but a conservative regime might not.

Outright *exclusion* of "opposition" news services from a national wired electronic news-delivery system would seem to be too much at variance with American traditions to be a possibility. But the effective steps taken by Richard Nixon to see to it that adverse content was kept out of the public television programming and downplayed on commercial networks are too strong a memory to allow us to say, categorically, "It can't happen here."

The Nixon administration used the threat of a license challenge under the Fairness Doctrine to intimidate licensees who opposed it. This is the chief problem I have with a federal agency's regulation of broadcast content: it provides a legally sanctioned opening wedge for later, more direct control of all media of communication, once they are merged into an electronic system. In fact, the Supreme Court itself has set down a dangerous precedent that could be used to justify government interference in electronic news operations. In 1978 it ruled that law-enforcement officers may enter a newspaper without warning and search its files for evidence concerning suspected criminal activity of third parties. The case arose when police in Palo Alto, California, obtained a warrant to search the offices of the Stanford University student newspaper for photographs of persons at a campus demonstration in which nine policemen were hurt. The 5-to-3 vote reversed two lower court decisions that held the police could subpeona records of the paper, but not conduct an unannounced search.* The dissenters, Justices Potter Stewart, John Paul Stevens, and Thurgood Marshall, argued that unannounced police searches of news offices would seriously hamper reporters' and editors' ability to maintain the confidentiality of information.

Jack C. Landau, director of the Reporters Committee for Freedom of the Press, declared the ruling was "a constitutional outrage to the First Amendment rights of every news organization and to the citizens they serve.

"It allows police," he said, "to break into newsrooms, riffling through unpublished articles, confidential documents, correspondence, internal memos, reporters' notebooks, and film files, and the news organization, its reporters and editors are helpless to protect their information from seizure by the government."

In a computerized system to which the government had access, it would be possible for prosecutors to search a newspaper's files without entering the premises. Reporters' private notes for their articles, customarily entered into storage through their VDT's, could also be scrutinized. Videotape "out-takes"—pieces edited out of visual stories prepared for television news programs—could also be accessed, if they had been entered digitally into the computers. It has long been a matter of journalistic principle for reporters to protect the confidentiality of their sources, as well as their notes and "out-takes." But this principle could be overridden by government investigators who had the key to the system's computers and used it to go on electronic fishing expeditions.

WHO WILL SET JOURNALISTIC STANDARDS?

Although newspaper editors have defended their own First Amendment rights with a passion, they have not been strong defenders of the freedom of the electronic press. To some extent, the First Amendment protections accorded newspapers give them a competitive advantage over broadcasting, which they see as a rival medium. If they do not get involved in videotex, they are not likely to fight *its* First Amendment battles, either. Yet if they stay out, they may see

* *Zurcher* v. *Stanford Daily*, No. 76–1484. The majority opinion was written by Justice Byron R. White.

themselves become an anachronism, superseded by electronic news services run by others over whom they have no influence.

Conceivably, these services could be provided by any one of a number of institutions: the phone company, a media conglomerate, a cable MSO, a television network, a superstation reaching cable systems by satellite, one of the wire services, or a national newspaper oriented to the change to electronic distribution. The quality of the news and information produced would be influenced by the approach of whichever of these entities brought an integrated news service into being. Because of their journalistic traditions and orientation, operation by wire services or newspapers would be likely to provide news services of most benefit to the public. I have worked on newspapers and in commercial television news. I found the people I worked with on newspapers the more dedicated to presenting news and information that will serve the public good. More than in television, they get support for this dedication from management. This is probably because top executives on newspapers are usually journalists who have risen from the ranks or are members of a family that has run the paper for generations and consider themselves journalists.

Because they feel it is their responsibility to inform the public, newspaper executives normally are more willing than are television executives to publish controversial stories just because they are true. They want to make a profit, but their outlook does not usually begin and end with profit.

In commercial television, the executives' outlook begins and ends with profit—rather, audiences ratings that they see as the direct generators of profit. They are salesmen, not journalists. Almost every television station general manager has been a time salesman first and then sales manager, on his way to management control. They look on news programs—literally—as "profit centers." Having come out of a tradition where the concern for selling entertainment was paramount, they see news in show-biz terms. The morning after an excellent digging report on the station's news program, the general manager does not say to his news director, "Gee, that was a great story, how did you get it?" He says, "How did the show do on the overnights?" The news is always a "show" whose sole purpose is to attract ratings. A television general manager is happiest when a new and prettier "anchor" (male or female) brings in an extra rating point; a newspaper editor, when his paper has broken an important and exclusive story on Page One.

It would be disastrous if the public's supply of news and information were dependent on an integrated system run by commercially oriented televison managers, rather than by journalists. In that case, text would be provided as an adjunct to the video pictures, not as an information facet of the system equal in importance to the televised news. In a drive for a mass audience, salesmen-managers might try to impose show-biz values on the print news as well as on the video. On the other hand, electronic news stories that grew out of print journalism could have a salutary effect on the content of the video side of the operation. Accuracy and completeness, not hallmarks of commercial television news broadcasts, could be markedly improved if reporting practices routine to newspapers were installed in the video newsroom. I offer one illustration to make the point: no good newspaper reporter would think of writing an important story without checking for background material in the paper's morgue or its reference library. Few television reporters feel this is worth the effort—almost no television station has a morgue and very few have reference libraries worthy of the name. (At WCBS-TV in New York, the salesman/manager was willing to approve an eleventh film crew, at a cost of $125,000 a year, but he considered $1000 to *begin* a reference library a needless expense.)

In the Scenario, another deleterious practice of broadcast journalism has already crept into the Newscom operation: stories are being fed into the system and across the country *unedited.* Everyone needs an editor: it is very hard to catch your own mistakes. Yet in television and radio news, editorless reporting has been a way of life from the beginning. A reporter in the field does an audio actuality or a video "stand-upper" ad-lib or from a script written on a notebook on her knee. These stories are put on live, or on tape, by producers pressed for time and pressed by their managements to use their reporters, on the air, every day, to get the most out of their show-biz potential. It is too *difficult,* the producers say, to stop the proceeding and ask a reporter to do the piece over, just to correct an error or fill in a gaping hole in the story.

Very few stories prepared in-house are subjected to anything more than cursory checking, if they are checked at all. In Boston, I asked the news director of WEEI, the all-news radio station owned and operated by CBS, why I saw no editor working an afternoon shift. Copy was being shuffled to an on-air anchorman who had been an announcer, not a newspaperman, once himself. "We used to have an editor on each shift," he told me, "but we cut that out, to save money. We find it works out very well. Now each writer is responsible for the accuracy of the stories he gives to the anchorman. Besides, the anchor often catches errors, on air."

(I've heard such catches—they sound more like bobbles. And they recall a highly paid television anchorman I knew in New York who prided himself in his *sight-reading* of every news broadcast. He would come in a half hour before the broadcast, "loosen up" in the hall by having a softball catch with a soundman, then shuffle through his script for five minutes before air, and proceed to sight-read. Until a page dropped out. Then the producer would shout "Take the commercial" to the director, run into the studio, and say, "No, Jim, look—it goes *this* way.")

Listening to egregious errors and unanswered questions in WEEI's news broadcasts, the lack of editing became glaringly apparent. But its *ratings* were high, because it was the only all-news station in town. And, unfortunately, the listeners, from long experience, know they can't expect from radio and television news the same accuracy they would demand from their newspapers. The attitude of many news reporters and producers in television and radio is: "Who's going to catch us? It's all gone by in a second."

Is that the attitude of the woman reporter in the Scenario who balances her electronic typewriter on the speakers' stand and types out a story that appears instantly on subscribers' screens all across the country? Probably not—if she came out of the print tradition. But I don't know any reporter on a newspaper who has not at some time made an error that was caught by a copy editor, and been thankful to that editor for making the catch. In the broadcast tradition, there are seldom editors to make the catch.

Print journalists may also lose out in the long run to nonbroadcast entrepreneurs whose only concern is to turn a buck by supplying information "product" to meet the public's growing demand. They may operate solely as "umbrella" organizations that shovel news and information into the computers without concern for quality, originality, accuracy, or source of the material being provided.

There is a danger that the local newspaper function—assembling the day's news and knowledge into a comprehensible package for a reader—will fall apart. Editors might be replaced by computer indexers who assemble "menus" of related stories and information pieces supplied directly by governments, business and labor lobbyists, special-interest groups, or community organizations that want to get their messages directly across to the readers, without the intervention of reporters or editors for a news service.

In some ways this could lead to the availability of a greater diversity of information and opinion. But what would be lost in this indiscriminate variety package would be a critical intelligence dedicated to assessing the truth or falsehood of self-serving statements by people and organizations who want to present themselves or their causes in the best possible light.

If the newspaper editors' function survives into the electronic news service, people with something to say could still have direct contact with the public by putting their "commercial" or "public service" messages directly on the computer for anyone to access at home. These messages would also be taken into account by editors and reporters for inclusion in news-service stories that related the information to an assessment of its meaning.

One advantage of the print media, the Aspen Institute Project on Communications Policy pointed out, is that they supply a high level of editorial service: "People are willing to pay something to avoid the task of sifting data for themselves, and editors compete for the readership market by compiling packages that suit the tastes of individuals. Indeed, in the Age of Information, editors assume an even greater importance; people will pay *not* to be deluged with unedited data."[16]

This editorial service gives the national news agencies an observable advantage in the electronic system over, say, "umbrella" services that send out information diverse providers pay them to transmit to cable system computers. Local newspapers have an even greater jump on becoming the dominant information provider for the electronic distribution center in each city and town. They have by far the best information-gathering and processing organization in each community. Therefore, they can provide a mass of accurate data on their areas at lower costs than information wholesalers who might want to enter the field because they now have equal access to the means of distribution.

But editors who still look at the world from under green eyeshades often come up with arguments against electronic dissemination:

"It won't happen."

"Even if it does happen, you aren't going to wean people away from a habit of a lifetime—they are going to want to *hold* the newspaper, the way they always did. They are *not* going to want to get their news out of a box."

I can hear a town crier in Boston, on being urged by an early printer to put some of his news down in a printed newsletter, saying, "Oh, come off it—people want to *hear* the news—they're not going to pay to read it on paper."

Editors with more open minds about an electronic newspaper feel there are many problems to be surmounted before it becomes practical. Some who have watched the Prestel development in England think that in its present configuration the system could be used only as a supplemental news service. The Indiana Center's survey indicated the editors believed that, to become viable for the dissemination of news content, later versions would have to transmit photographs, provide easily read video pages with far more than 150 words to a page, and have a simple method for the reader to secure "clippings" of the stories they wanted. All these improvements are, of course, technically possible.

It is usually those with vested interests in technologies of the past, especially those whose careers have been spent in mastering those techniques, who fight most strongly against new technologies that may force change. The long battle of the typographical unions, whose vested interest lay in setting copy in hot type on a cumbersome machine, to keep cold type out of newspapers is the most obvious case in point. In the United States, that battle was not over until *The New York Times* negotiated a precedent-setting contract with the International Typographical Union in 1975. That step reduced the people required in the process from nine hundred to six hundred, but gave, in effect, lifetime job guarantees to ex-printers on the paper who would have to be retrained to do the new functions.

"We were proud of being printers," said a printshop supervisor. "I was proud. Now the computer does it for you."[17] It is a very human concern. It was the same feeling that copy editors had when the newspapers they worked for began using heads whose lines were flush with the left-hand margin, rather than stepped heads whose top line was exactly balanced with the bottom line. Some copy editors at the *Times* berated the change at other papers with the comment that anyone could write flush-left heads—all the professional skill had gone out of it.*

* The *Times* still uses stepped heads, and I must admit I hope that is a creative anachronism that will never change, even when the paper is printed out by facsimile.

But the complaint lost sight of the fact that content, not form, is the important thing in communicating the news. The whole drive in editing the *Times* is to make news and information understandable to the readers, and leave no unanswered questions. Unfortunately, that does not seem to be the *raison d'être* of copy editors at a number of other papers. But it is a drive that should be translated into the electronic news services.

TOWARD A CUSTOM-TAILORED NEWSPAPER

Rather than jump directly into electronic dessemination of news, planners at some papers suggested that the way to stave off the new information providers was to attach computers to the presses and give readers papers tailored to their personal desires. The way for this had already been paved by the production of "zoned editions" aimed at specific communities in a newspaper's distribution area. The *Middlesex News* got a hold on Boston's western suburbs by zoning its editions so that a story of interest only in Wayland would not appear in the edition zoned for Framingham, and vice versa. Inserting "zoned" pages during a pressrun obviously saves newsprint because a paper does not have to print all of its locally originated stories in every edition. Now a means has been devised to extend this concept to the individual reader.

In standard operations, the presses must be stopped intermittently and the photo-offset plates used to print the pages must be changed to give each zone a different content. With ink-jet presses, the computer can alter the pattern of the fifty thousand tiny drops of ink squeezed out each second, and literally print a different paper for each subscriber. In this system, individuals can indicate for the computer the categories of stories in which they are particularly interested. They can say whether or not they want special sections or sports or home building, for instance. There is no need to waste space for a column on woodworking for a subscriber who lists gardening as his sole avocation. When the subscriber's tab pops up in the addressing machine, the computer follows its standing instructions to select among the stories and special sections the paper has prepared for that day. This concept, obviously, is transferable into an electronic delivery system.

Critics of the idea worry that people will suffer a loss if they read only what they actively select and are not exposed by serendipity to "unwanted" information—as happens when your eye falls on an interesting item in the newspaper you have spread out as a drop cloth while painting a chair. There may be a social justification for building into the system easy ways for people to fall upon some news or information by accident.

COMING: "THE PERFECT MEDIUM FOR NEWS DISSEMINATION"

The custom-made newspaper is a fascinating idea, and, for the immediate future, it might keep readers from turning to an HCS for the specialized news they want. But the physical distribution problems will not have been solved: When there is a heavy snow in Boston, the suburban subscriber will still go without *The Boston Globe* for that day.

In the meantime, other electronic information providers will steal a march on reaching subscribers.

A snowstorm in Indiana provided a glimmer of the public's acceptance of a video "newspaper." A snow emergency in Bloomington kept *The Herald Telephone* from being delivered. So the paper persuaded the public television station of the University of Indiana to broadcast its news for ninety minutes in the late afternoon. For the first half hour, people at home could read headlines on the screen. For the next hour, they could phone in to have stories and picture captions read to them on air. (The print on the regular newspaper was smaller than that provided on a videotex screen.) More viewers turned to the station that day than ever in its history. But the surprising thing was that when the station repeated the ninety-minute broadcast the next day, after the emergency was over and the paper was being delivered to homes again, the audience size and the call-ins were greater than the day before.[18]

The development of high-resolution, nonglare color screens on which print can be read as easily in the daytime as when the room is darkened, plus easy reproduction of stories on reusable, paper-thin plastic sheets, may well lead to public acceptance of videotex news. But the amount and quality of information available will probably have to be *superior* to that now provided by conventional newspapers, and the cost will have to be at least as low.

In an address at a journalism school dedication, Robert M. White III, editor of a small daily in Missouri, attempted to define the perfect medium for news dissemination.[19] The medium, he said, should have five basic qualities:

- Its every story would have to be continually updated.
- Its every story would have to be available to the reader or viewer when he wants it and where he wants it.
- Its story selection and story length would be in sufficient quantity to satisfy the changing and varied interests of a general readership or viewership.
- Its every story could be preserved for as long as the reader or viewer would want to preserve it.
- It would cost the customer very little, if anything.

To that, I would add the capability to see, live or on tape, televised, visual versions of most of the stories in the videotex bank.

A combined video and videotex service such as Newscom in the Scenario could have these qualities. How rapidly such an electronic news service will develop will depend on how quickly the service can be brought within the financial reach and desire of everyone, creating a large market of subscribers.

Assuming an electronic news service was desired by all, could it be afforded by all? Consumers, through the purchase and repair of television sets, have been willing to assume a greater percentage of the total cost of television than they assume for newspapers.[20]

With mass production and continual reduction in the costs of electronic circuitry, it is possible that an HCS may in time cost no more than a moderately priced television set. Since distribution costs of former newspapers would go down, advertising might be used to cover the entire cost of producing the paper. Promoters of the service would then tell viewers that the service of videotex was "free," just as broadcasters promote the idea that their programs are free. The consumer, of course, pays the *total* cost of the advertising that keeps programs on air, because these costs are added directly to the price of the products advertised.

Some who fear the power of advertising to influence the news have suggested that the electronic newspaper may present the first realistic opportunity for news publishers to free themselves from the constraints (implicit or explicit) imposed by advertisers. Through newspaper subscription and newsstand purchases, newspaper readers pay about 30 percent of the costs of producing a paper; the advertisers, about 70 percent. As in television, the readers ultimately pick up the entire cost of this advertising.

Advertising represents about 60 percent of all pages printed in newspapers, and is more expensive to handle than news. A study by the RAND Corporation estimated that if newspapers eliminated all advertising and the selling and production costs associated with producing it, and delivered newspapers containing only the 40 percent devoted to editorial matter, subscribers would have to pay only about 70 percent more than they normally do now for their newspapers.[21]

In the computerized system, by charging for only the material a person wanted to read, rather than for all the wide-ranging matter the reader now gets in his paper and never looks at, costs to him might be no more than he had previously spent on the traditional newspaper. The chances would be increased if production costs were reduced dramatically. This seems likely to happen. At a time when the costs of almost everything, including newsprint, are rising annually at double-digit rates, the costs of electronic materials and transmission facilities have been *dropping* at triple-digit rates: more than 100 percent a year.[22]

Still, the cost of the set might bar such a service to the poorest citizens, who would otherwise be expected to buy a newspaper. This, however, did not follow when television came in as an alternative to newspapers. By the time television reached nearly 100 percent saturation of American homes, newspapers were reaching only 80 percent. It may be that, as in the Scenario, government subsidy will be needed to supply an HCS to the small percentage of people who could not afford to buy them.*

Such subsidies would not be a startling precedent, even in the United States. Congress has subsidized airline and rail travel—both forms of communication—partly because it was thought to be of social benefit to do so. For years, newspapers received an indirect subsidy from the government in the form of preferential postal rates. Television stations received a subsidy of inestimable financial value when the FCC granted them free use of the public's broadcast spectrum.[23]

Taking all these potentials into account, it would appear to be a realistic possibility that electronic news services can be provided to everyone who wants them at a reasonable cost.

* I am speaking now about the developed nations, not the less developed. In poorer countries, community-center access to "home" communications facilities will likely be more the norm well after the system is in general home use in the richer countries.

A THREAT AND AN OPPORTUNITY

The reason that newspapers in Britain, Canada, Japan, Finland, Norway, and Sweden showed serious interest in the videotex option before those in the United States is probably that those countries began testing with the system before the Americans did.

In Sweden, which reports the highest newspaper consumption per capita in the world, six newspapers, working with the Swedish Central News Agency and the Swedish Newspaper Publishers Association, signed up to take part as soon as the test services were announced. I asked Karl Henrik Ekberg, director of the association, why they had plunged in. He replied, simply: "To protect ourselves."

Swedish publishers think videotex will be a supplementary service in the first decade of its existence, he said, but may become a fully developed facsimile news service by A.D. 2010. That view is supported by a two-year, proprietary study conducted by Arthur D. Little Inc. for a group of newspapers, newsprint producers, broadcasting companies, and electronics manufacturers. Electronic information systems will not be a serious threat to news publishing through the 1980s, Donald F. Sparrow, the project director, told me. "But by the mid-1990s their inroads into the home could substantially impact the news industry." The study saw four possible scenarios for how this might come about, each with a different element of the present media becoming dominant. "In all four scenarios," said Sparrow, "a home information center with diverse electronic information capabilities tends to evolve." Whether this will become a threat or an opportunity depends on the newspaper publishers themselves, he believes. "The ones who become broad-based information providers will find new channels for marketing the news and information," he said.

Robert G. Marbut, chairman of the telecommunications committee of the American Newspaper Publishers Association, agreed. In a symposium on the future of newspapers conducted by the ANPA Research Institute, he said:

"The same technique is available to all information providers. Thus, in the future, traditional newspapers cannot rely solely on the uniqueness of their product or the habits of readers to insure success.

"These principles dictate that we put the need of information consumers first, that we define our business not in terms of the product we produce [the newspaper] but in terms of the needs that we meet. Newspapers really perform the function of meeting the needs of information."[24]

In an electronic news service, the essentials of newsgathering by editors and reporters would not change: getting the facts (who, what, where, when, and why, and sometimes how), checking them for accuracy, analyzing them for meaning, putting them in logical order in a story that tells a reader or viewer what happened and what it means. The process should, in fact, be improved by the reporter's capability to check facts and previous developments from an encyclopedic array of background material available instantly in the news organization's data bank. Editors would have the added responsibility of seeing to it that translations of the story into other facets of a combined news service—video, audio, "headline" teletext—preserved its original meaning and accuracy.

Perhaps electronic news services, with their capacity of supplying much background and consumer-oriented information in addition to headline stories reporting conflict, can develop in readers a whole new mind-set about the press. More and more, newspapers and news broadcasts have been seen primarily as the bringers of bad news. Newspapers began to recognize and react to this criticism in the 1970s by providing more "useful news" and "life-style" information in special sections. These could easily be adapted to a two-way system in which the subscriber probes the service for information he or she needs. Asking for and receiving such information, the subscriber develops an identity with the news services that may help defuse the idea that "they" are the bad guys who give us only the bad news. And in this way, the consumer of news may drop the growing tendency to want to kill the messengers—because, in an interactive electronic "newspaper," the consumer becomes one of the messengers.

5 | VIA SATELLITE FROM APPALACHIA

Since 1975, public schools in the United States have been required by federal law to provide "free and appropriate" education for all handicapped children.[1] This education must be provided in the "mainstream"—the regular classroom. The underlying concept was that each child should have the opportunity to learn at her or his own pace and to the limits of her or his own capacity. One problem this presents is that most teachers have had little or no training in teaching physically or mentally handicapped children. Overcoming this obstacle was particularly difficult for many poorly financed and isolated school systems in the Appalachian region—the thirteen states from New York to Alabama transversed by the Appalachian mountain range.

The Appalachian Regional Commission tried to remedy the problem by offering in-service training on teaching the handicapped to grade-school teachers via satellite. Setting up separate classroom courses to instruct small groups of teachers at dozens of sites along the thousand-mile Appalachian Range would have been inordinately costly. But using NASA's Sixth Applications Technology Satellite (*ATS-6*) so that an instructor in a studio classroom at the University of Kentucky could reach groups in thirty-four communities at once made the training economically possible. In 1978, 270 teachers of children three to eight years old received instruction via this system. Enrollments at individual sites ranged from one in Hazard, Kentucky, to twenty-four in Greenville, South Carolina.

Most of the sessions were "downstream" presentations in which film and tape segments were used to show the teaching of handicapped children in actual classroom situations. But four were live, interactive sessions in which students at diverse locations could phone in questions to teachers in the studio. (Other applications of this technique have used direct, two-way satellite exchanges between students and instructors.)

Development of the course was funded by the National Institute of Education, which supported the commission's Appalachia educational satellite program. In 1974 the program began transmission, from an earth station at the University of Kentucky using *ATS-6*, a series of teacher-training, professional-updating and consumer-education courses to forty-five sites in the region. Four years later the project adopted the name Appalachian Community Service Network (ACSN) and offered its programming nationally, via satellite transmissions to cable systems and other organizations that maintained earth stations to receive them. By 1980 courses had proliferated on the five-day schedule. They included continuing education for people at home, volunteer firefighters and policemen, as well as courses for credit from more than a dozen colleges and universities.

Under an edict from President Carter, *ATS-6* was to be the last U.S. public-service satellite the National Aeronauts and Space Administration (NASA) would launch. As a consequence, when *ATS-6* died, the Appalachian network was forced to transfer to a commercial communications satellite—*Satcom I*—paying the standard tariffs charged by its owner, RCA. ACSN built a ten-meter parabolic dish antenna on the University of Kentucky campus, to beam programs to the satellite.

THE TREND TO THE PRIVATE-INTEREST SATELLITE

People who wanted to see communication satellites used for nonprofit services such as education thought the government should operate such satellites and provide their facilities to nonprofit public-interest users, at cost. As the United States entered the 1980s, however, the trend was in another direction, based on a deliberate policy to favor private interests in operations of satellites. This is how that came to be: Although, or rather, because, the Soviet Union beat the United States into space by launching *Sputnik* in 1957, the American government became preeminent in the field of space technology and satellite development. President John F. Kennedy decided the race to the moon was necessary to recoup American prestige. In addition, the Department of Defense (DOD) wanted to develop rocket, missile, and satellite capabilities that would be superior to anything the Soviets could contrive. The DOD knew that not only could rocket-powered missiles carry a hydrogen bomb but so also could satellites. Within a year the United States had one-upped the Russian accomplishment by putting two small satellites, *Vanguard* and *Explorer*, into orbit.

Communications tests became an early priority in these space shots, in large part because the DOD wanted an alternative to overseas cable and radio for its international military communications network. Building on this technology, NASA put into orbit a communications satellite—*Telstar*—that could receive, amplify, and retransmit messages back to earth. The launch itself was paid for by AT&T; it wanted to test a satellite that could handle a thousand phone calls at a time, a capacity that seems primitive now. But this was a low-orbit vehicle that circled the earth every few hours. It could be used only by complicated earth stations that tracked it across the sky, then lost it when it went over the horizon. What was needed was a communications satellite that would hang there, apparently motionless, receiving signals from an earth station aimed permanently at one spot, and retransmit those signals to other distant stations across the world. This was accomplished in 1963 by a "synchronous" satellite, *Syncom I.*

Following a principle proposed by the British futurist Arthur C. Clarke in 1945, this satellite was sent into orbit at an altitude and orbital speed—22,300 miles and 6875 miles per hour—that would keep it in equilibrium at a point directly over the equator. From the earth, the satellite appeared to be stationary in the sky. A message could be sent across the continent by beaming it from an earth station in New York to a satellite, which in turn beamed it down to a receiving earth station in San Francisco. The technique could replace overseas transmission by underwater cable, and overland transmission by regular long-distance telephone lines or microwave relay stations. (Because microwaves travel in a line of sight, and do not follow the curvature of the earth, it takes hundreds of microwave towers to relay a telephone call across the continent, moving from point to point, between towers that are in sight of each other, along the route.)

As Clarke had pointed out, only three synchronous satellites, positioned at longitudes 120 degrees apart, were needed to communicate with the entire earth outside of the polar regions. A message could be sent around the world by relaying it from one satellite to the next.

Syncom I was capable of carrying a television channel, as well as telephone voice circuits.

As a rationale for the space program, the American people had been assured that it would produce "public dividends." But obviously, there were profits to be made in relaying telephone calls and television pictures over vast distances of the earth. Now that the practicality of using satellites had been demonstrated and the research and development paid for by the government, AT&T and other communications carriers wanted to take over and reap these profits. But a fight developed in Congress. Many senators and representatives thought the dividend ought to go directly to the public, without commercial companies creaming profits off the top. They wanted to keep space communications (those not already preempted by the Pentagon) in the hands of civilian federal agencies, to build a satellite system that would provide for the country's domestic and international communications needs. Early drafts of their bill called for an independent agency that could develop the new technology without the commercial restraints imposed by a built-in requirement to protect the older technologies. One of these old technologies was the terrestrial system of telephone lines and microwave relays established across the country by AT&T. The telephone company did not want to replace this network, which could last forty years and was providing it a healthy return as part of its rate base, with a satellite network that could bring about a reduction in tariff charges to the consumer. But AT&T did not want to lose control of satellite communications, and its lobbyists pressured the administration and Congress to hand the system over to it lock, stock, and barrel. Or, when that idea failed, to set up a communications satellite corporation it could control. When the satellite bill came to be marked up, the Bell System and the other carriers had the votes. Congress established a commercial corporation— Comsat—to operate the country's first satellite communication system.

The president was allowed to appoint only three of the fifteen members of Comsat's board of directors. The act permitted AT&T, RCA, and Western Union to own 50 percent of its stock, with the other 50 percent to be sold to the public. The "public" included other corporate interests. AT&T, with 29 percent, was the biggest stockholder, and its managers thought this would be sufficient to give them control. But, as it turned out, it did not, and Bell later sold off its interest when it found it could not call the tune on all of Comsat's business operations.

Congress placed two additional restrictions on Comsat: it was to operate only in international communications, thus protecting the AT&T investment in its Long Lines terrestrial network from the new technology. And Comsat was to be a carrier's carrier: only profit-making retransmission companies, and not nonprofit public-interest groups, would buy the use of its facilities, in blocks of time on the satellites. These companies would then resell the capacity at retail, becoming middlemen to business users and other consumers.

Comsat then established the International Telecommunications Satellite Consortium (Intelsat), a space-transmission corporation that eventually was owned or leased by more than one hundred countries around the world. Comsat owned about 27 percent of its shares. By 1980 its revenues had reached more than $200 million.

U.S. taxpayers received none of the revenues in the form of public dividends for their $80 billion investment in the space program. On the contrary, they were asked instead to contribute further to Comsat's profits: Intelsat charges Comsat for use of the telephone channels. Comsat marks up the figure it charges AT&T to lease the channel. AT&T marks up the figure it charges to the New York Telephone Company (or another local phone company), which marks up the figure it charges you to make a call.[2]

If you have made such a call, you probably did not know whether it was being carried to London by satellite or by one of AT&T's underwater cables. Rather, it was Intelsat's television capability that first made the people of the United States and Western Europe aware of communications satellites. Its first satellite, launched in 1965, became famous as *Early Bird,* which transmitted television news pictures across the Atlantic live to home television sets, usually with the words Via Satellite superimposed across the bottom of the picture. That same year, the Soviet Union launched two low-power communications satellites to extend the direct television programming reach of the central government to Siberia and Outer Mongolia.

By 1969, when NASA carried out Jack Kennedy's promise that the United States would be the first to put a man on the moon, Intelsat had become the world's predominant commercial communications satellite network. In 1974 the Soviet Union founded Intersputnik, a satellite network offered originally to nine nations in its sphere, and modeled on Intelsat. In 1979 the People's Republic of China negotiated with Comsat to establish an extensive system for its domestic use.

More than a hundred space vehicles had been placed in geostationary orbit by 1980—half of them owned by the United States and the Soviet Union. It has been estimated that of all man-made objects placed in space, 90 percent were for military purposes—put there by the two superpowers and NATO.[3] About 5 percent are used for meteorological, maritime, and earth-sensing applications. The remaining 5 percent are telecommunications satellites and of these the DOD is by far the biggest single user. According to William H. Read of the Harvard University Program on Information Resources Policy, the Pentagon has become enamored of satellite communications technology, in large part because satellites are relatively inexpensive in comparison to other long-distance communications. "Indeed," he said, "it may be argued that the military is becoming dangerously dependent on communications satellites."[4] Satellite transmissions, he pointed out, are subject to Soviet eavesdropping (as are phone calls transmitted by microwave). And the satellites themselves are vulnerable to being destroyed by "killer" satellites developed by the Soviet Union.

That the commercial carriers were successful in capturing the nonmilitary satellite communications in the United States was a victory for a propaganda campaign begun twenty years before by corporate fronts such as the National Association of Manufacturers and the private power company lobby to implant in the populace two ideas:

1. "Free enterprise can do it better and more efficiently," and

2. Government interference or competition with private companies is socialism, and therefore evil; using the people's taxes to subsidize profit-making corporations (as in the satellite giveaways and the bailing out of poor managements such as Lockheed and Chrysler) is in the best tradition of free enterprise, and, therefore, good.

That the American public bought this contradiction is a tribute to the press agents and ad men who managed the campaign. One delicious irony is that the costs of the private power company ads that led the way in promoting "free" enterprise were added to the utilities' rate base, which in turn permitted these companies to charge us for our own brainwashing.

Of course, it was not all won by ads and coordinated pronouncements by top company executives. The formation of corporate political action committees, judicious contributions to congressional campaigns, and direct corporate assistance—often "informational" and sometimes financial—to government officials were used as well. Support for the "free enterprise" argument from the Reagan, Carter, Ford, and Nixon administrations also helped.

In the area of satellites, the campaign was aided dramatically when Richard Nixon's Office of Telecommunication Policy called for the FCC, supposedly an independent agency, to adopt an "open skies" policy, in which anyone who had the technical equipment and the funds to do it could put up a domestic communications satellite. The FCC complied. The public interest would be served, so the Nixon White House said, by "free and open competition" in the satellite area. Such competition was obviously ruled out for public-interest groups, since the launching of satellites ran to many millions of dollars. As a consequence, large corporations were the chief beneficiaries of the government research and development program, and they quickly preempted the domestic communications satellite field. First came Western Union with its *Westar* in 1974. Next up was RCA, whose chief interest was in interconnecting cable television systems into satellite networks over which Home Box Office and other companies could deliver pay television films and entertainment programs. Then AT&T and GTE joined Comsat to put up the Comstar series of telecommunications satellites. This experience paved the way for a huge communications satellite enterprise—Satellite Business Systems (SBS). This was a new corporation owned jointly by IBM, Comsat, and Aetna Life and Casualty Co.

At an MIT symposium on satellite communications, Ronald Stowe, an SBS attorney, argued that this line of development was justified because, in the United States, the private companies, acting as an informal conglomerate, were providing the backbone structure for the country's communications.

"Industry has a bad reputation for selfishness and self-interest," he said. "But people in government should recognize that representation of private self-interest is not necessarily against the public good."[5]

The corporate view was the prevailing one, in the America of the 1970s. Nevertheless, a corner of the populace and a minority in government felt that the game should not be thrown to corporate executives who wanted it all. They had one victory among the defeats: they persuaded Congress to permit NASA to build into its *ATS-6* the radiated power necessary to conduct two-way communications experiments that could serve public-service uses. All previous satellites had been low-power, requiring large and costly earth stations to pick them up. The large corporate carriers wanted it kept that way: then users could not afford to build their own earth stations, but would have to lease them from the carriers themselves.

Individual educational or medical institutions or other public-service users would be effectively barred from leasing transponders* on such commercial satellites, first because the volume of their traffic would be too low (in comparison with that of a multinational corporation) for the commercial satellite carrier to lease them directly, and second, the prices charged to a single public-service user would be prohibitive.

Rather than continue this inequitable situation, public-interest groups wanted high-powered satellites that could be picked up by small, inexpensive ground stations on the premises of public-service organizations that could not afford to lease transmission from the commercial carriers.

NONPROFIT USERS BECOME ACTIVE

In 1975 some public broadcasters and other potential nonprofit users of satellites formed a Public Service Satellite Consortium (PSSC). It aimed to become a service agency that would help service agencies learn how they could use satellites effectively and "provide coordination and technical support for experiments that will *eventually move members into regular operation on commercial satellites.*" (Emphasis added.)

At about the same time, another organization, the Public Interest Satellite Association (PISA) was formed with a political objective—organizing the public-service sector to bring about the establishment of a low-cost satellite communications system tailored to serve the noncommercial needs of society. Its founders, Andrew Horowitz and Bert Cowlan, drew support from such disparate groups as the Consumers Federation of America (Consumers Union), Action for Children's Television (ACT), the National Conference of

---

* A transponder receives a signal from an earth station and retransmits it to other earth stations. Each communications satellite has a number of transponders.

Christians and Jews, and the South Dakota Indian Education Association. From the beginning, it fought an uphill fight.

The public-service consortium, meanwhile, began helping user organizations set up trials on the *ATS-6* satellite. These led directly to the establishment of the Appalachian tele-education project.

The National Institution of Education also made a grant to the state of Alaska to use *ATS-6* to transmit educational programs to remote Indian villages. Of the seventeen remote communities in this experiment, thirteen could receive video and audio and transmit audio, and four could receive and transmit video and audio. Interactive programming included health education for elementary school students and a topical "Alaskan Native Magazine" for adults.

In 1976 the *Hermes/CTS** satellite, designed and built in Canada, was launched from Cape Canaveral, under the cosponsorship of the Canadian Department of Communication and NASA. The most powerful communications satellite that had been launched, its mission was to conduct experiments in the 12 and 14 gigahertz (GHz) †
bands, which permit the use of low-cost, transportable ground stations.

One of the American experiments was put to an emergency operational test. The American Red Cross had planned tests of a small, highly transportable ground terminal with a 1.2 meter disc antenna for use in establishing communications in a disaster area. The terminal, constructed by Comsat Laboratories, had been in use in two simulated disasters—an Ohio River flood-watch and a Texas hurricane simulation.

Then on Saturday, July 23, 1977, the Red Cross in Pennsylvania requested emergency communications for the disaster that became known as the second Johnstown flood. The terminal was flown to Pittsburgh and transported to Johnstown, a city of 43,000 on the Conemaugh River, one of the tributaries of the Ohio. In the flooding, the phone system had broken down. So two voice channels were established between Johnstown and nearby Clarksburg, West Virginia, which routed them into the telephone network. The terminal also carried voice and facsimile traffic for the American Red Cross Disaster Relief unit at its Washington headquarters, and to many other

---

* CTS stands for "Communications Technology Satellite."
† *Hertz* is the standard term for measurement of radio frequencies in cycles per second. Thus, 100 kilohertz (KHz) is 100,000 cycles; 42 megahertz is 42,000,000 cycles; and 12 gigahertz is 12,000,000,000 cycles.

points. Red Cross workers transmitted requests for emergency supplies and messages to notify families of flood victims. On Monday the Johnstown telephone plant, which had restored some operations, had to be evacuated because of an explosion nearby, and the satellite link became the only means of communication into the area.

Besides the Moose Factory telemedicine experiment I described in Chapter II, Canadian projects included tests of satellite-cable linkups. One of these, called Project Intercom, linked two widely separated towns in Quebec—Buchanan and Saint Raymond—for five days for two and a half hours in the afternoon and two and a half hours at night. Both had active community television stations, carried on the cable system, and the people could view or participate in the exchanges from the studios or from their homes. On the two-way video test, people exchanged ideas on common problems in their homes and in the communities.

The *ATS-6* and *Hermes CTS* satellites demonstrated that the technology could be useful in delivering services to the public. Public-interest groups began to move to get a satellite to allow nonprofit organizations to provide these services at a cost they and the public could afford.

NASA and PISA, supported by nonprofit activist agencies such as the Communication Commission of the National Council of Churches, in New York, developed a plan to launch a public satellite and disperse inexpensive ground terminals to minimize the "entrance fee" for those who wanted to become involved in public-satellite use. The plan rested on a technological finding that large savings could be realized by using multibeam satellites with large antennas that concentrated radiation into small areas of the earth's surface, referred to as "footprints." One NASA report proposed a satellite with a 210-foot-long Large Deployable Antenna strung out into space that could provide seventy-seven beams. By using, for instance, frequencies in the S Band (2.5–2.69 GHz), sixty-two simultaneous television channels could be provided for each of the seventy-seven beams. This could provide 4774 channels of broad-band communications. In place of each television channel, many more channels could be used for transmission of voice or data circuits that take up less spectrum width. The report calculated that such a system, if used continuously, could provide these channels at a cost from 1/500 to 1/200 of the amounts charged by the commercial carriers for channels on their satellites. The key to inexpensive operation of a dedicated public-service satellite is the generation of enough traffic to make the unit costs very low, and thus accessible to almost any public-service group that wants to use it.

PISA, in a plan made public in June 1978, proposed that the way to make efficient use of such a satellite would be to coordinate the project through the most likely candidate for beneficial use of small earth stations: the Instructional Television Fixed Service (ITFS). This service, which began in the late 1960s, provides point-to-point microwave delivery of instructional programs for many schools and hospitals throughout the country. The system allows teachers and students to talk to each other via interactive television; it can transmit educational material digitally, as well. It uses line-of-sight microwave in the S Band. In 1980 it covered an area with 50 percent of the U.S. population. By adding the satellite capability, instructional television could be made available to every part of the country, to the worldwide army educational network, and to ships in the navy and maritime service.

If the ITFS traffic were combined with the public-service users already requesting use of the facilities, the PISA report suggested, the satellite could be made cost-effective immediately. Such a system would reduce transmission costs to ITFS, and provide many more channels over which its members could receive a greater variety of programming.

PISA said that the cooperation of ITFS was absolutely essential: "A viable Public Interest Satellite system can only emerge if it is built on the foundations already laid by a licensed system owned and operated by the schools, hospitals, and other public service entities throughout the country."

(An Arthur D. Little study written a couple of years before had suggested another alternative, growing out of the same considerations: A public-interest satellite would come about against the opposition of the commercial carriers, it said, only if the Defense Department wanted a high-powered communications satellite for its own uses, rather than ride the commercial satellites, and was willing to back the establishment of a government satellite it would share with public-service users.[6])

To develop such a system, further experimentation would be necessary. To facilitate this, NASA proposed to use the space shuttle to launch a Large Deployable Antenna. Without such continued experimentation, the National Academy of Science warned, public-service uses of satellites would fall by the wayside.

The plan got some congressional support: On September 11, 1978, Representative Richard L. Ottinger, Democrat of New York, introduced a bill to direct NASA and the NTIA (National Telecommunications and Information Administration) "to develop a low-cost, interactive satellite for public-service uses." But then came the kick in the head: the Carter administration would have none of this. Spending money to develop uses of satellites in the public sector was out of the question. The Ottinger bill did not pass. Instead, on October 10, 1978, Jimmy Carter issued Presidential Directive NSC-42, mandating NTIA to collect public-service users and deliver them to private satellite entrepreneurs. "NTIA will form a policy to assist in market aggregating, technical transmission, and possible development of domestic and international public satellite services," the directive said.

Taking its cue, NTIA in January of 1980 put out a request to the private satellite carriers for a proposal to develop a management structure "to aggregate the public-service market and provide these services via the commercial satellite market." NTIA offered to give the corporation that proposed the best commercial marketing system several millions of dollars in subsidy in which to develop it. I asked one of the overseers of the program what the basic intention was.

"We hope that in a few years' time, someone in the industry, possibly one of the regular commercial carriers, will be making a living aggregating public-interest uses and providing these services for a fee," he said. When I asked him if anyone in government was still supporting the idea of a public-service satellite, he replied he knew of no one.

I found someone at NASA (although, of course, he could not be thought of as a disinterested party in the fight). A high-ranking official who had worked on public-service satellite project experiments said, "I think we should subsidize satellite communication for social purposes until it becomes so generally used that the public can afford it. It will take a lot longer to get going, otherwise."

Andrew Horowitz felt the battle had been lost. "You can't even get people in government to talk about it with you," he said. "NTIA says, 'Don't expect the government to do it for you—we are not going to be an advocate for public-service uses. It should be done privately'—which means leaving it to a very few corporations that can compete in this area."

PISA was disbanded.

The Public Service Satellite Consortium, on the other hand, felt it could live with the turn of events.

"There won't be a dedicated public satellite," Elizabeth Young, its president, told me in Washington. "Western Union, RCA, and the others don't want the government to do what they want to do commercially." She said she felt the needs could be met by service-based organizations, if they would band together to buy blocks of time on the commercial satellites. "People are willing to pay for these services," she said. "Everyone wants to stay well—if you want to beef up medical-data exchange, for example, the funds are available to do that."

PSSC also expected to get government funds to help public-service groups move onto the commercial satellites. Since these will sell transponder time only in bulk on a long-term basis, rather than piece-by-piece, PSSC or a profit-making aggregator of users will have to act as middlemen, buying time in bulk and selling to individual users.

PSSC found a great deal of interest in its service from the health community. Both the American Hospital Association and the American Dietetic Association, for example, used it to buy time for continuing education courses for professionals in various locations. Programs were sent to the satellite from the earth station operated by PSSC in Denver. It had been suggested early on that PSSC might eventually put up a public satellite of its own. Its president did not see that as a possibility. "The costs of building and launching satellites are so enormous that I think for the consortium ever to have its own, at least in the present state of the technology, is unrealistic," she said.

In 1979, when the FCC lifted a long-standing ban on AT&T's entry into satellite communications, Bell stepped forward with a promise to provide the kind of satellite service public-interest groups could use. This came in a proposal to launch a high-capacity satellite that would provide data-transmission service to small businesses, nonprofit users, and householders who would not be served by the low-powered satellites proposed by SBS.

"Big data communication users don't need us," a top AT&T executive told me. "But just as the objective fifty years ago was universal telephone service, probably the thrust of the future is universal data service. The only company around to do that is Bell." For this purpose, AT&T could become the "aggregator," he said. He added, however, that the company could not provide satellite service for an educational system at a cost that would not be profitable. The question was, could public-service users afford AT&T's prices?

PUBLIC TELEVISION GETS ON THE "BIRD"

The trend toward the use of commercial satellites by public-service organizations was foreshadowed by a decision of the Corporation for Public Broadcasting (CPB) to go that route. A public satellite for broadcasting had been debated since 1966, when the Ford Foundation proposed creation of a Broadcasters Nonprofit Satellite System to link stations of the Public Broadcasting Service (PBS) network. After a decade of argument and an FCC inquiry into such a system, CPB chose instead to lease four transponders on Western Union's *Westar* satellite. By getting on the "bird," by 1978 PBS was able to transmit as many as four feeds to its 264 stations simultaneously, rather than the single, take-it-or-leave-it feed that could be supplied over AT&T's terrestrial system. Live public television service was possible to Alaska, Hawaii, and Puerto Rico for the first time, replacing videotapes sent to them by mail. In 1980 the Public Radio Satellite System, also funded by CPB, completed interconnection of 192 public radio stations via *Westar*. Several of these stations had "uplink" capacity to feed programming into the network from their earth stations.

The economic justification for CPB to use satellites was there: although it cost the corporation $40 million to set up satellite-receiving terminals at public television stations, the savings of this form of transmission over the charges imposed by AT&T made it possible to pay off the investment in a very few years.

Pressed by other public-service organizations, CPB agreed to share unused time on its *Westar* transponders and ground stations with nonprofit users who would pay for their operation at cost. This made it possible, for example, for independent journalists to arrange coverage of a national event and offer it to PBS stations via satellite. This was done for the first time on May 6, 1979, when, for a few thousand dollars, a group of young videotape producers, organized as Public Interest Video, provided national coverage of an antinuclear rally in Washington. (Later that year, in the interests of liberal-conservative balance, the same group covered an antiabortion convention in Cincinnati. More than a dozen public television stations carried the program live and dozens more monitored it on the system, for excerpting in news broadcasts or later time periods.)

Ironically, the coming of satellites and the ability of independent organizations to establish satellite networks for the distribution of programs was seen by some as a threat to the survival of public television in the United States. Many of public television's critics have accused the stations and the national entities that support them of an elitist approach to programming. The stations and PBS have largely featured and promoted "cultural" programs—opera, drama, the dance, and high-quality dramatic series produced by the BBC—rather than national and local news and public-service programs. The reasons for this were twofold. First, and most important in the thinking of public station executives, has been the fact that the viewers who help pay the station executives' salaries *have been* an elite that wants to see cultural programming on public television that it cannot see on commercial television. This elite consists of middle- and upper-class viewers who make the larger contributions during the stations' fund-raising drives. National funding for cultural programs is also heavily supported by underwriters such as Mobil, Exxon, and Gulf who want to be looked on favorably by this elite.

Cultural programming of this type is a necessary alternative on television and should be provided for those who want to watch it. However, they can now get such cultural programming from other sources. Rather than contribute to public television stations for a potpourri of programs that they might possibly want to watch, they can (or soon will be able to) subscribe to satellite programming services that supply exactly the category of programs they want to watch for a monthly fee, or a specific program they want to watch on a pay-per-program basis. (They can, of course, also buy many of these programs for their home videodisc or videocassette players.) With this capacity developing, some critics contend, the primary justification used by the public television establishment for its continued existence no longer exists.

Which brings us to the second reason why cultural programming was favored over news and public-affairs programming: cultural programming does not arouse the popular and political opposition that news and public affairs can arouse if they are done in a hard-hitting way that plays no favorites, yields to no pressures, and protects no sacred cows. Most public television managers, like commercial television managers, like to play it safe. Most would swear to the FCC that they are deeply into public affairs. Most would say they are deeply involved in their communities. On examination, this involvement is not borne out, either in the number of programs presented or the depth of reporting or probing into events they present. Almost all such programs shy away from investigating issues in such a way that would make it possible to offer conclusions about what has been learned. If you dig too hard, you may *find* something, and that may rock the boat. Rather, they are on-the-one-hand, on-the-other-hand exercises that leave the viewer, if she watches them at all beyond the first five minutes, in what is known in the news business as the MEGO-state (My Eyes Glaze Over).

At the great majority of stations, news programming gets even shorter shrift than public affairs. Public television managers who are against doing news on a daily basis will usually tell you it costs too much, and besides, the commercial stations do it well—both arguable assertions. News does not have to be expensive; it does have to have a commitment from station management to do it in ways that will mean something to the people of the area; it requires a willingness to do the kind of digging reporting that a good local paper has traditionally been willing to do. Beyond that, it requires a willingness to do what a local newspaper *cannot* do—present hot debates at council meetings and hearings on controversial public questions *live*.

It has been lack of this commitment, not money, that in most communities has prevented public television from making a significant contribution to informed discussion among the populace. If it is done intelligently, news of local people and events can lead more people to pay attention to the station than cultural programming aimed at an elite minority.

And although the capability exists within public television to put together large minority-interest audiences (ethnic music performances, nationality-interest topics), this has seldom been done because minorities and those in lower-income groups have not been seen as public television's main constituency.

Yet if public television stations did become deeply involved in covering their community's affairs and the PBS network did actually serve the interests of the *deprived* minorities—rather than those of the *affluent* minority—public television would have a rationale for its existence that no new technology could take away from it. Such a commitment would not only be socially responsible but an insurance policy, as well. Public television would be staking out an area of service that commercial television has done poorly or not at all. And doing this would amply justify public funding that is now being questioned.

To continue the community services implicit in the original *idea* of public broadcasting, it will be necessary and beneficial for stations and the PBS network to make use of many of the new technologies of communication. For example, videotex could be used imaginatively and effectively in conjunction with these stations' formal daytime school programs and informal adult education programs. These screen-text supplements to television teaching could be carried either over the air or on cable channels associated with the stations. The PTV satellite facilities could make the best of these offerings available to stations across the country for incorporation into their own instructional television efforts.

This again points up the need for satellites dedicated to nonprofit public uses.

CANADA SUPPORTS PUBLIC-INTEREST USES

Throughout the 1970s, as I have said, no government policy existed in the United States to promote the use of domestic satellites for public service. The major problem this presented to nonprofit users was that none of the American commercial satellites could relay powerful signals that could be picked up by those who could afford only small (one meter) dishes on their rooftops.

The Canadian government, on the other hand, recognized this need and acknowledged there should be a public dividend for its research and development in the satellite field.

Canada was the first country in the world to launch a national communications satellite independent of the Intelsat system. In 1969 the Parliament set up Telesat Canada, owned 50 percent by the federal government and 50 percent by telecommunications carriers— such as Bell Canada and the provincial (public) telephone companies—to establish a system of satellite communications across the country. In 1973 it launched a satellite called *Anik*—an Inuit (Eskimo) word for "brother"—to provide national phone, television, and data transmission service.

Following its joint *Hermes/CTS* project with the United States, the Department of Communication (DOC) decided it was necessary to continue subsidizing public-service experiments. Learning from the *Hermes* experiments, Telesat designed later vehicles in the *Anik* series so that, although they were not so powerful as *Hermes,* they would still be able to meet tele-education and telemedicine requirements. The DOC leased four channels on the *Anik B* satellite, to provide time free of charge for further public-service experiments, and made twenty ground stations available for the purpose.

In addition, the Canadian government lent fifty rooftop dishes to residents of rural communities and began testing direct-to-home television broadcasting for those who otherwise could not receive transmissions from local television stations.

(Direct satellite broadcasting of a commercial nature was proposed in the United States by Comsat, which in 1980 formed a subsidiary, Satellite Television Corp., to present its application to the FCC. This ran in the face of long-standing FCC policy that direct broadcasting should come from the transmitters of local stations, not from national transmitters. As expected, the proposal was met with stiff opposition from conventional broadcasters. However, the policy of "localism" had been dented, if not breached, when Ted Turner helped set up a satellite carrier, Southern Satellite Systems, to transmit "local" programs—mostly movies and sports—from his "superstation" in Atlanta to cable systems across the country.)

In announcing the plan to use *Anik B* channels for continued testing of public services, an official of the DOC remarked: "There are plenty of examples in regard to field trials in the public-services sector where support ceased too early and therefore all early initiative and positive development were lost." As opposed to the Carter administration's position, the Canadians said that "in specific terms, the Department of Communication will support the public-service sector" in satellite communications. This did not mean, however, that the DOC intended to launch an operational public satellite, rather it would attempt to get priority treatment for public-service users on Telesat's service.

There were, however, those who feared that in the long run, public-service interests in Canada would go the way of American commercialism. At a symposium on what was learned from the *Hermes* experiments, Dr. William H. Melody of Simon Fraser University in Burnaby, British Columbia, pointed out that in its satellite operations, Telesat leased service only at satellite-channel band width, thus excluding any users other than the telephone companies and the television distributors. Alphonse Ouimet, Telesat's chairman, replied that the limitation could be removed. "Some way will be worked out so that there are no limitations on smaller users," he said.[7]

For all the talk in North America of providing channels for

public-service uses by aggregating markets or by other means, there is little or no concern for these users in the area where it counts—the commercial satellite corporations themselves.

Dr. Anna Casey-Stahmer, who coordinated the *Hermes* experiments for the DOC, pointed out that the requirements of the public-service sector did not enter into the planning of these systems. More than that, she said, public-service users "are dealing with communication entities which have not participated in the earlier process of applications experimentation and therefore do not appreciate fully the requirements." The technology tested in the projects—small earth stations, remote video origination, and transportable terminals—is not available in operating systems or only available at a high price, she pointed out.[8]

COMMERCIAL OPERATORS BATTLE
FOR THE SPOILS

The commercial operators, naturally, are aiming for the greatest returns, and those will come from other business users of satellite communications services. It appeared that nonprofit users would be barred from the biggest commercial satellite of them all—Satellite Business Systems. When I asked a company executive at SBS, headquartered in McLean, Virginia, if public-interest groups might use the service, he told me this was not likely: "The tariff will be too high," he said.

SBS, of which IBM owns 40 percent, was formed with the approval of the FCC to give AT&T a competitor in the long-distance communications business. The SBS plan was to sell private networks to business customers in a way that would bypass Bell Long Lines completely. It appeared that IBM, which next to the federal government had been the largest user of AT&T telecommunications services, would now become the largest customer of SBS. (The FCC, frustrated by years of unsuccessful attempts to control or even understand Bell's long-distance rate structure, decided to allow competition to promote marketplace "regulation" of these charges to the customers.)

The system SBS designed made it likely that only the largest corporations would be users: large earth stations were to be built on the premises of the businesses themselves, at costs higher than $500,000 each. A geographically dispersed corporation can use the satellite channels for telephone service, data communication, facsimile, transmission, and teleconferencing among a score of company offices at the same time. Video teleconferencing was the sales gimmick used at first to promote the service. An SBS description of this service said: "By bringing together facsimile, voice, and data transmission and adding video, a novel idea evolves: business conferences across a continent that permit people not only to hear and see each other but to conveniently transmit the hard copy, visuals, and data they may need to work together in a conference situation. In this way, teleconferencing can replace much of the costly and exhausting travel that characterizes so many business lives. People will be brought together immediately to solve problems, and that will be a significant benefit."

The company planners held out the possibility that the service would one day include projecting holographic images of those taking part in the teleconferences—to make it *appear* that distant participants were actually standing or sitting in the same room.

Even before the first SBS satellite got off the ground, however, the company shifted its marketing emphasis to voice—long-distance satellite telephone transmission—at rates lower than AT&T was offering to business.[9] It also decided to allow companies to share earth station terminals to increase the number who could afford them. The idea was to try to turn a short-term profit while it was trying to generate demand for the full range of data communications it wanted to provide.

AT&T offered its own form of video teleconferencing, called Picturephone Meeting Service. In this, however, participants had to go to "electronic" meeting rooms in a particular city, from which television images of people present, graphics, and text could be transmitted to similar meeting rooms in other cities.

IBM, working with SBS, was in effect designing a globe-spanning "automated office," in which computers, electronic typewriters, facsimile machines could "talk to each other" via the satellite network. The automated office machines would not be supplied by SBS. The idea was that most of them *would* be supplied by IBM.*

AT&T began offering a similar thing through its Advanced Communications Service (ACS) and Dataspeed computer terminals. In

---

* IBM saw business applications for videodisc systems. In 1979 it formed a joint company with the Music Corporation of America to develop and market videodiscs and playback units, mainly for use by industry as sales and training aids. This was the closest the business machines giant had yet come to the consumer business.

the Bell arrangement, the company supplies both the machines and the facilities. Although this was set up first as a land-based service, it is equally workable on Bell satellites.

At AT&T headquarters on lower Broadway I asked William Sharwell, vice-president for planning, if the corporation now considered itself in head-to-head competition with data-processing companies.

"We will provide anything that anyone else does," he said.

I wondered how AT&T could do that in light of the agreement with the Justice Department that forbade it from engaging in data processing. "How will you get around the consent decree?" I asked.

Sharwell, a gregarious, expansive man in late middle age, smiled, and then explained: "I'm smiling" he said, "because I spent all morning working on that subject."

Congressional legislation could kill the provisions of the consent decree, he pointed out. The decrees included an understanding that Bell could not be in any business, such as computers, that cannot be regulated. One way around that, he said, would be for Congress to allow Bell to set up a subsidiary that could be competitive with IBM or other computer manufacturers, while the main corporation continued to operate as a monopoly in transmission of computer data.

Shortly after I talked with him, the FCC approved a ruling that appeared to accomplish this without congressional action. By 5 to 2, the commission voted to give Bell the right to enter the data-processing business. The only restriction was that the competition with other computer manufacturers would have to be carried on through a subsidiary, so that telephone profits could not be used to subsidize AT&T's data processing business. The order, to go into effect by 1982, appeared to kill the consent decree. Bell officials were wary, however, that this interpretation might be challenged in the courts, by its competitors or by the Justice Department itself.

The fact that AT&T could begin to operate openly in the data processing area even before the consent decree was annulled points to the fusion of computers and communications that confounded FCC efforts to keep the two lines apart. IBM called AT&T's system out-and-out data processing; AT&T said No, it was merely efficient transmission of data between transmission links.

At any rate, by 1980, these two corporate giants—AT&T with 100,000 employees, assets of nearly $100 billion, and annual sales of nearly $40 billion; IBM with 300,000 employees, assets of $19 billion, and sales of nearly $20 billion—were facing each other for what many industry analysts thought would be the corporate joust of the century.[10] At stake was domination of the satellite communications market.

In 1956, when AT&T signed the consent decree, computers were computers and they belonged to IBM; telecommunication was telecommunication, and it belonged to AT&T. As the 1980s began, computers and telecommunications had become one, and the one was up for grabs. To many in the administration and the Congress, this was of no great concern so long as competition between the two giants was maintained—and augmented by others getting into the field. The FCC decision on "open skies" seemed to guarantee such competition in the satellite area. What it did not guarantee was the admission of nonprofit public-service agencies to the field. If you accept the premise that only profit-taking entrepreneurs, rather than nonprofit agencies, should be allowed to provide services, setting up a competition between private companies probably does help to keep profit-added prices in line. Except, of course, where the companies get together secretly to administer prices, or where the industry leader is big enough to set prices for the whole industry—as when a price increase by Big Steel (U.S. Steel) is mimicked immediately by Little Steel (all the others). Then, however, government abdicates its role of *regulator* in the public interest and becomes *referee* to see to it each of the commercial competitors is assured a fair fight for the consumer's dollar.

In this limited way, the FCC as a referee may have more beneficial effect than the long-drawn-out antitrust actions against AT&T and IBM. On and off, the Justice Department has been fighting suits against AT&T, charging "conspiracy" to monopolize the telecommunications market, since the 1880s—with little tangible result. AT&T has usually had the money and legal resources to battle the government to a draw.

The Justice Department's latest and largest effort to penalize the corporation for unnecessary roughness in dealing with its competitors appeared headed for another out-of-court settlement that would leave the communications giant essentially intact. AT&T spent $250 million of corporate funds to insure that result. With other corporate giants such as IBM/SBS allowed to enter the telecommunications lists, AT&T began to have fears for its monopoly never induced by the antitrust actions.

Among the major competitors, Xerox announced an integrated

telecommunications system called *X-Ten*—the same, but not the same, as SBS's: companies would send their communications between Xerox earth stations, from which they would be transmitted to rooftop antennas of company offices by microwave relays. Texas Instruments Inc., RCA, ITT, and Exxon Corp. also became contenders in the business communications market.

Companies pushing the automated office idea center much of their planning on the word processor. The word processor, with its VDT screen, looks and acts very much like a VDT editing machine in a newspaper office. It could easily be adapted to the Prestel-type videotex operation. The device stores typewriter strokes in its memory and can reproduce the text for editing. It can send the content between terminals—on the same floor or, by satellite, to a branch office across the country. It can retype letters more efficiently than a human secretary, then file copies more efficiently than a human file clerk. Computerized data banks to which word processors are connected can store company records at the home and branch offices. A home office executive with the proper clearance can access a branch office manager's sales file daily, for example, to see how the manager is doing. Using an HCS terminal, a business executive could do some of her work from home.

The system is sold on the basis of increasing office efficiency and management productivity. How automated offices, tied together by machines and people who talk to each other across great distances, will actually affect managers and the lives of the people who work for them is a subject of debate among corporate and university sociologists. The system will, say the telecommunications company brochures, reduce manpower needs in the office. People in clerical unions are worried about that promise. Will the system mean loss of jobs, or will it open more interesting and productive jobs elsewhere for secretaries and file clerks who have been displaced by automation?

Depending on how it is used, a satellite-based system can either centralize or decentralize corporate control. In fact, one reason that fears of multinational corporations are increasing around the world is that the growing satellite networks give corporate headquarters the power to extract information from—and instantly communicate decisions to—its subsidiaries anywhere on earth. Some national governments believe that such centralized control provides a method for international corporations to manipulate markets in ways that are beyond the ability of the local governments to regulate.

Bruce MacKenzie, a communications management consultant based in Boston, told me he thinks the global information system can have a decentralizing, rather than a centralizing effect on multinationals: "With more and more up-to-date information available to managers at every level," he said, "I think we are beginning to see a more horizontal dispersion of decision-making. There is a change that gives increased authority and resources to divisions and branches. Most users have opted for new approaches that are decentralizing in spirit.

"At the same time, better communications tend to make decentralization less risky. Wrong decisions can be spotted earlier and responded to more rapidly. Thus, there is less risk of a segment of the business running out of control. The satellite-based systems may give organizations the best of both worlds—the advantages of decentralized decision-making without the major risk that errors will go uncaught."

But making such a system work depends on the corporate management's intentions. If, for example, the head of the São Paulo division thinks his boss in New York is looking over his shoulder every day by electronically accessing his records, he can defeat the purpose of the system by putting into the machine only that information that will make him look good.

In the era of new communications, do even persons in business have the right to privacy in the daily conduct of their business operations? They do—only if a corporation is willing to trust them to given areas of autonomy. If not, we get back to Winston and the monitoring telescreen. We can also get authoritarian central control that will eventually lead local governments to decide the only safe thing to do is expropriate the multinational's local subsidiary.

The issue of privacy is raised for corporate managements themselves, but from another perspective. Transfer of messages between company terminals is, in effect, a form of electronic mail. Can industrial secrets, or even confidential business discussions, be preserved if most company communications are not placed in envelopes and sent through the regular mails, but typed into a terminal or fed into a facsimile transmitter, sent by satellite, and reproduced on another terminal or facsimile machine in a distant office? Some in business believe encryption of this traffic is necessary. It is known, for example, that both the United States and the Soviet Union have the capability of intercepting telephone messages or data communications transmitted via communications satellites.

The SBS executive declared its system was *safer* than the mails: "It's a secure system because it provides *bulk* encryption," he said. "You would need to know the earth station codes for addressing and transmission, and you can change the key to those at will. The Defense Department could break the codes if it wanted to spend millions of dollars to do it, but it would be pretty hard for another firm to do it."

(However, another firm did it to the DOD. In an evaluation test of vulnerability, a team from the Mitre Corporation cracked an "ultrasecure" Pentagon computer system in less than a day.[11])

POSTAL SERVICE STARTS ELECTRONIC MAIL

The development of private electronic mail obviously presents a major challenge to the U.S. Postal Service, with ramifications, in fact, that threaten its very existence. Several of the satellite carriers want to take over business mail service, which accounts for 73 percent of all first-class mail and is obviously the mainstay of the postal system.

It was estimated in 1978 that 23 percent of all mail was potentially deliverable to end-users by telecommunications, and 23 percent more was deliverable to post offices.[12]

Private communications companies want potential money-making aspects of electronic mail to be reserved to themselves. These include electronic delivery to business end-users, and electronic transmission of mail between post offices. Most are conceding home delivery by hand to the Postal Service, because this service loses money.

The Postal Service thinks it will either have to get into electronic mail delivery or be driven out of business by private competition. Its studies show that, if electronic mail is handled in bulk, via satellite, the price per piece can be as low or lower than the price for physical transport of mail in envelopes.

So in the late 1970s it drew up plans to test two services:

1. Intelpost—a system designed to transmit facsimile messages via satellite between the United States and countries in Western Europe, post-office-to-post-office, and

2. EMSS—Electronic Message Service System, designed to convert hard-copy letters to digital form, send them via satellite, cor-

vert them back to hard copy, and distribute them through the regular postal system.

In 1979 President Carter issued a policy statement backing the proposed service. But he endorsed competition in delivery of electronic mail and directed the Postal Service to purchase transmission services from the private companies, rather than build a transmission network of its own. However, private entrepreneurs and their supporters in Congress immediately proposed laws to block these services and to preserve them for commercial enterprise. The FCC jumped to the support of the private companies. It claimed jurisdiction over electronic mail, and indicated its intention of barring operation of such systems until they could be regulated to permit competition from the private carriers. The Post Office said it was willing to compete, but that its regulations had to be set by the Postal Rate Commission, and not the FCC. In its report the same year, the USPS said that with electronic mail delivery, it could reduce substantially the handling costs associated with regular letter mail. It pointed out that, unlike private electronic mail services, it was required to pass these savings on to the mailer. By 1990, it said, the projected cost for an average piece of electronic mail should be about two-thirds the cost of regular first-class mail.

In Washington, Peter Boyd, who supervised the original testing of Intelpost facsimile service between postal headquarters there and London, showed me a technique that would help keep this mail private. Once my message was transmitted from Washington to the BPO test center in London, it was wiped off the memories of the computers at either end. Nevertheless, this was somewhat less secure than a piece of regular transatlantic mail because, he pointed out, "It has been seen by human beings putting it into the machine here and taking it out over there." Sensitive mail would still be sealed in envelopes by the sender. It is more difficult for someone to open private mail, copy it, and send it on its way without the sender or the receiver noticing that this has happened. Direct addressing of electronic mail from the home via HCS would increase privacy because postal employees could not view the message (or its "envelope," unless they had deliberately tapped into your home lines). But such service will come later than post-office-to-post-office service.

At the other end of the U.S.-British satellite linkup, I found enthusiasm for an Intelpost service across the Atlantic, but a less optimistic prediction concerning domestic electronic mail. At BPO headquarters near Saint Paul's Cathedral, Ray Watkins, the administrator in charge of new technologies who had been looking into the possibilities, told me: "Our feeling is, baldly, that a major impact on conventional mail is still some way off." Business mail is delivered anywhere in the country overnight, he pointed out. But someday, electronic mail could be cheaper for business. "I don't think there's any doubt that most people in the Post Office in the U.K. accept that, in the long run, electronic mail will make up a large part of our business." Same-day service between countries, which Intelpost would provide, is worth pursuing now, he said.

Watkins spoke from a more comfortable position than his colleagues in the United States—knowing that his postal and telecommunications service was a government monopoly, and no private companies were going to be in a position to try to drive it out of business. If people in Britain realize that they can send mail via an electronic link between private offices, he said, that's all right: BPO will supply the end-to-end transmission link, a service Carter forbade to the U.S. Postal Service.

Meantime, in Sweden, facsimile mail service was already in operation between post offices and major cities.

In reporting in Western Europe, I found that the public and the legislatures support the idea that government must compete with private companies to keep them on their toes, and to prevent them from monopolizing communications markets. In the mixed economies of the social democratic states it works both ways. Some years ago, for a documentary I was producing for public television on power blackouts, I interviewed the head of the Swedish State Power Board, which provides a national electricity grid that serves both the public and private local distribution agencies. "I think it is a good thing that my engineers have some competition from the private companies' engineers," he told me. "It keeps our system efficient." And the president of the largest private power company said to me, "I think the State Power Board has worked as a yardstick, regarding rates, and I think it has worked rather well. For the customers, it is good, and also for the companies—the competition."

From the standpoint of the governments and the managers of the post and telecommunications agencies, however, the chief concern is maintaining the national telecommunications monopolies. The bogeyman I heard mentioned as a threat to these monopolies was not AT&T or ITT, but IBM. SBS, the combination IBM has put together with Comsat and Aetna, is seen as the most dangerous vehicle of this threat. In answer to a question about this, an SBS official told me, picking his words carefully, I thought, "We don't have it within our business plan to offer the service on the international scene." Industry analysts predicted, however, that IBM, via SBS, would offer a "cradle to grave" information network—a worldwide communications system for voice, data, facsimile, video—driven by computers.

According to Alain Giraud, chief of communications research for the Centre National d'Études des Télécommunications (CNET) in France, the PTT's are worried that if large corporations want to install ground stations on their premises and connect with the SBS satellite system, they are going to have the political and economic power to do it, whether PTT managers like it or not. The answer of the European PTT's, he said, is to develop their own systems to offer business communications that are competitive. Partly for this reason, the French PTT in 1979 persuaded the government to launch *Télécom I* and *II,* national satellites providing all the transmission services envisioned in the SBS system.

Although it has a terrestrial television network that covers France completely, Télédiffusion de France (TDF) got approval for the direct broadcast satellite, which can transmit programs to rooftop antennas. West Germany also decided to put up a direct broadcast satellite, called *TV-Sat,* to broadcast television and radio programs from its regional public networks.

These projects were pushed by aerospace hardware manufacturers who wanted their countries to get into the satellite business. The clincher in France came from the argument by the government broadcasters that if they did not put up the satellite, then commercial interests in neighboring countries would do so, and "invade" their national territories. Given the choice, the French public might indeed choose to watch commercial programs with slick production values, rather than the duller offerings of the TDF.

In the late 1970s Compagnie Luxembourgeoise de Télédiffusion announced its intention of supplying a European-wide satellite television service, financed entirely by advertising. (Commercial television stations in San Marino, Andorra, and Monte Carlo also transmit ad-supported programs across national borders.) This idea was anathema to the Western European national television services, which predicted that commercial competition in television would reduce programming to the least-common-denominator fare offered to the public in the United States.

The French and West German public systems permit commercials bunched together, usually before and after the news. State systems in Sweden, Norway, and Denmark permit none at all, and governments there are adamantly against commercials supporting any service coming directly into their countries. And they do not want programs containing commercials to "spill over" from other countries into their national territories.

Spillover is both a technical and political problem. At an international conference sponsored by the International Telecommunications Union in 1977, each European country had been allocated five national satellite channels and positions over the equator for placing communications satellites in orbit.

The beam from a direct broadcast satellite can be restricted to an ellipse (called a footprint) that covers an area about the size of West Germany. Since many countries in Europe are smaller than this, beams aimed at any one of them would overlap others. And even a satellite beam pointed at West Germany could not be made to follow the contours of a border. So some spillover would be inevitable.

So, at the 1977 meeting, regulations were adopted that said "unavoidable" spillover was accepted for these television channels, but that countries placing satellites in orbit should try to avoid it.

Whether all countries would abide by this rule is a matter of doubt. Sweden, Ghana, Britain, the United States, and the Soviet Union, to name a few, have ignored limits on radiated power from their transmitters in an effort to get their messages heard in distant countries they would not otherwise have been able to reach.

France, because of a desire to spread its language, is apparently delighted with the inevitability of spilling talk shows across its borders. It is happy with the idea that the direct broadcast satellites will extend domestic television programs to its former colonies in North Africa. West Germany is pleased with the notion that its television will be seen throughout East Germany.

Other countries actively *desire* spillover from another's television—Switzerland, for example, wants German, French, and Italian television for people in its three major language groups. But some countries actively oppose invasion of their territories by foreign television, calling unwanted transmission a violation of their cultural integrity.

Swedish Social Democrats, who like West German commercial values as little as they do those of the United States, are particularly concerned about West German programs, including commercials, being picked up by Swedish sets. They would prefer to exchange programs among the Scandinavian countries by their satellite, *Nordsat.* But even then, some Swedes fear that providing more channels than the two now existing would only mean set-owners could opt out of cultural and public-affairs programming, switching instead from one American movie to another on the "extra" services provided by her Scandinavian partners. For the most zealous, this translates into a desire to give the people what is good for them. In their attitudes, there is an overlay of feeling that Sweden should be a guided democracy—an idea that would be suspect among Americans concerned with freedom of choice. This notion is especially dangerous, not when it comes from democratically inspired ideals, as it does in Sweden, but from authoritarian nationalist ideas among emerging nations.

That coin has another side, as well. Less-developed countries almost everywhere object to the Westernization, and some to the Sovietization, threatened by direct broadcast satellite transmissions from the industrialized nations. At their insistence, UNESCO in 1972 adopted a declaration that stated it "is necessary that states, taking into account the principle of freedom of information, reach prior agreements concerning direct satellite broadcasting to the population of countries other than the country of origin of the transmission." The United States, casting the lone dissenting vote, contended this was a violation of the principle of free flow of information among nations.

Some totalitarian countries can combat the spillover problem by forbidding their citizens to have rooftop antennas aimed at the satellites of countries whose politics they disapprove. But that is not possible when countries are adjacent and the totalitarian country—East Germany, for example—wants to put up a satellite for its own citizens. An East German satellite would have to be placed roughly in the same orbital position as West Germany's satellite, and thus, an East German citizen's rooftop antenna would inevitably pick up pictures from both.

EUROPEAN SPACE AGENCY BACKS
A PUB SAT

Late in the 1970s the European Space Agency, which provides research and development for most Western European countries' satellite programs, developed plans to launch an *H-Sat*—a heavy direct broadcast satellite that could also be used for public services. (The project, proposed as a joint venture of France and West Germany, was delayed when each country decided to launch national communications satellites of their own.)

Calin Rosetti, one of the designers of the *H-Sat* system, promoted the project specifically because dedicated channels could be used by less-developed countries in Africa. For one thing, it could give these countries an alternative to Western cultural fare: "What will our television do for poor people?" Rosetti asked. "What if it shows them Western goods to buy if they have no possibility for work?"

But public satellite communications would obviously have appeal for developing countries—Nigeria, for example—where terrestrial communications networks are nonexistent and difficult to build. A national direct broadcast satellite, or leased satellite channels, could provide telephone, voice radio, and data communications. It could present educational and medical instruction programs transmitted from urban centers to community centers in remote areas. In many cases, satellite *radio* would be more practical than satellite television, Rosetti pointed out. Home television sets are scarce in most of these countries.

"Radio makes it cheap to produce programs," he said. "You can receive them on cheap receivers, and solar power is possible—you put the radio in the sun, and it will recharge."

A two-way educational network and voice teleconferencing would be possible with such a system. Using satellite radio, remote medical diagnosis could be accomplished between a nurse practitioner at a distant clinic and a physician at a base hospital. Radio would be somewhat less effective than television for this particular use, however.

Third World delegates to the general World Administrative Radio Conference (WARC), held in Geneva by the International Telecommunications Union for ten weeks in the fall of 1979, were aware of the benefits—and dangers—of satellite communications. They sought to have frequencies and "parking spaces" in orbit reserved for their use, as a defense against having all of them preempted by the industrialized countries. The United States, on the other hand, wanted the allocations to be made, as before, on a first-come, first-served basis, rather than country-by-country. This meant U.S. communications corporations would get most of the available slots. The question was finessed temporarily by permitting slots and frequencies to be assigned country-by-country in Europe, Africa, and Asia, and postponing the decision for North and South America until later conferences. This gave competing private companies in the United States a chance to go ahead with their satellite plans, with conflicting claims of Canada, Mexico, and other American countries to be settled through international negotiations.

Most of the less-developed countries would like to keep telecommunications as a government monopoly, on the grounds that communications must be made to serve national development. With this goal as justification, many Third World governments seek to control information available to their own people, information about their countries that is being transmitted to the First and Second Worlds, and information being siphoned (some say *stolen*) from their countries by industrialists and governments of the developed countries.

But unless they can control the communications satellites, this will not be possible. Colombia, an equatorial nation over which satellites ride, claimed the orbital parking spaces directly overhead, and said no satellite should be placed there without its permission. Since it would be impossible for Colombia to shoot down satellites over its territory, this claim was seen primarily as a negotiating ploy.

Nonsynchronous satellites circling the globe have "invaded" other countries' national space for years, beginning with military satellites used by the United Sates and the Soviet Union to sense missile launchings and other military developments. Since 1972 a NASA *Landsat* vehicle has carried out remote sensing of resources over all countries of the world. The *Landsat*s have "prospected" for mineral resources and oil deposits and provided imagery for crop production forecasts. NASA sells that information to private industry and to other governments, including the Soviet Union. Dr. Cees Hamelink of the Netherlands, who has conducted studies in the "cultural imperialism" of the new communications, remarked:

"Remote sensing is applied to agriculture, forestry, hydrology, oceanography, and mineral exploitation. Where its application is totally controlled by a few 'haves' it raises for the 'have nots' urgent questions about the potential loss of national sovereignty due to 'data drain.' The technological advantage of access to superior means of data-collection, transmission, and processing can easily be translated into a substantial economic advantage. Think of the implications of early information about mineral deposits or crop diseases."[13]

With remote sensing, he pointed out, the "sensed" countries are more vulnerable than they are in the case of direct satellite broadcasting, because technical defenses against receiving transmissions from satellites are more effective than those against having one's own resources *sensed* by satellite.

Surprisingly, at the WARC, the U.S. delegation was able to persuade LDC's that remote sensing was good for them. I asked Wilson Dizard, a delegate to the conference from the State Department, how the United States was able to get these countries to go along with its proposals for continued sensing by *Landsat* and later satellites.

"I think NASA laid the groundwork for overcoming their objections by inviting eighty countries to take part in its experiments," he said. "There was a great deal of discussion of 'What's in it for me?' A lot of countries perceived that they were getting a lot of benefit from the *Landsat* project, and so they overlooked the fact that the United States would get the most."

Remote sensing of resources is only one use to which high-resolution cameras, infrared heat-sensing devices, and radar in satellites are being put. In the late 1960s, the Central Intelligence Agency used intelligence satellites to spy on American students engaged in antiwar demonstrations.[14] A CIA document procured under the Freedom of Information Act disclosed this, but did not say whether the satellite pictures were used to estimate the size of demonstrations or were enlarged to identify individuals taking part. Cameras in American spy satellites, orbiting the world at altitudes higher than one hundred miles, are reported to be sharp enough to tell on which side a person on the ground parts his hair.

"FAR OUT" APPLICATIONS FOR THE NEAR-TERM

"Outlook for Space," a study made for NASA by Ivan Bekey and Harris Mayer of the Aerospace Corp.,[15] suggested a number of other "far out" applications for communications satellites that are now within the state of the communication art, and could be introduced at any time. I have described some of the more intriguing applications in the paragraphs that follow:

- Large, high-powered communications satellites could be used to receive and route messages between large numbers of people wearing wrist radiophones about the size of digital wristwatches. The authors predict such "Dick Tracy" wristwatch radios could be mass-produced for $10. Bekey and Mayer point out that such radio telephones would be ideal for use by police patrolmen—with their messages scrambled for confidentiality. (The Citizens Band radio phenomenon is a haphazard precursor to the personal radio telephone. And in the late 1970s AT&T installed in Chicago a "cellular" system for car telephones that could be used for personal telephones, as well. The mobile phone sends out a low-power radio signal that is picked up by transceivers situated in the particular "cell" area of the city through which the phone user is traveling. The call is then transmitted into the regular phone system network.) A personal satellite navigation system could be built into the wrist radios giving someone who is lost position coordinates that correspond to coordinates (A-5, H-7) on local or regional road maps or street guides.

This system could be used in reverse: both policemen and private citizens could use a panic switch on the phones to call for help— the device would signal the coordinates of the person calling to the nearest police cruiser or police station. Getting a fix on your personal wristphone would *also* make it possible for a satellite to track you anywhere in the world. Governments could use this to keep track of political dissidents or wanted suspects. Private investigators might pay the service to monitor the whereabouts of someone in whom a client was interested.

• "Intrusion alarm" devices, sensitive to footsteps, could be placed around your house (or factory). These would relay the presence of a prowler, setting off an alarm in the building and at the police station. Similar devices—weighing one pound each and disguised as rocks—could be placed along a country's boundary lines to send signals to monitoring satellites, reporting "intrusion" by illegal immigrants coming across the border.

• Railway cars, and even packages en route in the mails could be pinpointed so that they could be efficiently routed—or found, and put back on the track, if they had been misdirected. Stolen goods— including weapons-grade nuclear fuel, for example—could be tracked down, if unobtrusive radio transmitters were incorporated in the goods at the time of manufacture.

• Using a wrist-radio–satellite-computer connection, millions of people could be polled by the government instantly in time of crisis. (This, of course, raises the bandwagon-effect dangers I have discussed concerning two-way cable television.) If identification instruments (voiceprint recognition, for example) could be built in to insure that the user is a qualified voter, the devices could be used as portable voting booths in an election. This would be bound to increase the voter "turnout."

• High-powered satellites could extend the "hot line" network now existing between the United States and the Soviet Union into a system connecting heads of states of all countries of the world. Terminals could be made easily portable so these officials could have the system available wherever they went.

Bekey and Mayer see the use of satellite telephony as a public service—and a money-maker for private operators: "With this type of service, the vast majority of our citizens would personally benefit from space in the course of their everyday lives. Billing would be automatic, in a fashion not unlike today's telephone operations. Revenue would be tremendous. Thus the industry could develop and operate the satellite system as a public utility." So, obviously, could a public corporation.

As I have indicated, the technologies described in the Bekey-Mayer study hold specific dangers for individuals as well as the benefits the authors describe.

On the large scale, the chief danger in the developing satellite picture lies in the assumption in the United States—the country that is by far the most advanced in operation of satellites—that the only justification for their use is economic. (In this context, I ignore the military justification, in which the public interest gets little consideration.) Certainly, it is a dangerous public policy that says no public services should be provided that do not return a profit. If we allow that to continue to be our guide, then some needed public services that could be provided by communications satellites will never see the light of day.

6 | PRIVACY: HOW SWEDEN PROTECTS ITS CITIZENS FROM THE COMPUTERS

Personal data banks fed by interactive communications networks are becoming the new back fences for gossip. The use of computers in the investigation of citizens' financial, medical, mental, and moral status is a major—and growth—industry. We have little control over what the computers are saying about us, and to whom they are saying it. Investigating reports are being transmitted from computer to computer across the United States by communications satellites.

The computerized dossiers are being produced mainly by credit-rating bureaus, which collect "hard" data such as the size of your bank balance and salary and how promptly you pay off purchases made on credit, and consumer-investigation firms that collect "soft" data, such as a neighbor's estimate of your moral fitness. Hard data is normally assembled for retail businesses to whom a customer has applied for credit. Soft data is usually collected for life-insurance or automobile-insurance companies that want information to help them evaluate you as an insurance risk, and by prospective employers who want to check into your background and probity. Computerized government files are a major source of this information.

Equifax, Inc., which describes itself as the largest "business information" firm in the private sector, gathers both hard and soft data on consumers through various of its 13 subsidiaries. These include The Credit Bureau Inc. of Georgia, which does credit ratings, and Equifax Services Inc., of Atlanta, which does consumer investigations. The system's 13,000 employees, working out of 1,800 offices in the United States and Canada, produce 25 million reports a year. Its files contain more than 50 million dossiers on individuals. It sells the information in these files to 62,000 customers, among them the agencies of the federal government. The company is grossing about a third of a billion dollars a year by selling personal information about you and your neighbors.

I visited the Equifax, Inc. headquarters on Peachtree Street in Atlanta (almost every business in Atlanta is on one or another of its Peachtree streets). The outside of the building looks like a white, twenty-first-century mausoleum. Inside, the dark wood paneling gives you a feeling of old-line respectability (after all, the managers tell you, "We've been around since 1899"). At the reception desk, a guard asked me to register my name, address, and place of business; the person I wished to see, and time in and out. He then issued me a pink plasticized security badge marked "V" for Visitor, and I was escorted by a pleasant, self-assured secretary to administrative offices at the end of a wide corridor. Although the thermostat had been set, in the Atlanta summer, at eighty degrees to save air-conditioning energy, every man I saw was wearing a conservative jacket and tie.

What I found, in talking to the public-relations director and the general counsel, was a great sensitivity to the issues of individual privacy and the accuracy of information in the files, and the rights of consumers to have those files corrected if they are wrong. In today's climate of concern, this may just be good business. I suspect part of the sensitivity arises from three things: the Fair Credit Reporting Act, which requires companies to divulge the "nature and substance" of the report on a person the company has investigated if that person properly identifies himself or herself at the door; lawsuits by consumers who feel they have been "burned" by false reports about them by the company; and the decision of a law judge of the Federal Trade Commission that the company had been violating the act in the way its field representatives collected material about consumers.

Robert Ellis Smith, editor of *The Privacy Journal* in New York, charges that Equifax is cavalier about the facts it provides through its investigations, some of which have involved "pretext interviews"— inquiries made under false pretenses.

From his own inquiry, he reports: " 'Investigation' is a misnomer, because Equifax does not at all conduct methodical inquiry into facts, using several persons with diverse investigating skills.

What it does typically is send a young man in his twenties, who will stay with the company five years or so, to talk to the individual involved and as many neighbors as possible in twenty minutes or less. He may make inquiries by telephone or, if pressed, draw conclusions based on a person's zip code, neighborhood, last name, or age." The consequences to you are pretty bad, Smith points out, if the Equifax man picks the wrong neighbor to ask about your character, habits, finances, medical condition, and driving abilities. He quotes this excerpt from a report on a Mississippi woman as typical of the "drivel" insurance underwriters use to help them make decisions:

> TRAITS: Mrs. _____ is regarded as an aggressive type person and in stable (*sic*) in her work. She is also known to be a "straightforward" person. She says what she feels like saying. Sources state that she is an odd sort of person.[1]

Not surprisingly, Hal Arnold, the Equifax public-relations director, had an entirely different view. Arnold told me he himself began with the company as a field investigator, and that most people join the concern at this entry-level position and work their way up. The average field representative, of whom there are 4200, he said, is thirty-five years old, has 2.3 children, two years of college in the liberal arts, and has been with the company ten years. They are skilled investigators, he said.

"As an investigator, I know when a neighbor of yours is telling the truth. When a neighbor bad-mouths you, says you drink too much, for example, I don't care how honest he is, I'm required to confirm it with another neighbor." He smiled. "We just want the facts, ma'am."

Some of the investigators are free-lancers, the company says: "Housewives, teachers, and retired persons who want a second career to supplement family income." They are paid piecework rates. The products of their labors are kept usually for thirteen months as are all such files. The noninvestigative credit reports—those that supply information on your bill-paying propensities, are compiled from information provided by the consumer, from credit grantors, and from government records such as those reporting bankruptcies. Arnold said that credit-rating reports are never co-mingled or cross-referenced with the investigative consumer reports. They could be— no law says you have to keep "hard" facts separate from "soft" data in personal files in the United States. But it is less costly for Equifax's separate companies to do separate reports, which usually have to be done fresh on each request for information, according to Arnold.

As for consumer access to records, it has been company policy since 1976, he said, to show consumers the files that are kept on them and permit them to enter corrections. Some 250,000 persons inquire about their files every year, the company reported. Actually, having consumers check their files acts as a quality control, Arnold said, by pointing out which field representatives are filing inaccurate information.

"If you complain about material in your file," Edward D. De Vaney, Jr., the company's general counsel, told me, "we could very well tear it up in front of you and throw it away, to end the argument. But we could then simply go ahead and get it again, for a later investigation."

Equifax's investigative consumer reports are not kept in a central file, but in district offices nearest the consumer. Credit reporting files, however, are centralized in the computer in Atlanta for instant access to company offices anywhere in the United States and Canada.

"That's the reason for the security measures here." Arnold said. "We have information worth millions of dollars to us in that computer, and somebody could try to sabotage the computer."

Suppose I came in and wanted information from the computer about a friend of mine, I asked him, would the company sell it to me? No, he told me, the company will sell its reports only to businessmen with a permissible purpose for information. (That, incidentally, is what the law requires.)

"For instance," Arnold remarked, "I couldn't have access to your file and say, 'I want to find out about him because he is coming down here for an interview. . . .' Oh, I *could*—I have enough friends in the company to let me do that, but heck, I *wouldn't*."

I think that sums up one problem about computers and privacy—the machines are secure only until some human being chooses to violate their security. In the case of a consumer-rating agency, it would be reasonably easy for your neighbor to print up a letterhead as a prospective employer, and send along the $15 or so charged for a report on you as a "job applicant" or "credit applicant." As two-way systems spread, your neighbors may be able to get the gossip they want *directly*, by accessing the information provided by the investigating company through their home communications sets. They may be able to, that is, unless some legal safeguards are built into the consumer-investigations field *and* the electronic transferral of information from personal data banks.

The personal information–gathering process is being speeded up by the new communications. In an annual report, an executive of Equifax said: "We are moving rapidly to expand our uses of telecommunications. We are looking at a communications network that can move data rapidly and that will also enable us to place the services we now render to insurance companies and other customers in electronic form."

That means that every private investigation will be in the Equifax computers for immediate electronic access to any Equifax customer anywhere in the world.

Already, electronic communication has become the established way of life inside the personal-data field. A national trade association linking the major credit-rating companies has made it possible for them to query each other's computers and exchange information. Stores and restaurants they serve have interactive computer terminals so that they may check credit ratings of new customers electronically and continually update credit information on customers with whom they have continuing dealings. Each supplies information back to the consumer-credit service that provides the ratings on its customers.

Obviously, these ratings and investigating agencies could get additional information on customers with the help of a two-way cable operator who is willing to supply information that has been revealed, sometimes inadvertently, by the cable subscriber "interacting" with the two-way system. That information, augmented by the data already in the consumer investigating company's computer, could then be retransmitted over the cable or videotex system to businesses and individuals who pay the advertised fee.

Some private citizens I have talked with about this possibility have said, "I don't care what the system knows about me—I have nothing to hide." Perhaps not. But Professor Arthur R. Miller of Harvard had an interesting comment about that:

"There is the view (presumably advanced by those who fancy themselves as emotional Spartans) that informational privacy is an unnecessary ingredient in the life of an honest, clean-living, and God-fearing citizen. Adherents of this position typically believe that those who oppose increased wiretapping by law-enforcement agencies, the proliferation of data banks, stop-and-frisk legislation, and widespread use of lie-detector tests are trying to hide something or are simply the product of a guilt-ridden society. This incredibly insensitive attitude completely overlooks man's need for individuality and ignores the variousness of the human condition. It is a typical reaction, however, among those who believe that many of our civil liberties are outmoded in a scientifically based society that needs complete access to data for decision-making purposes."[2]

One man, after I had presented the issue at the Cambridge Forum in Massachusetts, said to me, "I think we should just get used to the idea that everybody will know everything about us." And then he added, "The only thing I don't want people to know is my private thoughts."

But that is precisely what people can now begin to know as computers analyze all the actions and opinions you put into the system, correlate them with all the "factual" information it knows about you from other sources, and intuits your motives from the synthesis. Surely this is a violation of your inner space that is just as great as if a stranger came up to you on the street and asked if you have ever beaten your spouse.

"We want to know and be known by those whom we choose to share our intimacy," wrote John Curtis Raines in his book *Attack on Privacy*. "But in order that we may choose, we must defend ourselves against forced disclosure. The zone of personal privacy preserves this possibility of intimate community. Its trespass, if sustained, exposes and withers the experience of intimacy and leaves us more public and surface persons."[3]

Professor Edward Bloustein, writing in the *NYU Law Review*, takes this idea a step further: "The man who is compelled to live every minute of his life among others and whose every need, thought, desire, fancy or gratification is subject to public scrutiny, has been deprived of his individuality and human dignity. Such an individual merges with the mass. His opinions, being public, tend never to be different; his aspirations, being known, tend always to be conventionally accepted ones; his feelings, being openly exhibited, tend to lose their quality of unique personal warmth and to become the feelings of every man. Such a being, although sentient, is not an individual."[4]

Quite apart from these philosophical concerns, information transferred from computer to computer can cause specific harm. Material may be innocuous in one context but harmful if it is used in another. The fact that you had tuberculosis, from which you were completely cured as a child, might be important to a physician evaluating your medical history. But that information, accessed and transmitted to a prospective employer, might be the fact that tilts the decision against her hiring you.

People in general do appear to have a growing awareness of the intrusiveness of information-storing and -transferring devices in their private lives. In a poll conducted in 1979 by Louis Harris and Associates Inc., nearly two-thirds of the citizens queried responded that they were concerned about threats to personal privacy in America. The growing realization that computers contribute to this threat was shown by a seventeen-point increase in this perception between 1976 and 1979. By 1979, 54 percent of those questioned said present uses of computers were a threat. Eighty percent said computers made it easier for someone to obtain confidential personal information about them improperly. As a result, 63 percent said they agreed with the statement: "If privacy is to be preserved, the use of computers must be sharply restricted in the future." Interestingly, when asked if they agreed that "Most people who complain about their privacy are engaged in immoral or illegal conduct," those surveyed rejected such an idea, 64 percent to 27.

In announcing the poll's results, Louis Harris commented: "If one wants ample evidence that in this country we do not live by bread alone, then this burning privacy issue is a prime example. The concept of human dignity, the right to be your own person, to have a broad range of personal activities, to be immune from being slotted in some mindless way into a computerized data bank and then to have your personal history available for that moment when you are brought under question is both obnoxious and critically wrong to the vast majority of Americans. Make no mistake about it, close to the essence of quality of human experience these days is to have that precious right to be a private person without harassment or worse from Big Brother in any form."[5]

The privacy poll showed that the public has a deep sense of vulnerability, according to Dr. Alan F. Westin, professor of law and government at Columbia University and an authority on privacy, who isolated the issues to be surveyed. "Basically," he said, "they [the public] feel too weak and powerless in the relationship with information collectors. They feel they are losing control over the way the vital personal details of their life history are circulated from organization to organization."[6]

The chief concern relates to the transfer of false information or gossip, by whatever means. It would be disastrous, for instance, if you went for a job and the prospective employer, relying on false information provided him by an investigating company, said to you, "I hear that you have a drinking problem." How do you counter that? Tell him, "Well, yes, I do drink a little, socially, but *I am not a drunkard*"? A computer network is an excellent medium for transmission of such information.

As people in the developed Western democracies have come to recognize the dangers, they have been increasing their demands for protection from computers. They have asked that brakes be placed on the amount of information collected about them by government and industry; that regulations be adopted to insure the accuracy of the information collected; and that restrictions be placed on the handling of the information and its transfer to third parties.

But in the United States and most other countries the laws have lagged behind the technology—to the disadvantage of the individual citizen. One country that has tried to get ahead of the technology is Sweden. Acting in the early 1970s, it became the first nation to take comprehensive legislative action to protect its citizens from intrusion by computer.

THE SWEDISH DATA INSPECTION BOARD

Like most citizens of Sweden, Stig Bjerström filed his income tax return in February and sat back to wait for the Taxation Board to send him a check for the 1000 kronor owed him on his return. December came, and with it, two computerized notices from the Taxation Board. One said he would get back 800 kronor. The other said he owed the government 8000 kronor and if he didn't pay up, the government would collect by attaching his salary. Bjerström wrote the income-tax people that there had been a mistake. The tax computer replied with a notice to his employer to begin deducting what he "owed" from his salary.

Bjerström got as mad as anyone who finds he can't make an impression on a computer that is toying with his life. But instead of carrying on a futile fight with the machine, he took another action, available to citizens in Sweden since 1973: he appealed to the Data Inspection Board. This agency, which regulates every computer data bank in the country that collects personal records, got right on his case. It notified the Taxation Board that, on investigation, it had found that Bjerström's tax records were in error, and asked the board to correct them. The tax computer promptly informed the Data Inspection Board that its records now indicated that Bjerström was dead. Its verdict was given credibility when Bjerström's wife began getting junk mail expressing sympathy for her recent widowhood, one direct mailer offering her a special price on a hot-water bottle to keep her warm on cold winter nights.

Jan Freese, director general of the Data Inspection Board, thought it was time for human intervention in the mechanical routines of the income tax computer. "We called up the people at the Taxation Board and told them we could show this man in flesh and blood, and we told them to correct the information in the computer." The tax people complied, and Bjerström, whose name I've changed to protect his privacy, got back the 1000 kronor that was owed him.

The Data Inspection Board has the power to do that—direct the keeper of a computerized file to correct or drop false information it contains on individuals. The power covers not only government agencies such as the Taxation Board but also private concerns such as consumer and credit investigation services. "We can go into police headquarters and check the records to see that they are being handled properly," Freese told me. "Even Intelligence Service files are no exception. Why should they be—these are the most important files, aren't they?"

Freese (pronounced Fray'seh), a former judge of the Swedish Court of Appeal, is a friendly, low-keyed man of forty-odd who gives the impression of being a quiet bulldozer. He has been given a lifetime appointment, under the Swedish Data Act, to protect his board from political influences. I interviewed him in an unprepossessing building in a pleasant, older part of Stockholm that houses a number of government offices.

In Sweden, as elsewhere, Freese said, concern over personal records and privacy has been building since the 1960s, when advances in computer technology made it easy to collect extensive dossiers on everyone and computer networks made it possible to cross-reference them with other dossiers held anywhere in the country. And now, with satellites, it is possible to exchange such information with computer data banks around the world. Freese thinks these developments increase the threat to individual liberty. In 1972 Sweden became the first country to pass national laws against the threat from computers in both the public *and* private sectors. Since then, other Western European countries have adopted similar protections. Rules on the handling of data by private companies were included in a package of privacy-protection bills the Carter administration submitted to Congress in 1979. In Sweden, as in the United States, the main worry expressed about personal data banks was that machine-processed dossiers, which have regularly been shown to contain serious errors, were being used to determine actions harmful to individuals: decisions not to hire a person, refusals to issue life insurance, refusals to grant a loan, and so on.

Thousands of such decisions are made daily, based on reports from the computerized files of large commercial concerns that "investigate" consumers for other commercial concerns—and for the government.

Swedish citizens became increasingly aware that private investigating companies were using personal information about them in the interest of profits, and that they were getting the help of government agencies in doing so. Government commissions had surveyed automatic data processing in the public sector. But the major part of computer processing of personal information is in the private sector. And private companies found they could use one of the constitutional laws—the Freedom of the Press Act—to gather information about Swedish citizens. This act, promulgated in 1766, guarantees the public free access to all documents produced by public officials or received by them. (Exceptions are specified to protect secrecy, for example, in some documents dealing with national security and crime.) Under this act, a wire-service reporter can walk into the prime minister's office and ask to see and publish the correspondence that had arrived on his desk that morning. Any citizen—or company—has the same right to enter a government office and make use of the information found there. Companies began obtaining personal data, such as annual salary and amount of taxes paid, from the government's income-tax files (which, following the access principle, are also open books) for use in consumer credit evaluations and the like. They used the government's magnetic tapes to transfer this information directly into their own computers' memories. Citizens complained that information they were required to submit to government agencies was being disseminated for other purposes to private data banks to which they had no effective access. This concern came on top of the general unease among people in the developed countries that too much information was being assembled in computer files by government and private agencies.

The government's response—a typical and often effective one in Sweden—was to establish a commission to study the problem of privacy as it related to computers, as well as the Freedom of the Press Act, and propose legislation to protect its citizens. Its two years of public deliberations brought into focus a need to strike a balance between conflicting interests: the right of the individual to be left in peace, versus the demands for effective use of computer technology in recording, storing, and retrieving information. From its review, the commission came up with a significant conclusion: augmenting the secrecy rules to prevent personal information from getting into private data banks would eviscerate the principle of free access; therefore the remedy is a data act that protects citizens by regulating the way every computerized file in the country collects and transfers personal information.

Parliament agreed. In 1972 it enacted laws to permit citizens to get at their records even when these were in the form of electronic bits stored in a computer. It gave them the right to see printouts of files kept in any data bank and make corrections in these files if they were in error. And it set up a Data Inspection Board with powers to license private data banks, set conditions for operation of government data banks, and enforce the provisions of the Data Act.

In its first six years of existence, the Data Board licensed 35,000 "responsible keepers" to operate personal data banks whose subject area is the 8,200,000 people who live in Sweden. In granting permission to maintain computerized files on people, the board is required to determine that there is no reason to assume that undue encroachment on the privacy of individuals registered will arise. It is directed to consider the nature and quantity of the information in the data bank, the purpose for which it is being collected, as well as the *attitude* that those who are registered can be expected to adopt toward the data bank.

The public's attitude has become an important consideration in the board's decisions. Soon after it began operating, social scientists in Stockholm sought to ask Turkish immigrants about their sexual mores, to gain an understanding about how best to persuade them to accept *Swedish* sexual mores. The Data Inspection Board refused permission to use the Turkish addresses from a public data bank for this purpose. Since the Turkish community had not been asked about the project, the board reasoned the Turkish immigrants would be likely to resist it. This made the social scientists unhappy, but the board stuck by its finding: This would be an improper use of a data bank.

"As a member of a community, one must be prepared to accept a certain amount of intrusion," Freese remarked. "The protection of personal privacy is therefore restricted to what can be considered improper."

Under the act, it is considered improper to keep a private bank containing information that anyone has been convicted of a crime, about a person's illness or mental health, or about his or her political or religious views.

Freese thinks it's best to take an informal approach to what is proper and what is not, in the operation of a data bank. "If a file-keeper comes to us and wants to set up a file and we think it's bad," he said, "we try to devise a constructive alternative. Usually, we work it out."

But sometimes it doesn't work out. A credit card company wanted to keep deep individual statistics about the use of its cards in restaurants: "How often you went, how many guests you had, what you ate," according to Freese. "We said, 'You may do that, but only if you get permission from every one of your cardholders to use these statistics.'

"Well, that one made the papers. The credit card company manager was critical—he told the press that the Data Board is too bureaucratic. But we *will* force responsible keepers to talk to their clients."

The board thinks that even junk mailers should keep a "client" ("occupant") informed: because of Sweden's open-documents principle, it can't prevent direct-mail firms from going to state agencies to get names and addresses, but it requires them to print the source of its list on each mailing.

In granting a license to a Swedish firm, the Data Board has the right to issue specific regulations concerning the handling of personal information in its bank. For particularly sensitive files, it can direct the responsible keeper to send file disclosures to recorded persons each time the file is updated or transfered to a third party.

Every citizen has the right, once a year, to inspect any computer file that is kept on her or him and to have a written printout of that information. If the person recorded finds an error in the file, the file-keeper is required to check the accuracy of the questioned item and, if necessary, correct it or exclude it from the data bank. The correction must be sent to anyone to whom the information had been transmitted previously.

If the record-keeper refuses to correct the file, a citizen may appeal to the Data Inspection Board. The board, if it judges the file to be in error, doesn't need a court to enforce an order to make a change—it has the power to revoke a data bank's license.

A record-keeper—or a private citizen—can appeal the ruling of the Data Board to the Ministry of Justice, and ultimately, to the courts. This has seldom happened, because the board is determined to work out disputes by negotiation. "We haven't had the situation where anyone has refused an order to expunge," Freese said.

He said complaints to the board were increasing, because citizens are more aware of their rights. By 1980 the board was getting more than a thousand a year. Most of them are solved by a phone call or a letter to the record-keeper, Freese said. About three hundred go through a more detailed investigation process. In one such investigation, the board was asked to find out why one man was having trouble with his personal references, although his background appeared to be without major blemishes. The board found out why: a second man, arrested by the police, had "proved" his identity by presenting a document belonging to the first. The arrested man, who was later referred to a psychiatric ward, was recorded in several sensitive consumer investigation files under the name of the man who was "clean." Through its enforcement powers the Data Board was able to get each file corrected, along with other files to which the false information had been transmitted.

The right of a citizen to see the information in his files has led to improvement in the reliability of this information, Freese believes. Open files make successful prosecution of damage suits arising from misinformation more likely. The penalty of a fine or a year in prison for violating the provisions of the act is also thought to have improved the quality of record-keepers' dealings with their subjects. Prosecutions have been few because record-keepers are maintaining their files with the Data Board in mind, the review commission found.

"The Swedish public likes the Data Inspectorate," said Kersten Anér, an influential M.P. and head of Sweden's Commission on the Future. Anér a big, feisty woman who is known for her strong opinions on individual freedom, pointed out that the Data Inspection Board was set up under the Social Democrats, but the Liberal Party, of which she is a member, strongly supports its protection of privacy. "Americans don't understand how we can give so much power to an agency," she said. "But to us, it is still quite natural to trust government." Besides, she said, "Everything has to be licensed in Sweden, even the shooting of elks."

To ensure this kind of trust, the eleven-member board, with Freese as chairman, contains representatives from each of the major parties, labor unions, industry, and the public sector. The Data Board, said Anér, has only one enemy—the social scientists. "They would like to be free from inspection entirely," she said. Social scientists in the universities are afraid that the board will censor their research, and they cite the refusal for the use of public files to check on Turkish immigrants as a case in point. It is a delicate issue.

In such research, one social scientist pointed out, you often have need to follow information concerning specific persons over a period of years. "The Data Act blocks that," he said, "by a rule saying you can't identify people by name." It has been suggested that researchers could use statistical methods that do not identify subjects by name, but this specific issue has not been resolved.

When the Data Act was set up, Parliament was thinking about excesses of corporations in their handling of data, not of data kept in university computers. So Freese and the Data Board seem to have adopted the "middle way" with regard to social-science research: Beyond suggesting to researchers how their files could be kept without intruding on individual privacy, they have pretty much let universities go their own way. "The board only wants to make them live up to standards for record-keeping set down in the law," said Anér.

Freese commented that he thought some social scientists were seeing "unexisting ghosts." Board practices concerning research have been accepted by the review commission and Parliament. "We look on science as a part of society, not something beside the rest of society," he said. "But this does not mean that we are piloting the direction or contents of research."

Polls have shown that people in Sweden have fears about the combining of personal files into one big data bank or the linking of files so that information stored anywhere could be cross-referenced for the use of a government agency or a keeper of a private file. Parliament, in adopting the Data Act, said such links should be discouraged. In the words of a committee that studied the problem: "Today there are no technical obstacles that prevent computer storage of all conceivable types of information about a person. Even if each item of information may be considered harmless in isolation, the totality of accumulated information may still constitute a serious threat to privacy. As a result, each individual can legitimately demand that no authority and no other individual shall be given complete information about him."

But government welfare agencies in Sweden have been pressing to cross-reference files to compare the income individuals declared for tax purposes to those they declared in order to be eligible for welfare benefits. I asked Freese: "Suppose the linking of two files could be shown to have a socially useful purpose—such as catching welfare cheaters—would you be for that?"

"Over my dead body," he said. "The road to 1984 is paved with good intentions. Besides that, you can't compare apples and pears— two data banks could have different rules for collection, and that can affect the quality of information."

A commission appointed in 1976 to review the workings of the Data Act reached the same conclusion. In 1978 it proposed, and Parliament approved, an amendment that said data that had been gathered by a public agency for one reason may not be used by another agency in a different context, unless the citizens have been told this in the first place.

Linkage, or cross-referencing, of personal files can be done most easily when an individual is registered in each file under a standard universal identifier. In theory, this is a number that is assigned to a person at birth and is used to record any of his activities requiring positive identification. All Swedish citizens have had personal identity numbers since 1947. The number is composed as follows:

Birth Date	Place of Birth	Number Sequence*	Technical Control Digit
33 10 28	04	9	2

When the identifier was introduced in the 1940s it was accepted without much public discussion. But now that it is being used in electronic data processing, many people are beginning to feel that it should be abandoned. Critics of the universal identifier have said that it could serve as the skeleton for a national dossier system to maintain information on citizens from the cradle to the grave, and make it easier to monitor and control behavior through records maintained on them by a wide number of institutions. Public concerns over the im-

* Your position in the order of births, by sex, in that place that day. Even numbers indicate females, odd numbers indicate males.

plications of a universal identifier have also been expressed in France, West Germany, the United Kingdom, and the United States. In Britain, the Committee on Data Protection, headed by Sir Norman Lindop, said that, because it would facilitate linkage, such an identifier poses dangers for data protection.[7] The committee urged that a personal identification number should not be allowed to evolve informally. If it is ever to be contemplated, it said, Parliament should pass special legislation to set it up in a way that would restrict its use. In the United States, the report of the Privacy Protection Study Commission urged against the evolution of the Social Security number into a universal identifier—a trend that has been furthered by states' use of the number on drivers' license identification cards.[8] If this number were to become a standard identifier, the commission pointed out, it could supplant credit card numbers, driver's license numbers, personal charge-account numbers, and all other identifiers. One correspondent of the privacy commission asked it to "prevent us from becoming our Social Security numbers." The report said "this concern seems to reflect a feeling that to label a person by a number, rather than by a name, is dehumanizing." However, after looking into the second concern—that linkge would be facilitated by such a number—the commission concluded that the Social Security number was a surrogate for the problem of linkage. Although the number is often used for record exchanges, it said, it is only one of the possible ways that computerized records are being linked, exchanged, and consolidated. Studies indicate that record-matching techniques using a combination of such identifiers as name, address, birth date, and sex are technically adequate in performing the linkages. Because the use of such identifiers leads to fewer errors, many government agencies now no longer use the Social Security number in cross-referencing computer data. Therefore, the commission said it failed to see how drastically restricting the use of this number would make much difference in inhibiting the linking of computers. Computers can go about the process of putting together the records of an individual from two different files quite easily without it.

Jan Freese said the same conclusion had been reached by the Data Inspection Board concerning the Swedish national identification number. "It is a psychological question more than a technical one," he said. "People should not be thought of as numbers." A new law will place restrictions on the universal use of the number with all record-keeping systems, he said, but the problem of linkage and "One Big Data Bank" will have to be attacked on other grounds.

The idea of combining separate dossiers in hundreds or thousands of files into one central population file has been opposed by almost everyone but the entrepreneurs of personal information whose profits would be enhanced if access to such a file, whether kept by government or the personal information industry, were available. Since in Sweden these companies have ready access to any government file, the Swedish government has acted to restrict the country's central file-keeping to nuts-and-bolts information such as name, address, and identity number under the control of a specific government data bank. Such limits, it hopes, will prohibit the accumulation in a national file of all manner of "soft" data about citizens that could then be transmitted to another big file, in Sweden or elsewhere. The U.S. Privacy Protection Study Commission opposed even this use of a national identifier:

"Any consideration of a standard universal label and of a record system approximating a central population register, should be postponed until society, through its legislatures, has made significant progress in establishing policies to regulate the use and disclosure of information about individuals collected by both the private organizations and government agencies, and until such policies are shown to be effective."

A report published by the Swedish Defense Department has expressed the fear that a potential aggressive enemy could be able to get hold of a comprehensive national population register and use it to pick out leaders or administrators for elimination, or to select a minority for extinction.[9] The Swedes point out that during World War II the Nazis used government records in various localities to help them seek out Jews in the populations of conquered countries. Their task would have been made much easier if there had been central population files. SARK, the Swedish government committee that produced the report, said the vulnerability to external or internal sabotage to *all* computer data banks and networks in the country was unacceptably high.

"Future development," it said, "will lead to an increasing vulnerability unless countermeasures are taken." One measure, it suggested, should be "to limit continued concentration and integration, and, instead, to try out solutions involving dispersion of data processing."

Even with the restrictions imposed by the Data Board, the government estimates that a couple of thousand registers of personal information are transmitted via telecommunications networks and satellites to computers located in other countries. The potential capability of a hostile government or multinational corporation of tapping directly into computers in Sweden linked to this network has not been overlooked. SARK pointed out that chaos could result from the sabotage of data banks in Sweden, either physically to the machines or electronically from someone tapping into the system. As one example to illustrate the concern, it pictured the consternation that would be caused by the scrambling of debits and credits in an electronic funds transfer system.

The Swedish Data Board has also been concerned about *legitimate* transfer of information on Swedish citizens to data banks in other countries. Sweden and the other Scandinavian governments, which now have similar privacy laws, have agreed to permit the movement of data only to countries whose regulations are compatible with their own. Although it has no control over the ways companies abroad handle personnel data, Sweden can prohibit its own concerns from sending out the information on magnetic tapes. The Data Act requires each such transfer to get the permission of the board and in several cases it has refused.

Through its licensing powers, the Data Board exercises some indirect control over the SWIFT* data network, which uses satellites to provide electronic funds transfer among banks around the world. The board obviously can't go to Brussels, headquarters of the SWIFT system, and dictate precautions it should impose on its international transfer of information. But it can look into terminals of the system in Swedish banks, and if it finds malpractices in the system it can block these banks from using the network. So it is in the interests of Swedish bankers to influence managers of the network to provide safeguards to protect the confidentiality of information being exchanged.

An official of Xerox concerned with international affairs told me Sweden had blocked his company from carrying out data transmission it considered essential. Top management of Xerox and chief executive officers of other multinational corporations, he said, feel they have a legitimate concern that they will not be able to transfer information necessary to the effective operation of their businesses in Sweden and other countries that have followed its lead. They are afraid it would be costly to change their information-processing sys-

* Society for Worldwide International Funds Transfer.

tems to comply with data-protection laws. These systems were not planned with people in mind—they just grew, as electronic "improvements" on older forms of record-keeping and information transfer. Once corporate managers give sufficient attention to the problem, it may prove that the changes necessary to protect personal data could be incorporated by fairly inexpensive rearrangement of methods. At industry meetings on the question, however, many American executives have damned the system instead of seeking a solution. They have charged that Sweden is hiding behind the privacy laws to restrict foreign competition with its information-gathering industry. But Swedish officials have a low opinion of the cavalier way American companies are allowed to handle personal dossiers and are not eager to have their citizens treated the same way. Obviously, international agreements are needed on the handling of personal data transmitted across national boundaries.

This is recognized by the State Department, which conducted a study of the problem in 1977. Rather than promote protection of privacy, however, its report focused on guaranteeing flow of information across international borders. This ideal, while accepted in principle by most nations, conflicts with ideas in Western European society that are oriented more toward guaranteeing individual privacy. It is a complicated question that can only be resolved through long and difficult international negotiations. The Council of Europe has conducted discussions toward reconciling the various European regulations by treaty. This could be extended to the United States and Canada through the Organization for Economic Cooperation and Development, of which both are members.

The government of Canada, however, has shown no great urgency about regulating data banks. Throughout the 1970s various government agencies, including the Department of Communication and the Department of Justice, made studies of privacy protection. A joint report by these departments suggested that "some type of surveillance agency combined with an ombudsman to handle specific complaints by individuals" might be useful.[10] No legislative action followed on that report, however.

One of the concerns of Europeans working in the field is that some fly-by-night regime might decide that it is to its financial and political advantage to ignore responsible regulations for the handling of personal data and offer multinational corporations "data havens" for ill-gotten information. This could be done in the same way that Liberia and Panama offer private shipping concerns "flags of convenience," permitting them to operate their ships without conforming to generally accepted safety regulations. Private computers in these "data havens" would be allowed to store "sensitive" personal data, based perhaps on wiretaps or other illegal surveillance, as well as hearsay "evidence" against private citizens, government officials, or executives of other companies. When needed, this information could then be accessed, across national borders—or oceans, for that matter—by companies tied in with the worldwide satellite-computer networks. And it would be hard for responsible countries to track such information as it moves through the system.

Nevertheless, Freese told me, Sweden is determined to try to protect its citizens from such abuses by restricting transfers only to those countries that provide similar protections for their own citizens. The United States does not do that: to the degree that it does not, it is thought of in Western Europe as a data haven.

The Swedish experience with data protection had a strong influence on the other Western European countries. By 1980 Denmark, Norway, Finland, and Austria had set up data boards. In West Germany, the states established data-protection agencies and the federal government appointed a "data ombudsman." Any firm that employed more than five persons in computer operations was required to hire a data-protection specialist, responsible to the government. A study commission in Britain proposed setting up a "Data Protection Authority," and a state committee in the Netherlands proposed a "Registration Board."

France placed privacy protection under an independent agency, the Commission Nationale de l'Informatique et des Libertés. This body was established as a result of a media campaign, led by the Paris newspaper *Le Monde* in 1974, to prevent the establishment of Safari, a system that would have used a universal identifier to tie all data banks of government departments together. Creating one big data bank in this way, *Le Monde* declared, could be the end of liberty. A temporary commission appointed to study the problem—and privacy in general—recommended a data-protection law and the establishment of a permanent commission to administer it. This group set up shop in an old, reconverted mansion on the Left Bank, whose high-walled courtyard once protected the privacy of a wealthy mer chant. Mme. Marie Georges, a tall woman in her thirties with a no-nonsense approach to defending the public's privacy, was put in charge of its staff.

"We are faced with a new problem about which we don't know exactly the limits," she told me. "The law says we are to be concerned with information *and* liberty. French law does not take the problem solely in the way of individual liberty. The way computers are used is also a menace to collective liberty." So, she said, the commission will try to learn "what's going on in our society because of computers," in order to propose legislation that will further protect the individual's privacy and the public's freedom. Access to such information is assured: no computer processing of personal data, public or private, may be established without the prior review of the commission.

As a first principle, the act concerning computers and liberty sets down that "No legal, administrative, or private decisions implying a judgment on a person's conduct may be solely based on computer processing of data to determine his aptitudes or personality." In most of its provisions, the French act follows the Swedish precedent. The commission's powers of enforcement, however, are less definite than those of the Data Inspection Board. If a data-holder refused to comply with a decision that a person's file must be corrected, the citizen or the commission must appeal to the courts for enforcement. Like Freese in Sweden, Georges believes the commission should act informally to try to settle such problems without going to the courts.

DEMAND FOR PROTECTION RISES IN THE UNITED STATES

Even with the toughest computer law in the world, the people of Sweden voted the threat to privacy a leading "public enemy" in an opinion poll conducted in 1977. In the United States, the privacy study conducted by Louis Harris and Associates showed that 76 percent of Americans believe the right of privacy must now be added to the list of fundamental rights for a just society. In the 1970s public expression of this concern has led Congress, and then the executive, to pay more attention to the problem.

The debate began in earnest about 1965, when the Bureau of the Budget proposed a "Federal Data Center" with a computerized system that would "end duplications" in agency record-keeping. Negative reaction in Congress, which reflected expressions of dismay from constituents, was so strong that the idea was dropped. In 1974 the General Services Administration proposed a similar data bank, to be called "Fednet." President Ford vetoed it. Rising concern about such proposals led directly to the passage of the Privacy Act of 1974 to regulate collection and storage of personal information by federal agencies. At the time, it was estimated that the federal government held 4 billion records on individuals, most of them stored in the government's eight thousand computers.

Under the act, personal information kept in one agency's files may be released to other agencies only with the individual's consent, as a result of a court order, for "routine use" compatible with the purpose for which the information was collected and in "compelling circumstances affecting the health and safety of an individual."

The law did not cover linkage of personal information banks in the private sector (an oversight that is glaringly apparent from the fact that the largest credit-rating banks in the country are linked together by their trade-association agreement).

The act did establish the Privacy Protection Study Commission, to look into protections needed in the private sector, as well as the public. The Privacy Commission, in its 1977 report, said that an effective policy should include "minimum intrusiveness" of the record-keepers, "maximum fairness," and the necessity to "create legitimate expectations of confidentiality."

Under "minimum intrusiveness," it recommended that individuals should be told what kind of information is being collected about them, how it will be used, and to whom it would be disclosed. Under "maximum fairness," it urged that a citizen has the right to correct a record and that the record-keeping organization be required to forward the correction to any past recipients of inaccurate information. Under "legitimate expectations of confidentiality," it urged that a record-keeper maintaining a confidential record relating to financial status, medical care, and insurance be placed under an obligation not to disclose the record without the consent of the individual, except in certain limited circumstances such as a medical emergency.

The Carter administration, reviewing the commission's work with a view to drafting privacy legislation, agreed with its recommendations in general, but rejected the idea of including teeth in the bill to make them directly enforceable. The commission, for example, had proposed that a "Federal Privacy Board" be established which, although it would not be granted the direct licensing and enforcement authority given the Swedish Data Board, would monitor compliance with the privacy legislation. President Carter decided there should be no independent entity within the government to monitor provisions of the act or issue regulations governing the operation of federal or private data banks. When I asked Harry Schwartz, the White House staff man following the privacy legislation, why a supervisory board had not been proposed, he said, "The President made a conscious decision not to create a new federal agency—these rights are self-enforcing, through the courts."

Whether an ordinary citizen harmed by incorrect data could get prompt and adequate redress through court action, much less afford the costs of going to court, seems debatable.

Carter's "conscious decision" ran counter to public opinion as expressed in the Harris poll. Sixty-two percent of those questioned said they thought it was "very important" that there should be an independent agency to handle complaints about violations of personal privacy by an organization. Nineteen percent more said that it was "somewhat important."

The management of Equifax Inc. did not think it was important at all. "We do not feel that a separate privacy board is needed," its general counsel told me, "because we feel that the Fair Credit Reporting Act is working very well. We are getting more government than we are paying for, now." He said he thought the president had taken a "very intelligent and balanced approach" to privacy.

The main bill proposed by the administration—the Fair Financial Information Practices Act—would give consumers the right to see and copy credit and investigative reports about them. Under the 1970 Fair Credit Reporting Act, they received only the right to learn the "nature and substance" of these records. A White House fact sheet on the bill said it "improves the consumer's ability to correct disputed credit and investigative consumer reports." One way it would do this, according to James Howard of the National Telecommunications Administration, who drafted the legislation, is to require the credit *grantor* to show the consumer the original of the report sent to it by the credit-rating bureau.

The theory, Schwartz told me later, was to insure that the consumer "has the right to examine the same records on which, say, a department store has made its decision not to grant him credit." However, he acknowledged, "We have not provided any means to get the record-keeper to change the record."

The Carter bill also ignored a Privacy Commission proposal that a company dealing in sensitive personal areas such as insurance and employment be required to send the applicant a copy of any investigative report it has made. "I suspect that would create a substantial financial burden for the companies," Schwartz remarked. "That would create a lot of paper."

Other parts of the package relating to personal privacy included provisions that:

• Forbid researchers to release information for nonresearch purposes.

• Allow persons to participate in decisions to disclose their medical records (which they may see) when the records will be used to affect them.

• Prohibit "pretext" interviews (interviews conducted under false pretenses) to gain information about consumers.

Its critics said the Carter package granted too many exceptions to the protections offered, favoring federal agencies' and private companies' convenience at the expense of the individual's privacy. Drafters of the legislation said they felt it was the strongest measure they could get.

Neither the Privacy Commission nor the White House staff appeared to have inquired into the practical experience of the Swedish Data Board in dealing with computers and privacy. Sweden, having formally reviewed this experience, has moved on to the development of rules relating to all problems of privacy and personal integrity, not only those arising from the use of computers. Jan Freese, in a national report on the Data Act, said that a general "Integrity Act" could be expected in Sweden in the long run. Such an act, the committee to review the data legislation suggested, would include fundamental ethical rules for the use of all personal data. Among these would be the obligations to improve the quality of "soft data" that consumer investigation agencies include in their files—judgments by one human being about another—concerning a person's family condition, behavior, social adjustment, psychic state, job performance, and the like.

"We have to be strict to see that opinions expressed in files are based on fact," Freese said, "because information is spread like ripples on the water."

Kersten Anér has suggested, for example, that "soft data" might not be entered into a file without provision for alternative judgments from other sources, or "equal time" being accorded to the subject herself.

"These laws would not be easy to write, but it is difficult to prove that they would not be necessary," she said. "Information is practically always used by the powerful against the less powerful, and misuse must always in principle be suspected and guarded against."

FREE FLOW OF INFORMATION VS. RESTRICTIONS

The Swedes have a penchant for reasonableness that seems to build in a guarantee that a powerful entity such as the Data Board will act with justice in the interests of protecting the people. The approach seems better than the essentially laissez-faire attitude toward data protection exhibited among businessmen and government officials in the United States. When Harris asked whether interviewees agreed with the statement: "If privacy is to be preserved, the use of computers must be sharply restricted in the future," only 31 percent of business employers, 36 percent of government officials, and 15 percent of executives in private investigations industries said they agreed. In contrast, 63 percent of the general public said they agreed.

In the United States, persons who oppose setting up a government agency to intervene in the protection of citizens' privacy do so out of fear that such an agency itself might become the vehicle for restricting individual freedom. Placing power to control data flow in the hands of a government agency involves dangers that might become more apparent in countries different from the social democratic state of Sweden. To Western observers, a board set up in a "socialist" country of the Eastern bloc to control how personal data was handled would be immediately suspect. Such a board established by a military dictatorship in Latin America or a police state in Africa or parts of Asia would be a major cause for alarm. Linking of computerized personal-data files via a unified communications system would give officials of authoritarian governments a weapon of considerable power in controlling the country's citizens.

In the democracies of Western Europe, it is an open debate whether control of computer networks, which use microwave, land-line, and satellite facilities, should be added to the monopoly control of the PTT's—the government-run telecommunications agencies. At

issue here is the same question faced in PTT control of videotex—
would giving the development and operation of *backbone* services for
computer networks to the PTT's inevitably lead to their attempting to
control the data that is transmitted on these networks?

In the United States, concern over the licensing of information
banks is based on First Amendment principles. Would the morgue
(clipping file) of a newspaper, when computerized, become subject
to licensing? Although the Swedish Data Inspection Board has not
sought to license newspaper files, a data bank of this sort would seem
to meet the Data Act's criteria of computerized files containing personal information on a large group of individuals.

For reasons quite aside from this, the Lindop Committee in the
United Kingdom suggested that licensing might become unduly restrictive if every data bank had to receive prior authorization. Instead,
it proposed that each data bank should be registered by the operator
with a "Data Protection Authority," which would set codes of practice
for the various types of data banks—government and private. The authority would have inspection powers, and could prosecute a breach
of its code through the courts.

Registration of data banks, rather than licensing, might fit the
American situation better. Newspaper files would have to be ex-
empted—as they probably would be in Sweden, if a test case should
arise in the future.

First Amendment principles have also led American journalists
to protest vigorously against the idea, advanced by developing countries and Eastern European countries, that governments should have
a hand in deciding what information about their nations should be allowed to be transmitted from within their countries in the form of
news. Third World countries are concerned about the handling of information, including personal data that is obtained inside their countries by outside journalists, sociological researchers, and corporate
investigators. Western journalists are concerned about "free flow of
information" across international borders. Translate that idea into information transferred for storage in computers and you immediately
have a serious conflict. Business interests point out that restrictions
placed on data transfer by "data-protected" countries can be a form of
censorship. They don't want the idea exported to the developing
countries. They fear that such countries, once data processing becomes prevalent, will impose even tighter restrictions on information
that companies need to operate effectively. On the other hand, offi-

cials in developing countries ask: What right have Western commercial enterprises to make money off of personal data (relating, for instance, to the availability of a cheap labor market) that can be drawn off by a computer network for commercial planning purposes in the industrialized center of the world?

Each provision of the data acts in Sweden, France, and other Western democracies has a logical and praiseworthy reason behind its adoption. And each provision would appear to add to the protection of an individual's liberty and privacy. But some of the provisions raise philosophical questions about broader freedom and the right of people to be informed.

So data protection in the information society, while meeting a real and present danger, is bound to be the subject of argument and negotiation. This debate has not yet come to the forefront of the public's concern. We should be moving toward a philosophy of privacy protection. That philosophy should be embedded in law, perhaps in a constitutional amendment that adds the right of privacy to those rights already guaranteed. Basically, this philosophy should guarantee protection against invasion of a person's private thoughts, including the extrapolation of those thoughts from computer data. It should include the right to keep one's personal interactions private, so long as they do not injure other individuals in society. The philosophy would address the following specific concerns:

A person must have the right to see any file kept on him or her by a computer, make corrections in that file if it is in error, and have the corrections transmitted to all third parties to whom information from the file has been sent. Beyond that, the individual has less-precisely definable rights that will have to be negotiated. These include the right to minimum intrusion by computers and their attendant investigators; an expectation of confidentiality concerning medical records, family data, and legitimate financial transactions; and the right not to have all information about the individual known and transmittable by One Big Computer, either governmental or commercial.

All these rights have been eroded by the computer, the heart of the new communications technology.

Confidentiality of information has become a gray area that will become even foggier, and less subject to control, as the ease of transferring confidential information around the system increases. *Does my neighbor have the right, for a fee, to punch up my private life on* his HCS, out of idle curiosity? I do not think so. But are we not moving toward a time when the general breakdown of confidentiality, deliberately perpetrated by the operators of computers, will make such a transaction seem commonplace? At the very least, it would seem that we have the right to expect that information legitimately collected by government or private investigators, or which we give the government or a lending institution for legitimate uses, should not be available on the system for anyone to put to semilegitimate uses such as mailing lists or irresponsible uses such as gossip.

Just the fact that the computer, with an infinite capacity for record storage is *there,* is a force driving entrepreneurs and administrators to fill it with "useful" information on their "clients" and their habits. But the rules we set for filling that gaping maw and regurgitation from that monstrous belly are likely to define the extent of our personal liberties in the years immediately ahead.

7 | BRAZIL DEVELOPS CONTROL BY MEDIA

The military police censor, working over the proofs of the week's edition of the newspaper of the Archdiocese of São Paulo, Brazil, came upon a quote: "You shall know the truth, and the truth shall make you free."

"Who wrote that?" he asked the editor. "It's not attributed."

"Saint John—he was quoting Jesus."

"I still don't like it." He struck it out.

In Rio de Janeiro, the news director of Rede Globo, the country's major televisioin network, received his daily call from a colonel in the Federal Censorship: "There are troop movements near the Uruguayan border. You are not to carry any reports about them." The news director obeyed.

At the editorial office of *Veja,* Brazil's largest news magazine, a story arrived by telex from the bureau chief of Brasilia, reporting on corruption among high government officials. Almost immediately, the editor received a call from the headquarters of the Federal Military Police. "You can't publish anything about corruption in Brasilia," said the colonel in charge. The editor realized the military were plugged into *Veja*'s telex lines.

In São Paulo, Wladimir Herzog, thirty-eight, a leading journalist and news director of the country's biggest public television station, was called in for interrogation by army officers about his contacts with the left. That day, he died in their custody.

These are incidents from the 1974–79 term of Ernesto Geisel, who was the fourth general to serve as president of Brazil since the military revolution in 1964.

As a visiting professor of communications in São Paulo, I was in a position to observe conditions in Brazil as the Geisel regime was ending. I want to present the situation at that time as a case study showing how an authoritarian government used its control of existing media of communication to suppress dissent. Then I want to show how the new technologies of communications could be used to do the job even *more* effectively.

The public furor over Wladimir Herzog's death in 1975 led to a change in tactics of suppression in Brazil. To the displeasure of the hard-line generals in the government, Geisel brought a halt to the harsher measures that had been used to keep journalists, priests, and academics in line—arrest, interrogation, torture, and death.

In the last year of his administration, the government dropped copy and page-proof censorship that had been imposed on the more outspoken newspapers. Censors' phone calls to news publications and television news departments generally stopped.

Many papers, especially those in the more liberal south, burst forth with long-pent-up criticism of the government, the governing Aliança Renovadora Nacional (ARENA) Party and, more dangerously, the army, which has ruled the country since its generals overthrew a progressive president, João Goulart. As the end of his term neared, Geisel, an authoritarian who had not permitted personal opposition from even his own military colleagues, began talking about an *abertura*—an "opening" to democracy and eventual restoration of civil rights denied the people under the continuing "state of emergency." Liberal newspapers and the Movimento Democrático Brasileiro (MDB), then the only opposition party permitted by the regime, picked up the word *abertura* and tried to further the idea. Ominously, hard-liners in the army warned that, despite all this talk of an opening, the people should expect no rapid return to democracy.

On March 15, 1979, Geisel handed the government over to another ex-general, João Baptista de Oliveira Figueiredo, former head of the secret police. Despite his antecedents, Figueiredo announced he would "implant democracy in Brazil in a year and a half, at the maximum."[1] This pledge came a week after Vice-President Walter Mondale, following a meeting with Figueiredo in Brasilia, told the head of the governing party he was "much impressed with the climate of a democratic opening in Brazil."

I was in Brasilia the day Mondale was there, and the feeling I got was otherwise. In reporting and researching the subject I came to believe that the *abertura*, particularly in the areas of freedom of speech and press, was more apparent than real:

• On television, entertainment, cultural, and public-affairs programs remained under previous censorship; before each program, television stations had to display on the screen a certificate saying it had passed the Censura Federal.

• Movies had to be submitted to the Censorship for approval of content and for a government ruling on what age a person must be to see the film.

• Theater scripts had to be sent to Brasilia for a censor's stamp on each page; two censors had to attend the dress rehearsal, to make sure that the actors' gestures and looks did not turn the meaning of the approved lines around.

• Book manuscripts had to be approved *in toto* by the Federal Police before the books could be published.

And a close look at the lifting of prior censorship of the printed press showed that restrictions on its freedom were merely shifted to two other areas—enforcement of the National Security Laws and the use of economic pressures to make the publications conform.

"The government has a thousand ways of pressuring newspapers," said Julio Mesquita, director of *O Estado de São Paulo,* the most prestigious paper in Brazil. This being true, self-censorship became the price of survival, except at financially powerful publications such as *O Estado,* which had the money to withstand litigious and economic attacks.

(When the paper wanted to build a large new building, the government refused to permit any Brazilian bank to lend it mortgage money; after a long delay, the management was able to finance the building through the First National Bank of Boston. Smaller papers were not able to find such financing.)

O Estado, with a circulation of about 250,000, had never willingly accepted prior censorship, the kind that was imposed elsewhere by phone calls from the colonels. So the paper had censorship imposed on it by force—a resident censor was implanted in the newsroom, to strike from copy and proofs anything he did not think his military superiors would like to see in the paper.

Reporters and editors at *O Estado* developed their own ways of protesting the censorship. A resident censor (described by an observer as weak but arrogant about what he crossed out) installed himself in an office at the back of the newsroom. One morning, after he had made a particularly odious deletion, reporters climbed on their desks and as he slunk through the newsroom, chanted *"Filho da puta, filho da puta!"* ("Son of a whore, son of a whore!") until he disappeared into his office.

At first, the morning daily tried to leave blank spaces in the place of paragraphs that had been killed. Not allowed. So the paper printed epic poems in place of the censored passages. Its afternoon paper, *Folha da Tarde,* printed recipes. Sometimes the recipes made inventive use of puns on "ingredients" to indicate the names of government officials who had been mentioned in stories that were not allowed to appear. Thus, a story about Laudo Natel, then governor of São Paulo state, became "Lauto Pastel" ("Rich Pastry") in the substituted recipe.

In one instance, the paper tried to get political commentary past the censor by burying it in sports copy—read assiduously by Paulistas, but until then skipped over by the resident censor. But the colonel in charge of the censorship office in São Paulo spotted the prohibited matter. Instead of punishing the paper's editors, he fired the resident censor for not doing his job properly. The new resident read the sports pages assiduously.

When I asked Mesquita and other editors why Geisel had lifted prior censorship of newspapers and yet retained it in television, I received this reply:

Newspapers in Brazil talk to a literate elite; television talks to the illiterate masses. No more than 10 percent of the country's 120 million people read newspapers, but more than half of them have daily access to a television set. Television reaches into the *favelas,* the shanty towns where live the poorest of the poor, and the homes of low-income agricultural and industrial workers. These are the people who can be influenced for or against the regime, so the regime believes; the educated elite who edit the papers for the educated elite who read them are already against the government, and they are talking to themselves. Therefore, Geisel reasoned, why have a hassle over direct press censorship from newspaper and magazine editors and the academics, when they have no real power to influence the general populace?

Editors mentioned another factor: President Carter's campaign on human rights. Modern Western industrial nations, including the United States, value press freedom as a central indicator of a country's standing in civilized society. In 1977 the U.S. State Department angered the Brazilian regime by submitting a report to Congress that criticized the country's record on freedom. But now Geisel could say he had restored freedom of the press, and thus brought Brazil back into the club of civilized nations.*

Officials of the new administration justified continued censorship of television programs and films in movie theaters by saying "this is cultural, not political." Such censorship was done, according to a presidential decree in 1970, to protect the public from broadcasts and films "offensive to the morals and good customs" of the Brazilian people.

Thus, said the government officials charged with censorship, children are protected from seeing sexually immoral acts portrayed on the screen, and adults are protected from ideas on television that would degrade their national culture. Surprisingly, several editors said they felt there was some justification for this kind of censorship. Roberto Civita, editorial director of Editora Abril, the largest magazine-publishing house in Brazil and publisher of *Veja*, said: "I think this makes sense. There must be a line drawn somewhere about everything. Who draws the line? An independent 'code office' might be better than having the government do it, but someone has to do it."

By all accounts, however, the government methodically used the "morals and good customs" rationale to edit out of television and films any political ideas it did not like. Indeed, at the time the decree was published, the minister of justice explained that the object was "to combat the insidious efforts of international communism to impose free love and dissolve the moral fiber of society."

For the most part, the country's intellectual leaders vigorously opposed censorship of any kind.

THE LONG HISTORY OF CENSORSHIP

Used to repression from dictatorial regimes over fifty years, the general populace did not cry out for its rights to freedom of speech. Censorship has had a long history in Brazil. The Portuguese regime

* Since then, the pressure from the United States in support of human rights has slacked off. As it took office, the Reagan administration signaled that it would not be so concerned with the human rights activities of regimes with which it was on friendly terms.

allowed no books to be published in its Brazilian colony until 1807, when a Portuguese king ruled the empire from Rio, his place of refuge from Napoleon.

In the area of morals, the Portuguese who became Brazilians were guided by the Roman Catholic tradition with its respect for authority. It would have been unthinkable for members of the Brazilian aristocratic establishment to read works on the Catholic Index of Forbidden Books.

The republic's first constitution after it became independent from Portugal in 1822 provided that there would be freedom of expression, without censorship. But the populace knew that, in practice, this meant "within the bounds of the mores"—and sometimes the politics—condoned by the ruling establishment.

As early as 1829 the government required that all theater pieces be submitted for prior approval by the police. This control has been in effect, with greater or lesser degree of stringency, ever since.

Press censorship was established formally in the 1930s when President Getulio Vargas, who had assumed dictatorial powers, set up the Press and Propaganda Department. Subsequent presidents controlled the press to the extent that they chose to enforce the decrees of Vargas that were still technically in effect.

But it was the generals of the 1964 revolution who, paranoid over real or imagined threats to their power, decided that ideas opposed to their own in all areas of expression must be suppressed. The constitutional guarantee of freedom of speech and press, modeled on that of the United States, was amended to include some interesting caveats:

> There is freedom of expression of thought, and of political or philosophical convictions, as well as freedom of information, free of censorship, except with respect to public entertainment and performances, either being answerable to the law for any abuses that may be committed. The right of reply is assured. The publication of books, magazines, and newspapers is not contingent upon authorized license. However, propaganda for war, *for subversion of order,* or for discrimination based upon religion, race, or class, and publications whose content is opposed to morality and good manners *shall not be tolerated.* (Emphasis added.)[2]

No law had ever been passed by the Brazilian Congress establishing *political* censorship of news, in print or on the air. In theory, such censorship is prohibited by the Constitution. Rather, political censorship was imposed under the "emergency" dictatorial powers given to the president in 1969 by Institutional Act No. 5. This act, aimed at the antigovernment urban guerrilla movement, gave the president the authority to close Congress, suspend citizens' rights, dismiss elected officials, jail citizens without giving cause in political cases, overrule the courts, deprive anyone of his political rights for up to ten years, and rule by decree. All this in the guise of protecting "national security." Although the academics, priests, and students who led the urban guerrillas were soon hunted down and killed, the act remained in force for ten years, until Geisel allowed it to expire on January 1, 1979. Before he did, however, he had the Congress, over which he had assumed control, pass a bill that gave him and succeeding presidents "emergency" powers similar to those under IA 5, except that they must be renewed every six months.

Prior censorship was one of the most formidable tools of IA 5 for suppressing dissent, and it was systematically and openly applied. The Federal Police, a military force reporting to the Ministry of Justice but usually controlled directly from the president's office, set up a Division of Censorship of Public Entertainment. Censors were trained at the Federal School for Censors in Brasilia. Secret guidelines were laid down for them by successive military regimes, but these were never revealed to the editors and writers whose work they controlled. The result was a suppression at base vicious and at best, capricious.

CARDINAL FIGHTS AGAINST REPRESSION

One focus of this suppression has been the Roman Catholic Church, which, in an abrupt turn away from previous support to authoritarian regimes, presented the strongest opposition to the violations of human rights. Its priests suffered in consequence: some were known to have been tortured and killed; others simply disappeared.

Cardinal Dom Paulo Evaristo Arns of São Paulo became a leader of that opposition, and as a result, the government systematically interfered with his right to be heard. This was done first by attacking the radio station of his archdiocese, which had developed a national audience.

From the first, the *Censura* let the cardinal know it did not want him to discuss social concerns on the station. He did not comply, and on October 30, 1973, the station's license was abruptly suspended. *O*

São Paulo, his weekly newspaper, was placed under resident censorship. Sermons by the cardinal and social pronouncements by the pope were killed in proof; the paper was forbidden to mention even the name of Dom Helder Camara, archbishop of Recife and Olinda, and another outspoken opponent of the regime.

In 1976 an old priest of the diocese, upset that so much of the paper was being censored, asked Frei Romeo, a Dominican who was the editor, to go with him to see the colonel of Federal Police in charge of censorship in São Paulo. During their first ten minutes in his office, Frei Romeo told me, the colonel explained to them that he was a good Catholic. Then Frei Romeo asked the colonel why the text of a speech by a political opponent of the regime had been stamped *Vetado* by the censors, when it had already appeared in the São Paulo daily papers.

The colonel smiled. "Okay, lets make an arrangement," he said. "You know what the government wants to be published, and you know what the government does not want to be published. Then you just follow this rule, and nothing will be marked out."

Frei Romeo spread out his hands. "This does not solve any problem," he said.

The next week, *O São Paulo* was more heavily censored than at any time since the censorship was imposed.

To avoid having a resident censor imposed upon it, *Folha de São Paulo,* which competed with *O Estado* as the leading newspaper in the city, decided to accept the telephoned and telegraphed edicts of the colonels on news it was not to touch. But under the editorship of Claudio Abramo, a respected journalist of the left, it pursued an independent course and often published editorials and commentary denouncing government suppression. For this, Abramo was interrogated and jailed briefly on several occasions. Then, in 1977, after a columnist wrote a satirical piece about an army hero, the military told the owner of the paper it wanted Abramo out of the editorship. Abramo was promptly kicked upstairs. The amount of dissenting "op-ed" comment was cut back, but the paper remained critical of the government.

After direct censorship of the major journals was lifted, *Folha* published verbatim transcripts with date and time, of 103 of the 286 censorship orders it had received between 1972 and 1974.[3] Here are some of the entries:*

* Translated by the author.

8/2/72 (9:30 p.m.) It is prohibited to divulge any news whatsoever referring to the imprisonment or disappearance of a journalist in Rio de Janeiro.

5/19/73 (5:16 p.m.) All news and commentaries about the explosion of a bomb in the American consulate [in São Paulo] are prohibited.

7/12/73 (9:44 p.m.) It is prohibited to publish the denunciations made by Senator [Edward] Kennedy about tortures in Brazil.

11/1/73 (4:58 p.m.) The following is prohibited: Commentaries, news interviews or critiques of whatever nature about political *abertura* or democratization; amnesty for *cassados* [unpersons]; editorials, commentaries, or unfavorable critiques in the field of economics and finance; the succession of the president and its implications ... transcriptions of debates in Congress or the [state] legislatures, in whole or in part.

11/1/73 (9:17 p.m.) By order of the Federal Police, editors are not permitted to raise the preceding communication for consideration.

2/5/74 (10:30 p.m.) Commentaries or reports about the confiscation, suspension, previous censorship and other methods, legal, preventative *and repressive* adopted against publishers, books, reviews, newspapers and television are prohibited.

Television showed none of the independence newspapers had shown in resisting this kind of suppression. Rede Globo, which has an overwhelming majority of the television audience, cooperated with the government censorship virtually without protest. The management in Rio did not see the need. Money can be made without freedom of speech.

"In Brazil, television is a government concern," a spokesman told me. "At any time, they can end the concession. We must be more cautious than the newspapers. Our 'Eight p.m. News' can change the views of forty million people—so this gives television more responsibility to see that this new process of *abertura* runs normally."

Normality, at Globo, included submitting for government approval twenty episodes at a time of all television *novelas*, the nighttime soap operas that are standard popular fare. (One *novela* on youth problems was vetoed because the government did not want to acknowledge that there *were* youth problems.) Until 1979 it included obeying telephoned prohibitions on news stories. After that, general warnings sufficed: self-censorship prevailed. During a strike of 154,000 auto workers in São Paulo, which the new Figueiredo government immediately declared illegal, the regime let it be known that it would not look favorably on extensive coverage by television. As a consequence, Roberto Marinha, who owned most of Globo's stock, reportedly edited news coverage of the strike himself, to see that it stayed in bounds.

"VLADO" HERZOG: A JOURNALIST DIES

News on public television received less attention from the government because its audience was small. Even so, TV Cultura, the modern broadcasting operation funded by the State of São Paulo, did not make waves; it even submitted segments of home study courses for censorship if they related to political or social subjects. The staff had internalized the warning given them by the death of Wladimir Herzog, who had been its news director at the time.

"Vlado," as he was known, was a left-leaning liberal whose views angered the ultraconservatives in the Second Army garrison, headquartered in São Paulo. The notorious Department of Internal Operations ordered him to present himself for questioning on Saturday, October 25, 1975, at its São Paulo headquarters, where several dissidents had been tortured to death. Another journalist, waiting in the anteroom to be questioned, testified later in court that he had heard shouts exchanged between the interrogator and Vlado, and then the interrogator ordering equipment for torture. Shortly after that, he said, Vlado's shouts ceased. Late that afternoon, the Second Army put out a statement that Vlado, having confessed to membership in the Communist Party, had hanged himself in his cell. Cardinal Arns, the head of the journalists' union, and professors of the University of São Paulo, where Vlado taught part-time, called the statement a lie.*

More than 30,000 students boycotted classes at USP; thousands attended an ecumenical service the cardinal conducted in São Paulo Cathedral for Vlado, a Jew. His death became a *cause célèbre* in the press of Brazil and around the world. On this story, the censors backed off. President Geisel saw the developing situation as a threat to his regime. He warned General Ednardo D'Avila Melo, commandant of the Second Army, that he would brook no more "suicides" at his headquarters. Two months later, a laborer died there under similar circumstances. Geisel promptly dismissed General Ednardo and replaced him with a less-conservative general, signaling to the rest of

---

* In October 1978 a justice in a civil court ruled that Vlado had been incarcerated illegally, that the subsequent investigation by the army did not substantiate the army's claim of suicide, and that Vlado's widow and two children had to be indemnified for his death while in army custody.

the army that he was dissatisfied with the way repression was being carried out. After that, no suspicious deaths of political prisoners were reported. Claudio Abramo told me he thought that so long as papers were free to report such acts, the army would not be able to resume torture and murder.

But the big question, as Figueiredo came to power, was whether the army hard-liners, who by now no longer looked on him as a dependable member of the *apparat,* would permit further liberalization in the areas of free speech and press. Within the new administration, officials themselves argued about how far it was proper—and safe—to go with the "opening" to democracy. The talk of relaxation was aimed in part at the United States, which was giving signs of wanting to smooth over its human rights "affront" to Brazil.

In the futuristic building of the Ministry of Justice in Brasilia, source of harsh repression in the past, I asked the chief of cabinet, Dr. Syleno Ribeiro, whether the ministry was committed to an *abertura*.

"What some people call *abertura,*" he said, "is merely the process of continuing the perfection of our national institutions that began when the country gained its independence in 1822." A woman lawyer sitting in as the ministry's counsel on human rights commented, "There is no opening in Brazil, because, since the Revolution, our institutions have never been closed."

After two such remarks, I saw that my questions on the future were not going to be answered in this interview. Ribeiro suggested that I write out my questions and said, "By tomorrow noon, at your hotel, you will have the answers, written by the Minister of Justice himself." The answers never came.

The minister, Petronio Portela, was at the time involved in a public exchange over censorship with an unrelated namesake, Eduardo Portela, the new minister of education and culture. One official of the new government had pointed out that only two countries censored books—Brazil and the Soviet Union. Petronio said that, really, books should not be censored by the Federal Police. His predecessor, Armando Falcão, had prohibited or burned five hundred books during the Geisel years. Books, said Petronio, should be censored by "fitting persons" in the Ministry of Education and Culture. Eduardo, a Rio professor and former literary critic, said he did not believe books should be censored by the Federal Police, but he did not want the responsibility, either. Eduardo, however, was part of the government. "If the government thinks we will have to have some kind of of censorship, then of course we will accept it," his chief of cabinet told me. "But it will be done by the Minister of Justice."

As a result of harsh repression in 1969, university educators had found they had to accept suppression of academic freedom—censorship in another guise—as the norm of life. Military police sat in on classes, and reported "subversive" remarks by professors and students. In the first days, dissident professors and students were likely to disappear. When I was in Brazil, the current form was to report their dissonances to the university administrations, which in turn dismissed students from the universities and professors from their jobs.

One dean told me of a devilish technique that reduced the necessity for having a policeman in each class: a military police captain came to the dean's office, identified himself, and announced that he would be monitoring some courses. "Other members of my detachment will be registered as students in other classes," he said. "However, they won't identify themselves as members of the Policia Militar."

One way to tell a military policeman, my dean friend told me, was to note the person in class who asked the most questions, and tried to draw you out on political and social issues—at this stage, a very un-Brazilian thing to do. "He will be the policeman in your class," said the dean.

ARMY HARD-LINERS WANT MORE

In the end, everyone agreed, the decision on all forms of repression would be made by President Figueiredo. And he had not yet shown his hand. The tugging and pulling reflected a dilemma in which Figueiredo found himself. On one horn, journalists, academics, and leaders of the opposition party were determined that there should be no turning back from the concessions to freedom they felt they had from Geisel. On the other hand, old-line generals did not want to permit open criticism of the army. At base was their fear that, should a democratic civilian regime win control of the government, they were in danger of being made to account for past excesses at a Brazilian "Nuremberg trial." "Before we are allowed democracy," said one disgruntled editor, "the last general must die in bed."

The fear was reflected in the prosecution of *Veja* by the Supreme Military Tribunal. In February 1979 the news magazine published two investigative reports by Antonio Carlos Fon in which he gave times and places in which dissidents had been tortured and killed over the years, the names of army officers who had committed the torture, and the names of colonels and generals responsible for permitting it to happen. For this, the army prosecutor brought charges that the articles were "subversive in the extreme." Their sole intent, the indictment said, was to "turn public opinion against constituted authorities," a crime punishable under the National Security Laws. Punishment for conviction by the military on this charge brought by the military, was five years in jail.

I asked a source involved with the defense why the military, which was inseparable from the government, had decided to prosecute *Veja* at a time when government leaders were talking about an opening to freedom.

"What I think the military is saying," he replied, "is this: We are not going to stand trial for what happened between 1968 and 1976. *Veja* is as good a place to give that message as any—it's big and it's middle-of-the-road. If you say it to *Veja,* it's clear to everyone."

Since he did not intervene, Figueiredo, whose whole life has been devoted to the army, apparently wanted the message to be sent. The *Veja* case was an exception to what was reported to be the official strategy he had laid down: avoid confrontation with the major organs of the press, but prosecute vigorously publications of the alternative press. This was an obvious bow to the army ultras who were angered by the probing of these dissident papers. Actions for violations of the National Security Laws were instituted against *Pasquim,* a satirical weekly in Rio; *Tribuna da Imprensa,* a Rio daily; *Reporter,* a Rio monthly; *Resistencia,* a monthly in Pará; and *Movimento,* an investigative weekly in São Paulo.

The attack on *Movimento,* an influential journal of twenty-five thousand circulation set up in 1975 with contributions from journalists and professors, was a good example of how the government used the security laws and economic pressure to discourage opposition to the press.

I talked with Antonio Carlos Ferreira, its "Responsible Director" (the Brazilian title for top editor) on the second floor of a nondescript house in a middle-class section near the Cemetery of São Paulo. In the rooms around us, I saw men and women in faded jeans who could have been reporters, editors, and production people in any alternative paper in the United States—except that they were writing in Portuguese. The pressures on them had not been subtle. Three times the paper had been confiscated from the newsstands, even though the censors had approved the contents. Ferreira had been questioned many times by the Federal Police. "Certainly, our phones are tapped and certainly, we are being followed," he said. And now he was being called to answer charges in the Supreme Military Tribunal. The accusation, in effect, is that he endangered national security by writing about arguments within the ARENA Party over Geisel's choice of Figueiredo to succeed him. Ferreira, a man in his thirties who has a wife and two small children, was matter-of-fact about his prospects.

"I will be given a hearing before four military officers and one civilian judge," he said, "and then I will be sentenced to prison."

"Is that decided in advance?"

"Sure—they're the military, aren't they?"

"Can you appeal?"

"Yes, but I will be in jail."

(Ferreira spent the year that followed this interview undergoing hearings and periods of imprisonment and fleeing the interrogations of the political police. In the end, he was granted amnesty. The hardliners had turned to other methods of intimidation: firebombing the editorial offices of the alternative papers and newsstands that displayed their editions for sale. *Movimento, Pasquim,* and other opposition papers continued to publish despite the attacks. In August of 1980 a letterbomb killed a secretary of the Order of Advocates of Brazil, an organization of lawyers that had defended the human rights of publishers and editors of the alternative journals.)

Besides an interim editor, *Movimento* had to find a new printer. Its printer was driven out of business by government, which warned customers not to patronize the company so long as it printed *Movimento.* Banks were ordered to give the paper no credit and major companies warned not to advertise in its pages, Ferreira said. Most complied.

With *Movimento* in mind, I asked Julio Mesquita if he was satisfied with the state of press freedom in his country.

"I am happy because there is no prior censorship of newspapers, but as far as freedom of the press is concerned, I don't believe we have it," he said. "You would have to repeal the National Security Laws to have real freedom of the press."

The signs as the Figueiredo regime took over, indicated that freedom in Brazil had a long way to go:

• Twelve radio stations were fined for failing to carry "Voz do Brasil." From seven to eight each night, the government required every AM and FM station in the country to carry "Voz," a badly produced propaganda program touting the "miracle" of the country's advance as a major power. (All over the country, at 7:00, p.m., people turned their radios off.)

• The Brazilian Post Office refused to transmit a telegram of support from students of the University of Londrina to students of the University of Salvador (Bahia). Instead, postal officials made a list of the signers and turned the names over to the Military Police.

• In Curitiba, the Federal Censorship prohibited a children's play, "O Robo de Bobby," from being seen by children under fourteen. The reason given: the play mentioned the words "worker" and "strike."

• The government fined TV Guanabara in Rio $2000 for broadcasting an interview in which the governor of the state was criticized.

• Retired General Hugo Abreu was put in jail for twenty days for publishing a book "damaging to the Armed Forces." Abreu, a former top government official, had opposed Figueiredo's nomination as president.

So, by 1980, *abertura* in Brazil amounted to this: freedom of expression in one medium, the print press, boxed in by the threat of prosecution under punitive laws that meant whatever the military said they meant. For one of the country's leading academics, the auguries for wider freedom were not good. "People who read the liberal newspapers in Rio and São Paulo think there may be an opening to democracy," he said. "We who live in Brasilia think there will be a closed military regime for many years to come."

MAKING IT EASIER FOR THE AUTHORITARIANS

Brazil has known very few periods of democratic freedom since it became a nation in 1822. Rather, the traditional form of government has been authoritarian—marked in this century by military dictatorships. These have been reasonably successful in controlling the media as a way of suppressing dissent.

To show how the new technologies of communication could make things even easier for authoritarians of the future, I have built a final scenario on the premise that the hard-line generals have won, and imposed a strongly repressive regime on Brazil in the first years of the twenty-first century. And they now have an integrated, computerized, two-way electronic communications system to use as a tool for control.

SCENARIO: NEW YEAR IN BRAZIL

THE TIME: A New Year's Day in the first decades of the twenty-first century.

THE PLACE: Brasilia

The military dictatorship is smarting under the order, signed today by U.S. president Joanna Hampshire, cutting off all shipment of processed plutonium for using in fueling Brazilian nuclear power plants. President Hampshire signed the order because of a disastrous meltdown of Brazil's first nuclear plant, at Angra dos Reis on the coast between Rio and Santos. (The disaster had been foreshadowed as long ago as 1978, when the West German hired to supervise construction had quit in protest against unsafe Brazilian construction methods.) The plant had been plagued by a series of accidents over the years. Two days ago, when an explosion ruptured the containment building, a wind from onshore had blown the lethal radioactive cloud out to sea, but not before it had killed 1200 workers and their families living in the company town a kilometer from the plant.

Immediately after the explosion, President Oliveira, in his office in the Planalto, picked up the phone and ordered his minister of justice to block transmission of all news of the accident by satellite, electronic mail, and long-wave radio—the only forms of international communications now permitted. He forbade domestic distribution of the information on the country's integrated communications system, and told the minister to jam any covert short-wave transmission from foreign embassies and consulates in Rio and São Paulo.

Nevertheless, the U.S. consul in Rio, who had received word of the accident from underground dissidents, found a way to get the news back to the States. She dispatched a destroyer that had been on a goodwill visit to Rio out of the harbor so it could transmit on the relatively unjammable underwater array of extremely long-wave transmitters the United States had placed on the continental shelves to communicate with its submarines around the world.

President Oliveira now ordered that all information concerning President Hampshire's action be kept from the Brazilian people. The Censura Federal had already taken several restrictive measures:

It had programmed the computer controlling incoming satellite broadcasts from the United States and Europe to wipe out instantly from the receiving computers at the earth stations all digital pictures, audio, or teletext reports from outside the country that mentioned the words *Brazil, power plant, nuclear,* and *plutonium.*

This effectively blocked receipt of an AUPI story which said that President Hampshire had received word of the nuclear accident and had cut off shipments of nuclear fuel to Brazil. It also killed the story about the First-Night Celebration in which Hampshire shut down the Tucson nuclear plant and activated the solar plant.

Computers monitoring all telephone and telex transmissions from Brazil automatically cut circuits of voice transmissions and print stories containing these words, so that no news service reporter could get the story out of the country. Enterprising reporters, aware the cutoff would be in effect, tried to slip the word through in code. But they were blocked by censors in Brasilia. Using an intercept, the censors read teletext versions of all copy put into the electronic system by news agencies, before allowing the copy to proceed on its way. The copy was also fed into computers programmed to detect codes or ciphers even experienced censors might miss. Censors of domestic copy scanned all stories being typed into internal computers at electronic news services and at newspapers that were still putting out hard-copy editions. More are still doing that here, obviously, than in the United States. But all papers are required to write and edit stories on VDT's so that they can be censored from the central office in the capital, rather than have resident censors at each of the papers.

In the communications centers of every electronic news operation, newspaper, broadcasting station, videotex service, and cable system, an order appeared confirming what was already being imposed electronically:

Any news of the nuclear accident is prohibited; such information will be "wiped" from local news services' data banks by the computer overrides operated from Censura headquarters.

Just after the order was transmitted, an editor of *Folha de São Paulo,* noting that it referred only to news, decided to try to get the facts out in an editorial. Following normal practice, he typed his name, the slug line "editorial—atomic" into his VDT. Instantly, the keys gave him an electrical shock. As he jumped away from the terminal, a notice, addressed to him by name, appeared on the VDT screen:

Report immediately for questioning at Military Police Headquarters, Totoia Street, São Paulo.

Rather than have the Policia Militar track him down, the editor left the office and drove to the "Totoia Hilton," as the headquarters had come to be known. The police there knew he was en route, because they had locked into the tamper-proof black box installed in his car at the time of manufacture. (All cars in Brazil must now be built in Brazil.)

In Rio, an American correspondent was stopped at passport control as she was about to board a Varig supersonic flight to Miami. A magnetized strip in her Brazilian visa, sensed by the airport computer, had identified her as a foreign news reporter, all of whom had been ordered to remain in Brazil until further notice. The military policeman at the airport checkpoint found a typewritten story about the accident in her attaché case and informed her she was under arrest for violating the National Security Laws.

A young reporter for an alternative newspaper in São Paulo, walking overland to try to reach the area of the rumored nuclear accident on the coast, was spotted by a police helicopter that had been sent out to find him. The police in the copter machine-gunned him to death when he tried to duck into some low bushes. Knowing the monitoring satellite could obtain a fix on him through the signal his watch sent out, the reporter had deliberately left it behind at the office. But he did not know that his plastic identity card, which he was required to carry at all times, was transmitting his universal identifier number via a low-powered emission that could be picked up by the cellular radio-monitoring system that had been installed throughout the country. This device made it possible for the police to track suspected dissidents continuously by computer. (The safest thing for a person whose wristwatch radio signal fails is to go to the nearest police station and report in. Anyone who doesn't, or who throws the watch or identity card away in desperation, is hunted down through traditional police methods and eliminated. The word *cassado* is entered under his or her name in the Citizens Central Computer Data File in Brasilia, and the rest of the dossier is erased.)

Executives of commercial radio and television stations and cable systems had also heard rumors about the accident. But, recognizing it to be the type of information that was about to be vetoed by the Censura, they automatically dismissed the idea of checking it out. (The luxury of making that choice was not available to broadcasters of the Roman Catholic Church. Their stations had been closed down when the bishops of the church were placed under house arrest.)

In any event, the omnipresent monitoring computers would have killed the stories before they got on air; no program is broadcast live in Brazil. Even "live" coverage of Carnival around the country is now subject to seven-second delay so that human monitors can catch any infraction of rigid government restrictions on nudity and throw the kill switch. Because Carnival in Rio is now totally a tourist attraction to bring in foreign exchange, almost complete nudity is permitted by the *destaques*—the women "stars" of the attraction in the organized parades of the samba schools. The last bit of disclosure is forbidden, however, to protect "the mores and good customs" of the people. People are accustomed to the screens on their HCS's going blank during news broadcasts—they merely switch over to the video game channel or a government-approved telenovela. In fact, the news is little watched. "There's nothing we can do about what's happening," one homeowner remarked to an American reporter, "so why bother to know—it can only get you into trouble."

Books, which in Brazil do not come through the HCS, are scanned, page by page, by optical readers in computers that look for forbidden words or combinations of words that contain forbidden ideas.

In the early years of interactive communications, the police frequently employed the HCS to discipline citizens, because people had not yet adapted to curbing their tongues in their homes. The populace thought it was a great beneficence of the government to put at least one HCS (which actually aren't all that costly) into every home—then two in the homes of high-school graduates and three in the homes of college-trained families. But then they learned that the two-way audio and video capability was not for their information (for their *entertainment*, of course—the government wanted them to be entertained) but for the information of the Policia Militar. The local police headquarters spot-checked all homes in its district, turning on home sets at random to see and hear what the householders were doing and saying. People who express discouragement are summoned to the set and fined on the spot. The monitoring officer assesses the fine by transferring money from the culprit's account into that of the government. (Sales taxes on items purchased by the resident through the two-way catalogue services of the HCS are deducted automatically by government computers.)

People have been getting ridiculously cautious about what they say in private, the police report, since the time six months ago when monitoring was extended to the wristwatch radios everyone is required to wear, even in bed.

Audio and visual monitors have, of course, been required at all public or group meetings for years. Television cameras and microphones are installed in all university classrooms, doing away with the necessity of enrolling secret police personnel in classes to keep a check on professors' and students' attitudes.

The only exceptions—and they are *de facto* exceptions—are the board meetings of private corporations. Corporate executives have to pay officials of the government, from President Oliveira down to the lowest-ranking police monitor, for the privilege of private talks. Even then, they cannot be certain that their conversations are not being bugged surreptitiously. Multinational corporations have it best. Absolutely dependent on trouble-free telecommunications for their operations in Brazil, they make payoffs of monumental amounts to the officials, often giving them shares in the corporation or hiring them as "consultants" to the corporations. (It's in the great tradition in Brazil: as far back as the 1970s, the minister of justice was paid as a "consultant" to one of the commercial television networks.) Out of an enlightened self-interest, government officials take strong measures to see that "their" corporations' activities are not subjected to the monitorings and disruptions accorded to nonpaying citizens.

People, naturally, try to keep a low profile, and officials of the ruling ARENA Party generally like it that way. But the government does not want passive acquiescence. Every citizen over the age of twelve must take part in weekly public indoctrination programs conducted by two-way cable. (Younger children are thought to be sufficiently indoctrinated in the schools by interactive electronic sessions conducted by instructors from the Department of Education and Culture in Brasilia.) Reponse to questions raised in the government's "public affairs" programs is mandatory, via the multiple-choice buttons on the HCS key pad. If a citizen's "digital" responses do not show her or him to be sufficiently supportive of government policies, a Policia Militar interviewer appears on the screen and asks more personalized questions to determine whether or not the citizen will have to report for remedial sessions.

Public-affairs interrogation programs are presented on the home set at several convenient times each week so that all may "attend." Those who miss even these are required to punch up a computerized repeat of the week's questionnaire session before the week is out.

Those whose absence is noted are "visited" by police monitors via their home screens. Should the monitor fail to find the culprit within range of the set, police in the Morals and Good Customs Squad are sent around to the suspect's door.

Everyone is required to watch or listen to every speech presented by President Oliveira. Citizens indicate their attendance by inserting their plastic universal identifier cards into their sets. Questions are asked of the viewers afterward, to see if they have been paying attention.

Records of participation are kept in the Central Personal Data Bank in Brasilia, using the universal identifier number given at birth. The data file has dossiers on every person recorded to be living in the country. This record coordinates information from government registrations, military police files, the government credit-rating bureau, and its Reliability Investigating Service used for public and private hiring. To these files are added summaries of responses and transactions of citizens using their two-way communications sets. All the information, except that which the government wants to keep to itself, can be bought by anyone in the country, using the home or office communication terminal. Persons with derogatory information about their neighbors are expected to report it to the government via the HCS keyboard, or, if they are illiterate, speak it into the HCS mikes, after pressing the Government Monitoring Service button. Citizens have no right to correct derogatory items in their files—the theory is that any adverse material, true or false, puts the individual in the position of having to prove it wrong, if he or she is charged later with a violation of government decrees or a private corporation's rules.

The people of Brazil are told over and over again by their government that it wants them to be happy. Said *Voz do Brasil:* "You know what we want you to do and what we don't want you to do. All you have to do is follow your consciences by keeping to these rules, and you will have no problems at all—you can go about freely, living personally happy and useful lives."

And it is so. The great majority of the people do what they are supposed to do and they do not do what they are not supposed to do. And they are happy. They laugh, a bit nervously, when they tell of the disappearance of a friend or an acquaintance, but they go on with their affairs, confident it won't happen to them—because they are careful about what they say. The Brazilians are a happy people, except for those who openly disagree, or because of some quirky nature, think they can get away with some infraction of the rules. And, as the government points out with some pride, the numbers of these unhappy ones grow smaller every every passing year.

Some journalists, priests, and academics still try, once in a while, to resist control by communications. To give an immediate instance, here is an incident that happened today:

Carlos and Paula Ribeiro were driving northeast along the beautiful shoreline highway toward Rio, having just spent a warm New Year's Eve on the beach at Ubatuba. They were unaware that, two nights before and twenty kilometers farther along, there had been a disastrous escape of radioactive steam from the nuclear reactor at Angra dos Reis. As they approached a Policia Rodoviaria checkpoint before Parati, the engine in their car went dead, and they coasted to a stop outside the highway police station.

"Oh, the devil!" said Carlos, who happened to be driving. He realized the police inside the station had cut the car's engine by the radio-controlled black box built into it at the factory. "We weren't going more than sixty kilometers."

"They'll probably swear we were, though," his wife remarked.

A police lieutenant walked up to the car. "Professor Ribeiro," he said, glancing down at a computer printout and then at Carlos. "Didn't you hear on your Emergency Interrupt that the coast road is closed to all traffic headed toward Rio?"

"No—my radio isn't working." Carlos, hoping he and Paula could get away from outside contacts during the holiday, had taken a chance and disconnected the radio interrupt. "Why is it closed?"

"It is closed," said the lieutenant. "You know that having your Emergency Interrupt disconnected is a criminal offense."

"I was going to get it fixed as soon as the repair shops open."

"You shouldn't be driving with a radio that is not working," the lieutenant said. "I'm afraid you will have to stay overnight in our detention room so you can appear before the magistrate tomorrow. I think the fine will be very large." He looked at Ribeiro expectantly.

The professor had seen that look on military policemen's faces all his adult life. He shrugged. "Is there some way this could be taken care of today?"

"Why don't you step inside?"

At the interactive set in the station, Ribeiro entered the code number the lieutenant gave him, and transferred 10,000 cruzeiros—about a week's pay—from his own bank account to the lieutenant's personal bank account. The lieutenant assured him that the code would guarantee that no indication linking his name to the transaction would be transferred to Ribeiro's personal dossier in the Central Data Bank in Brasilia.

The professor walked out looking glum, got into the car, turned it around and drove back toward Ubatuba.

"How much did he want?" his wife asked.

"Ten thousand cruzeiros."

Paula Ribeiro shook her head, but did not say what she was thinking. Her husband glanced over at her.

"Well, it's better than the old days, when you had to hand them the money in cash," he said. "I didn't have ten thousand on me. If it hadn't been for the set, we would have had to spend the night in detention, for sure." He smiled. "You might say we've been saved by technology."

8 | CONCLUSION: TO GAIN THE PROMISE AND AVOID THE THREAT

In scenario after scenario since the 1960s, technological optimists have emphasized the wonders of the computer/communications revolution and passed over its inherent dangers. The danger is *present;* we can ignore it no longer.

The new technologies of communication *can* provide great benefits to society—I have no doubt about that. But unless we plan carefully for their arrival, rather than let them hit us head-on, the threats they bring with them may outweigh the benefits we may enjoy.

In the past, government administrations, corporate entrepreneurs, and the technocrats have encouraged us to believe that *they* are the ones who understand how the new technologies work, and that if we will just leave it to them—the professionals—all will be well. It ain't necessarily so. In the United States, we left broadcasting to the professionals, and we got a system as unrepresentative of the public interest as could have been devised if that had been the original intention.

The point is that the technology of the new communications is not all that complicated. We can understand both the technology and its implications, and we can make informed and sensible decisions about how it should be used.

In a field that is broad and changing rapidly, we may not be able to capture each piece of the new technology and fit it neatly into a Master Plan. But if we keep our eyes on the communications *services* the electronic developments can provide—regardless of whether they are provided by the Mark IV Fiber Communications Laser or the Mark VIII Light-Emitting Diode—it *is* possible to do some Master Planning.

If left to its own devices, the new system of communications will spread wherever commercial, political, or military forces make an opening for it. Attempts to control it in the public interest will be sporadic and thumb-in-the-dike. Such ad hoc policies are usually made only after the public realizes that some kind of crisis exists. For once it would be good if we *anticipated* the problems and took control of a life-altering technology before it takes hold of us. Public policies on so major an instrument of change will have to be enforced through government action. On the larger issues—such as control of the system, restrictions on freedom of expression, intrusions on privacy, and threats to individual liberty—policies must be debated and determined at the national level. Myriad other issues will have to be resolved, often through franchising action, at the local levels. In some cases, such as the free flow of information around the world, they must be negotiated at the international level.

Possible solutions to some of the concerns presented themselves while I was doing the reporting and research for this book, and I have suggested them in the chapters on specific parts of the emerging system. Where the experience has been so new that no obvious line of approach has suggested itself, I have tried to describe the problems that are foreseen by the people working in the pilot projects and the considerations that seem necessary to making decisions for future policy.

I don't have many definitive *answers,* and I found few people in the public-interest sector who do. Quite a few "answers" are already being offered by developers of the technologies and by those who have jumped in to use them for commercial, political, or military gain. What is needed now is action by those who are interested in the social consequences to the public of what is being done. Any such action will have to deal with the issue of control.

HOW SHOULD THE SYSTEM BE CONTROLLED?

An electronic technology that can merge all the media of communication into a unified system might appear to be a "natural monopoly." Such a monopoly could suggest economies of scale, as opposed to diseconomies from allowing competing organizations to operate side by side within the system, "duplicating" facilities. That reasoning appeared logical in the case of the traditional wired telephone system that developed first in the United States, then in countries around the world. But it does not necessarily make sense in the emerging communications system.

It is technically possible to base the new system almost entirely on communications satellites. These would be high-powered instruments, broadcasting the programs they receive, or retransmitting voice or text messages point-to-point, to small rooftop antennas on every home, business office, or government installation in the country. The rooftop antennas would relay incoming signals to the home communications set or automated office terminals at each receiving location. Since services provided thus would range from telephone to teletext or television, various operators could be using the "same" unified system, encapsulated in the HCS. In this arrangement, there would be no dis-economies of scale from competing facilities, so long as each satellite was being used to its capacity.

A satellite-only transmission system would probably be some technical generations away, however. It reckons without the historical fact of the huge network of landlines and land-hopping microwave towers that has been built by the communications carriers such as AT&T in the United States and the PTT's in Europe. These are surely not going to be abandoned, transferring all the traffic on the network to brand-new satellite networks.

"If you were charged with establishing a telephone system in Southern Rhodesia," said William Sharwell of AT&T, "you would start with a satellite. But this isn't the case in the United States. You use economics to determine the system."

But the cost savings to be gained from using satellites for much of this traffic are going to mean that satellites will be introduced into the existing setup in increasing numbers. So we are likely to have a hybrid system—a system combining satellite usage with point-to-point microwave, optical fiber landlines, and over-the-air broadcasting—well into the next century.*

Once you introduce satellites, the time-honored concept of the telecommunications network as a natural monopoly goes by

---

* "Satellite-microwave-optical fiber society" is not so neat a concept as the "wired society" that caught the popular imagination with the arrival of cable, but it is more accurate. Since computers are involved in all these technologies, "computerized society" or "information society" are better generic terms.

the boards. Even on the ground, this "natural" monopoly began breaking down when cable companies strung coaxial lines that paralleled the routes laid out for the telephone system. Cable companies and the phone companies have survived this "duplication" of facilities.

In the present state of the art, all telecommunications *could* be controlled by a single entity—but they do not have to be. Political or commercial pressures might push in the direction of monolithic national (or international) systems, but the technology could go either way. However, because government administrators and commercial entrepreneurs, respectively, now see the *possibility* of uniting the new communications as a monopoly under their control for power or profit, the fight among them to bring that about will be intense.

In Western Europe, as I have mentioned, telecommunications is considered to be a natural resource that should be provided by the government as a public utility. Most Europeans I talked to in and out of government seem to accept that as a given. They expect that this traditional model will be followed in the development of the merging electronic technologies. Some who believe in the concept, however, fear that the government operations will be taken over by multinational corporations now trying to get a foot in the door.

In the United States, the prevailing opinion is that the new communications will be monopolized, or at least heavily dominated, by AT&T.* In any event, it has seemed inconceivable, in the second half of the twentieth century, that the American telecommunications system would be operated by any agency other than private enterprise. I believe it is time now at least to *think* about the unthinkable.

A NONPROFIT PHONE SYSTEM IN THE UNITED STATES?

Philosophically, and totally beyond the political and pragmatic considerations, it does not seem right to me that anyone should make a profit from providing services that are essential to people's lives. I believe the new communications is such a service.

"Ah, but nothing good in life is free," the commercial operators reply. Even if I agreed with that, which I don't, there are many different ways for us to pay for our good. One way might conceivably be to

---

* Canada and Japan, the two other areas most advanced in the field of telecommunications, have mixed government and private systems that fall somewhere between the Western European and U.S. models.

set up public operating companies that provide services at cost, without automatically adding on a profit for those who provide them.

American businessmen justify adding on charges for profits by saying these give them the *incentive* to provide better and more efficient services than public agencies would supply. Actually, a strong case can be made that the profit incentive can lead service utilities down paths that are *harmful* to the public—as it did in the choice of the private power industry to build nuclear plants, regardless of the known and unknown dangers this technology might present to their customers. Profit incentive can also lead to higher costs to customers as in Bell's insistence on using landlines for long-distance calls long after it was apparent that satellite circuits could be less costly.

Despite these examples, I believe most business people are sincere when they argue that private enterprise can do it best. But that does not make it true in *every* case, as many corporate executives insist. A majority in Western Europe obviously do not believe it is true at all in telecommunications, electrical power, railroads, and other essential utilities. Our mindset should be changed so that we can consider this fact, and act on it, in our own interests.

Nor is it necessary, just because corporate executives may not be insincere, to turn over all decision-making in this area to those whose chief interest in providing services to the public is the *bottom line*. We need public, government, and corporate policies that make use of the new communications for the benefit of society, not only for the balance sheet.

Corporations and their managers are pushed each year by their chief stockholders and directors to maximize profits *now*, not five years from now or ten years from now. In trying to meet this demand and keep their jobs, top managers are tempted to take highly commercial shortcuts to achieve maximum short-term profits, without concerning themselves with the social problems these expediencies may cause. A good example is the push of electronics corporations to install computers for processing of personal data without building into them protections for the privacy of information they contain. Only lately have they begun to offer such protections as optional extras.

It is interesting that, *despite* the increasing pressure for profits, many industrial managers are discussing at industry meetings the idea that private companies *have* a responsibility to the public, and ought to become "good corporate citizens." Some of this comes from conscientious corporate managers who are concerned that they should be contributing something to society in *addition* to working for private gain. Some of it comes from the recognition that their customers, if they *do not* see some public dividend accruing to them from private operations, will finally, despite all the propaganda efforts of the corporations themselves, realize that they are being ripped off. As has happened in the oil industry, citizens may demand of Congress that the corporations be nationalized and run in their interests, rather than in the interests of the profit-takers.

Would it not have been enlightened self-interest for SBS and IBM to decide originally to build high-powered satellites that small customers (including providers of public services) could use, considering that small users might make up a large part of the market by the turn of the century? Instead, the announced policy of SBS was to build satellites that could service the needs of only the largest corporations in the country. (Within two years, when they found the huge companies were not beating a path to their door, SBS executives backed off from this idea, and began working on schemes that would let in middle-sized corporations as well.)

Supporters of the American profit system typified by the AT&T monopoly say that it has developed the finest telephone system in the world. Arguably, it has. But no one was permitted to test the idea that a government-chartered PTT, operated without profit, could not have in the same period of time produced a system equal to or better than the one the United States has now. One thing an American PTT could have done is what the European systems did do: moved sooner beyond the goal of an efficient telephone system to the goal of an efficient telecommunications system integrating all phases of electronic and computerized communications.

An American PTT would not have remained committed, for profit-maximizing purposes, to using outmoded electromechanical switching systems, ocean cables, and ground-line connections beyond the time when they constituted the most efficient ways to transmit phone calls and digital messages. (Old-timers at AT&T don't *want* to give up the land-based network. "We Bell System people have almost a love affair with the network," an AT&T executive told me. "What comes out as self-serving is really pretty deeply felt.")

And a PTT would have been quicker to provide needed telephone service to rural areas. Over the years, Bell companies have refused to do that on the ground that stringing lines to isolated homes is not a profitable thing to do, despite the needs of the people living in such homes. As a result, the federal government was forced, as late as 1949, to authorize the Rural Electrification Administration to provide phones for farm people that should have been included from the beginning as part of an integrated national service.

In a satellite network that included switched phone service, voice links to rooftop antennas on rural homesteads could be provided at no greater cost than providing service to a home in the Chicago suburbs. In a satellite phone system, it does not matter whether the long-distance phone call travels twenty miles or two thousand miles —the cost is the same. But you do not see AT&T letting the public know that, or offering to reduce their long-distance tariffs as they move on to satellite transmission of long-distance calls.

As I have said, the justice of providing a public dividend in the area of satellites is particularly great. However, despite the fact that United States taxpayers paid for the development of space vehicles, politicians in control of the federal government did not feel compelled to insure some public benefits by investing funds—all of which would have been recoverable in user charges—in a satellite system that would have made nonprofit services available. Minimally, NASA should be permitted to continue development of powerful, public-interest satellites that could provide educational and health services at cost. And a public corporation should be set up to provide services to small businesses and public-service organizations that are now effectively barred from using satellites by the high rates charged by the commercial operators.

Congress could do this by reorganizing Comsat into a nonprofit corporation that could develop facilities for these services. Congress had originally chartered Comsat as a privately owned, profit-making corporation to initiate the country's commercial satellite operations. In competition with private communications satellite operators such as AT&T, SBS, and RCA, a publicly operated Comsat could provide a yardstick for communications carrier services that would be offered to businesses and the public.

Although it has suffered a setback in the United States, the idea of constructing the new communications system as a "National Information Utility" has been kept alive by futurists and social planners. The core of their thinking, expressed in symposia on communications and in journals of communications, is similar to that expressed by one of them, Gene Youngblood:

Whereas the existing mass media constitute an advertising and marketing industry in which the mass audience is the product that's sold to the advertiser, the "National Information Utility" could be operated as a service industry providing public access to information specified by the user and public access to communications channels controlled by the user. I submit that this will not be possible unless the "National Information Utility" is operated as just that—a common-carrier public utility supported by public funds; a legal monopoly whose services, deemed essential for individual liberty and social survival, would by force of law be made available to everyone at standard rates, with ownership of the physical plant separated by law from the power to program it."[1]

If we accept sociological studies that show it takes about thirty years for a progressive idea to be implemented, it is conceivable that about the time of the last two scenarios in this book, the public and the government in the United States might be ready to reorganize the communications system, on which they are becoming more and more dependent, into an independent, nonprofit "Public Telecommunications Corporation." This organization could unite the electronic physical plant—including the core network and satellite transmission facilities—into a service utility. By that time, the "natural monopoly" view promoted by the telephone company might have become less sacrosanct, as people see competing forms of telecommunications offering many of the services they grew up believing that, by some divine decision, only the Bell System was *allowed* to provide.

Even with strong public support, the drive to do this would face tremendous political opposition from the carriers that would have to be absorbed and converted to noncommercial operations: AT&T, GTE, ITT, and the various commercial satellite carriers. Yet nationalization of the power industry took place in England and Sweden; those national systems are run far more dependably than the blackout-prone power industry in the United States. And while private railroads in the United States were deliberately ruining passenger service and running their companies into bankruptcy, the nationalized railways in Western Europe were developing into what is acknowledged to be the finest rail network on earth.

DANGER FROM AUTHORITARIAN REGIMES

The greatest potential disadvantage of a nationalized telecommunications utility is that an authoritarian regime might use it to control our lives. There always has been a danger—and there probably always will be—that a dictator will manipulate the national media to aid in repression of the people—Hitler's use of radio is the horrible example. The danger exists in the present, profit-oriented system. As I have pointed out, AT&T did not resist the Nixon Justice Department when Nixon wanted to install wiretaps on his opponents, real or imagined, or gain access to the records of phone calls made by "hostile" reporters. And the national commercial networks knuckled under to the administration when Nixon let it be known he wanted no more "instant analysis" after speeches he made to the nation by preempting those networks' prime-time programming.

Basically, resistance to such misuse must come from a public determined to protect its freedoms from an authoritarian president, prime minister, or chairman. But we can build in some protections in advance.

This can best be done by setting up the backbone transmission system as an independent public corporation, which would not be under the direct control of the government. Such a corporation, to remain independent, would have to be empowered to finance its operations primarily from some form of user charges, rather than taxes or direct government appropriations. The BBC is set up that way—it operates on a budget provided by license fees that go directly into its operating fund, rather than the national treasury. This gives it a great deal of independence from political pressures—which, of course, continue to exist, and will always exist, whether the system is public or commercial.

The activities of such a corporation are bound to be more open to scrutiny than would be the practices determined at closed board meetings of a commercial corporation that had gained control of the system. Investigative reporters would have the right of access to a public corporation's records that is denied them by the secrecy under which private corporations have been permitted to operate. And the fact that there is more expectation of openness in public agencies makes the climate more hospitable to "whistle blowers" than exists in tightly disciplined private companies.

One further—essential—provision is necessary to preserve our freedom under the new communications.

The backbone system, whether it is set up as a public corporation or evolves along commercial lines, must operate as a *common carrier*.

Under this arrangement, as I have said earlier, a public corporation or private operating company would provide the transmission facilities, and various individuals and organizations, public and private, would supply the messages, programs, and electronic services to be carried over the backbone system. Channels and circuits would be made available to all comers on a nondiscriminatory basis, and without interference by the carrier in the content that anyone wanted to transmit. The carrier itself would not be permitted to supply content, whether information, entertainment, or home-monitoring services such as burglar-alarm systems. It would not be permitted to monitor phone calls or any other transmissions on the system, nor would it permit the government or private investigating companies to install electronic surveillance or other eavesdropping devices.

This is by far the best defense we have against dictatorial control—whether by an authoritarian national administration or a domineering private corporation—over the communications that influence our lives.

As an added check we might construct the backbone network as a number of interlocking pieces, rather than as a single public or commercial entity, thus preventing one carrier from exercising power on a national scope. The technological system has to be interconnected and compatible, but it does not have to be run as a political or commercial unit. The national system could be composed of regional public carriers interconnected by satellite operators that provide long-distance transmission services.

The regional networks could themselves be composed of a number of local-area services, each providing a videotex data bank to meet the specialized needs of a particular community.

No matter how it is set up, the principle remains: technology must be kept separate from content. The question is: Will we act on principle?

As the people of the United States, influenced by the Nixon, Ford, Carter and Reagan administrations, moved to embrace the values of the marketplace, it has become unfashionable—palpably naïve—to insist that, in matters of public policy, we adhere to our philosophical ideals. Commercial expediency has become the most highly regarded political guide. Even where a course of action is ethically and morally right, and obviously in the public interest, the business community *expects* Congress, the administration, and the people to accept compromises to accommodate the "practical realities" of the profit system.

If we accede to commercial practice in place of the philosophical ideal of common carrier for the new communications, we put the future of our freedom in danger.

In the United States, the profit motive has decreed that technology and content should *not* be kept separate but combined in single commercial operations. This decree is wrong insofar as it affects the public interest. Control over content in the merging media by the operators of the system will mean eventual determination by the operators of what we will be permitted to know. As the system comes together, its domination by one or a few large private corporations or by a government authority becomes a real possibility. The dangers inherent in this situation can be forestalled only if the technical operator has no say in content but is required to open the system to a multiplicity of voices and services, without restriction.

Although I have keyed this argument to the situation in the United States, similar concerns about control apply for the systems developing Western Europe, Canada, and Japan—and they can be expected to arise as other countries move to acquire the new technologies. The *philosophy* of separation is embodied in the laws setting up the PTT's in Western Europe, so the *practice* should be easier to achieve there than in the United States, Canada, and Japan, where it is not.

Theoretically, in the United States, the FCC has the authority to keep the Bell System and new cable operators from providing the data bases for videotex operations.

To complete the separation, it would also be necessary for the FCC to order existing cable systems and multiple system operators to become common carriers, divesting themselves of their program-producing operations. These could be continued as separate companies that contracted with the backbone system for use of the facilities. Judging from past performance, however, the commission would be too weak to stand up to a challenge from commercial operators who wanted to remain in both the transmission and production sides of the business. It would almost certainly agree to "grandfather" existing combined operations—that is, permit those systems already providing both to continue to operate that way—thus defeating the purpose of complete separation.

Therefore, any shift to common-carrier status in the new technologies could probably be achieved only from a definitive policy of a national administration committed to that ideal, and willing to put it-self on the line before Congress to bring the change about.

To be in the best interests of the public, any such policy should encourage a move to nonprofit operation of cable and videotex trans-mission systems, as well. Where commercial cable operators had been providing programming as well as facilities, local or state govern-ments might be encouraged to buy out the physical plant for opera-tion as part of a municipal or regional utility, while the cable entrepreneurs continued to supply some of the system's program-ming. There is more money to be made, in any event, in pro-gramming, than there is to be made in operating the system.

The national policy should guarantee that everyone has access to put content into the system, and everyone has access to material that has been put into the system.

The first would require a graduated fee schedule for those who wished to present material. Nonprofit organizations such as univer-sities would be able to schedule input time at cost; profit-making institutions would pay fees sufficient to cover the costs plus an amount sufficient to provide some television "access" channels and videotex "access" pages for use without charge by private citizens and community service organizations. The idea that individuals, citi-zen groups and government, educational and welfare bodies should have free access was developed by public-interest groups when multi-ple channels on cable systems made this financially easy to provide. It should be continued as the system becomes a two-way medium for text as well as television, and the channels become even cheaper.

Obviously, freedom of expression in the new communications is going to be contingent upon a social policy that guarantees freedom of access.

So that nations will not be divided into the information rich and the information poor, some method of funding will have to be found whereby the basic home communications set will be available to citi-zens unable to pay for it themselves. In an integrated system, the cost of providing service to the indigent could be added to the overall operating costs.

It has been long-established social policy that public services—such as health care for the indigent—should be available to all with-out regard to ability to pay. Costs for providing such services via the two-way system should be built into the rate base set for general use of the system. Such costs might be subsidized out of regular welfare funds, since "electronifying" these services could bring a reduction in their traditional costs.

With costs of electronic installations dropping dramatically, it should not be too much to ask of a nation that has telephones in 98 percent of its homes to make the HCS possible in 100 percent.

CENTRALIZATION OR DECENTRALIZATION?

It is an interesting and significant fact about the new communications system that it can lead *either* to authoritarian centralization *or* democratic decentralization of our society.

The new technology makes *possible* a system in which a national (or international) government could extract from the people all the information it needed to control their lives, and transmit to the people only that information which would aid in that control.

It also makes possible a system in which authority can be spread across an enlightened populace. In this second model, communications is multilateral—two-way between government and people, and among the people themselves. Through it a vast diversity of information could be disseminated to give people the knowledge they need to govern their own lives effectively and make informed decisions about local and national policies.

Obviously, it is in our interests to move the system to foster decentralization. Here we are helped by the interactive technology itself. Decentralization is inherent in a system over which the *users* have control—the capability and the *right* to call up the information services and, indeed, the government, they need.

No prescription can be laid down that would guarantee this result. It depends a great deal on citizens understanding what is at stake and their willingness to influence government and corporations to adopt policies that will promote democratic decentralization and diversity.

IN THE UNITED STATES, THE PRESIDENT MUST TAKE THE LEAD

As a practical matter—given the American form of government, media, and education—the public is not likely to become sharply aware or concerned about this unless it is brought to its consciousness by the president. To do this, the president must himself understand what is at stake in the new communications system and be determined to shape its development in the public interest.

In the political turmoil of the 1970s, national administrations in the United States all but ignored the information revolution and the technological system that was emerging as its carrier. Communications policy was ad hoc, ad-libbed in many places in government. It was not influenced by a concerted administration policy because no such policy existed. For example, as the economy became a chief concern of government, successive administrations showed little desire even to understand the impact of the new communications in dramatically accelerating financial transactions across the nation and the world.

The economic impact alone would seem to be enough to motivate a president to try to shape its structure in ways that would benefit the public. Because of the commercial forces already at work in the new communications, this could probably be done only by setting up an agency with Cabinet-level influence—a "Department of Communications." Such a department would be mandated to devise a coherent national information policy and develop the methods and structures to carry it out. A base for this was laid by the establishment in 1978 of the National Telecommunications and Information Administration (NTIA) in the Department of Commerce. Although this office was instructed to pull together communications policy, there was little relation between its work and the government's operational activities in communications. (For example, NTIA had no jurisdiction over the telecommunications systems operated by the Defense Department or the General Services Administration, which provides telephone service linking federal offices across the country.) In addition, conflict existed between its role and that of the FCC, the Postal Service, NASA, and other agencies involved in communications. The respective roles of a new Cabinet-level department and these agencies would have to be clarified in any reorganization plan an administration would submit to Congress.

Into such a department might be integrated the Postal Service, including its electronic mail operations, and the telecommunications networks of the DOD and the GSA. The department should probably incorporate the policy-making and rule-making functions of the FCC, with that agency continuing to review rate-setting and equity questions relating to services offered to the public.

Working from its long-range plans, such an agency would be expected to develop and test new technologies of communications. This requirement would guarantee government investigation of technological developments that promise benefits to the public. It would avoid the embarrassment of seeing other nations put important technologies into operation, as the British did with videotex, before the U.S. government was aware of their importance.

The fact that the new technologies will have so strong an effect on our lives should make us demand that the president's appointments to top positions in such a department be based on quality and expertise, rather than their readiness to support industry interests, as has been the case in most appointments to the FCC.

Short of a Cabinet-level authority in the United States, we must still be concerned with policies promulgated by the FCC and other regulatory agencies. While monopoly forces continue to exist in telecommunications common-carrier service, and while scarcity continues to exist with regard to the over-the-air broadcast spectrum, it will be necessary to have federal regulations requiring the phone companies and the broadcasters to operate, in the words of the Communications Act of 1934, "in the public interest, convenience, and necessity."

As it has traditionally functioned, the FCC has clearly failed in its reponsibility to enforce that requirement. It should be reconstituted to make it responsive to the public's needs rather than to commercial demands. If it is retained as an independent agency, it has to be guaranteed sufficient staff, in quality and quantity, to cope with the army of lawyers and accountants that corporations can throw in against it, both at the hearings and in court challenges to its decisions.

Once the Bell System decided it wanted to compete head-to-head with IBM for control of the data-processing market, its lobbyists mounted an offensive to capture congressional committee staff members and FCC administrators to insure favorable legislation and regulation. The FCC was the first to buckle. On April 7, 1980, it said to Ma Bell, "Okay, you and IBM can fight it out."

The FCC has long admitted it does not have sufficient accountants and economists to understand cases for interstate telephone rate increases put before it by AT&T. Its expedient generally has been to grant the requested increases, discounted sometimes by the few percentage points that Bell had, in all likelihood, added onto its request in anticipation of the discounting.

This outcome almost became inevitable when you consider that, in such cases, Bell is in the enviable position of being the only provider of data necessary to making the decisions, while at the same time being able to pick and choose those records for a presentation that preordains the outcome it desires. Often, these records are produced in a volume that effectively buries the small staff of investigators the FCC can employ to review them.

Obviously, it would have a better chance to insure equitable rates to the public if it were being asked to review the rate proposals of a government corporation set up as a common carrier and whose books are open to public scrutiny under the Freedom of Information Act.

Beyond this, it is clear that the regulatory philosophy the agency evolved from the 1934 Communications Act will have to be amended as it applies to the new technologies.

First, the FCC (or any successor agency) must *not* be allowed to extend its over-the-air broadcast regulations concerning content to the new, abundant technologies, including cable television, videotex, and satellite networks, when these technologies become commonplace. When access to channels of communications is not limited by spectrum scarcity, the justification for intervention by the government in content ceases to exist. Even though they were inspired by laudatory purposes, the Fairness Doctrine, Equal Time Rule and Personal Attack Rule imposed on broadcasters have been in conflict with the First Amendment guarantee that "Congress shall make no law . . . abridging freedom of speech, or of the press." Freedom of the press, a principle steadfastly preserved while newspapers have been printed and distributed conventionally, should not be restricted as a consequence of newspapers' beginning to use electronic means of distribution. Government regulation of content has no place in the new communications.

Indeed, placing all transmission agencies in the emerging system under common-carrier status carries with it the implicit guarantee that the carriers would not be permitted to intervene in the content being transmitted. Providers of the content—television programming or textual information—may be held responsible after the fact for material that society has decided is injurious as a matter of law. But there may be no prior restraints upon its transmission on the system. To insist on any less absolute prohibition would be to abdicate our freedom to the government or to other organizations we have designated to run the technical facilities.

PRIVACY PROTECTION BOARD NEEDED

The development of computerized, interactive communication makes it essential that the government legislate and regulate in the area of privacy and threats to individual liberty. In Chapter VI, on data protection, I spelled out the ways the two-way technology can intrude on our lives. As I indicated there, national laws are necessary to protect us against specific threats. To see that these laws are carried out, I believe it will be necessary for Congress to establish a "Federal Privacy Board," as proposed by the Privacy Protection Study Commission in its report to the president.[2] As in the case of the Swedish Data Inspection Board, this agency should set guidelines aimed at protecting citizens' privacy, for operation of every personal data bank in the country. Rather than licensing them, the board should require private companies and government agencies to register their computerized files with regional offices of the board, indicating what steps they have taken to guarantee compliance. The board should have authority to inspect such files, to see that its directives have been carried out. Instead of making citizens sue in court to correct false records, they should be able to get direct administrative redress by applying to their regional office of the board. These offices should have the power to order a public or private data bank to expunge an improper or incorrect entry from a person's dossier.

The Privacy Board should also be directed to keep in touch with similar boards in other countries, and prepare international agreements for the president concerning transborder flow of personal data. In proposing further legislation in the United States and agreements with other governments, the board would have to keep in mind the potential conflict between protection of privacy and freedom of information. As the body of law and practice develops, there will be a continual balancing of these interests in the legislatures, the courts, and international bodies. Protection of an individual's right to privacy must be given high priority. At the same time, we must be careful that governments do not use "privacy" as an excuse for barring access to and transmission of information that the people have a legitimate right to know. Battles are even now being fought between those seeking information in government files under the Freedom of Information Act and administrators who are using "protection of privacy" as a shield to guard their operations from legitimate scrutiny.

Regulation of entertainment or information programming and general textual information placed in the computers of an interactive system is not the purview of government. Protection of citizens' use of the two-way system for *private* transactions *is* a legitimate concern of government. As the system develops, this concern could be most effectively addressed by local municipalities through their franchise agreements with cable distribution systems or other carriers providing facilities for the interactive services. The franchise protections should be based on national laws or regulations outlining minimum protections to be provided. The proposals made by Citizens for Privacy in Cable TV, outlined in Chapter II, seem to me to be excellent models for these protections.

If the concerns outlined in preceding chapters are to be met, other areas of the new communications will require legislation and regulation, as well. In the United States, policy for the new media will likely be shaped primarily by Congress, the FCC, and the National Telecommunications Information Administration or a successor telecommunications department. But other federal and state agencies will also be involved:

The Justice Department—Enforcing antitrust statutes and other federal regulations as they relate to cross-ownership of media, market dominance, and fair competition; acting in criminal cases such as computer embezzlement.

Federal Trade Commission—Monitoring marketing and advertising practices in the new services.

Securities and Exchange Commission—Regulating transfer of stocks and bonds via the system.

Copyright Tribunal—Protecting copyrighted material in the new information systems.

State public utility commissions, cable commissions, and banking commissions—Regulating activities within state borders.

In addition, the courts will undoubtedly play a major role in reviewing policies and practices, especially on questions relating to privacy, individual liberty, freedom of speech and press, and freedom of information. If they become sufficiently informed and concerned, citizens and public-interest groups can have strong influence in each of these areas of government activity.

GUARDING AGAINST DEHUMANIZATION

Finally, we should consider a danger against which it is well nigh impossible to legislate: that the emerging system will dehumanize us.

A recurring theme of science fiction is one of people "living" in communications cubicles, transacting all the business of living through electronic devices, in contact with other individuals (are they *human* beings?) only through two-way telescreens and the "feelies."

I do not think it is going to happen. I believe that our human nature is such that *nothing* is going to replace the feelings of love, excitement, satisfaction, or personal involvement that come from being in the physical presence of another human—or humans. All the communications technology humans have devised can never substitute for the emotional interchange that occurs between two persons in the same room at the same time—or among four, fourteen, or forty persons in the same room at the same time.

In fact, the nature of our persons is, I believe, going to make us use the technologies to increase, not diminish, that kind of interchange. We can *make* it work that way, if we are determined at each step along the way to preserve our humanity; to do, as individuals and with citizens groups, those things that will keep the system as our servant, not our master.

As I have pointed out, the essence of the new communications is *not* the passive observation and acceptance induced by mass-audience programming on television. Its essence is active intervention induced, for example, by the two-way interplay of the Reading, Pennsylvania, system, the personal-decision attributes of Prestel, or the capacity for personal exchange on the video telephone.

The people of Columbus found it personally interesting to take part in a public hearing when it was made available to them via two-way television. It will be even more interesting for many to be seen and heard, rather than have their views tabulated only by keyboard responses to preset questions, when the two-way video return tested in the Japanese experiments becomes standard equipment on the HCS.

These two-way experiments pointed to the likelihood that people who would *never* come out to a public meeting might become active participants in such a meeting via the system, as did hundreds of people in Qube's Upper Arlington zoning board hearing. Once they are hooked, human curiosity sets in: "I want to go down there, *in person,* and see what they are up to." Interaction via the set will likely lead to greater personal involvement in social and political activities. People in Reading who thought they were "too old" to take part in politics found the two-way system put them in the thick of things. Video discussion of their problems led to in-person meetings on the same issues in their housing units.

Rather than depositing people in front of their sets for hours, as with mind-numbing commercial television (it is not for nothing that commercial television producers refer to it as "the boob tube"), an interactive system has the potential for whetting their appetites for human interchange and pulling them out of their homes to make that happen.

It has happened in the field of entertainment before. When the stereophonic technique was introduced, critics said it meant the death of live concerts—people could hear all the music they wanted in their homes, at the same fidelity as in the concert hall. Instead, by increasing interest in music and the people who presented it, the stereo phonograph greatly increased attendance at concerts—classical, jazz, and rock. Listening at home was *not* the same as seeing a rock group or people in a symphony orchestra live on a stage. It still won't be the same when you hear the group in stereo on the HCS and see them on the set's large-screen component.

On the other hand, the ability of the set to present feature films on a large screen with good color definition plus stereo sound *will* lead more people to watch movies at home instead of in a theater. But this, I believe, humanizes a passive process that has, to some extent, been dehumanizing. People will no longer go out just for the privilege of sitting in a darkened cinema alongside strangers with whom they have nothing in common except that they are staring at the screen together. (My wife pointed out that the only time she feels the presence of strangers in the theater is when they laugh when she doesn't.) Instead, people (the family and friends) will get together in each other's homes to watch a feature film or documentary and then, inevitably, discuss it afterward. (Or, I hope in moderation, *during* the film. Laughing is okay, though.) One of the reasons you go to a movie with a friend is to exchange smiles in the theater with him or her—and then, best of all, to *talk* about it after it is over.

Doing that in the intimacy and relaxed atmosphere of your home could make it even more enjoyable. Getting *out* of the house is not a determinant of our humanity. There is nothing *wrong* with staying home for an evening of convivial conversation. It is much more humanizing than getting out for the sake of getting out.

There are lots of boring and not particularly humanizing things that I would just as soon accomplish from home using the set. I would be happy to do much of my routine shopping via the shopping channels, were that possible. Although I know many people who think shopping is fun, I don't. And I don't think that using the set to do my banking is any more mechanistic than *going out* to shove my money into a bank through a walk-up or drive-in teller's window—even when the teller tells me to have a nice day.

Obviously, people's psychic needs vary, and some need to get out and see people in a store or on the street more often than others. A change of environment is stimulating, and makes you come home refreshed. In any event, the two-way set does not *demand* that you sit in front of it for hours at a time. In fact, an interactive medium is likely to be less hypnotizing than the one-way television entertainment to which we subject ourselves today.

The ability of the system to provide first-run movies or first-rate slide-and-film presentations by a popular lecturer might encourage viewing-in-company more than past media have done. People might find it pleasurable and stimulating to gather at a community center to watch a documentary on a controversial topic and follow it with general or private discussions. It happens quite a bit in Sweden.

The system offers possibilities for human interaction beyond those offered by the earlier media. It provides a means for "respectable" introductions to new people across the city, across the country, across the world. You might find a new friend through an action as casual as typing in your request to be put in touch with someone who wanted to play a particular video game at a specific hour—someone you could see on half of the split screen while the game "board" was displayed on the other half. Or you could be matched up with someone who wanted to talk by videotelephone about breadmaking or the crisis in Outer Mongolia. This could allow people to check each other out over the system to see if a basis existed to pursue a friendship in person. If you and a person of like interests hit it off through sound-picture exchange and correspondence via the set, the *human-natural* desire would be to meet her/him in the flesh.

That suggestion raises an emotionally charged question: Can the *technology itself* serve the cause of humanizing our relationships in instances where we cannot be in the physical presence of others? I think the experience with the telephone in our personal relationships tells us that it can. Certainly it would be better and more human for me to see and hear my wife on an HCS when I am away on a long trip than *not* to be in contact with her, or only *hear* her on the phone. Certainly it would be better for her to be able to contact me on her personal radiophone when her car is caught in traffic and she wants to change the time we had agreed I would start the dinner—to say nothing about relieving my worry that she might be dead in an accident. The new communications gives promise of increasing human communication by making people accessible anywhere, at any time she or he is *willing* to be accessible. (I want to be able to *turn off* my wristwatch radio buzzer so no calls can get through, and no one can locate me by its signal, when I am skiing alone through the woods on a sunny winter's day.)

For people living alone, a fully interactive system of video, sound, and text can break the pattern of loneliness. For people who are bedridden or are too infirm to go out of the house, the HCS could be a godsend; it would keep them feeling alive and in touch with humanity. Elderly persons in Reading who were housebound reported that the coming of the two-way system had been the most important change for the better in their lives that year. Some of them had felt they were losing their personhood because they had been shunted out of the mainstream and left to drift quietly toward the grave. Now they could "get together" with their friends and acquaintances again, and become part of a life-giving exchange. They were responding to "telepresence," which assuredly was not so good as physical presence but much better than no presence at all. And who could say to them that what they were experiencing was not "human"?

Given the choice, would most of us substitute telepresence for real presence? Not very likely. But if we understood its potential as well as its limitations, we should be able to use telepresence to enhance our personal interchanges. People would have to be educated to realize they can use the system to extend their personal resources and add to their human contacts. The idea could be introduced in early childhood by teaching children to play video games* with other children across the tracks or across a culture, and developed later in interactive learning between children in schools a continent or an ocean apart. In secondary schools, in colleges, and through adult education, the aim would be to accustom people to use the system to become involved with the political and social life of their communities; to become less parochial by finding out, though interactive exchanges, what *other* people do, how *different* people live.

Given the nature of human beings, I do not believe dehumanization will be self-imposed, through substitution of electronic content for personal reality.

As I suggested by the Brazilian Scenario, I think it is far more possible that dehumanization could be imposed on us from the *outside,* through the use of the merging system of communications. This is a danger we *can* legislate against, if we develop a public consensus that this must be prevented from happening. It is essential, if we are not to lose our privacy and individual liberty, and thus a good part of our humanity.

It is part of the current wisdom to say that new laws cannot solve social problems. Laws in isolation cannot. It is necessary for the laws to well up from people's awareness of the dangers in a particular situation and their feeling that "something has got to be done."

The Swedish Data Inspection Board *worked* because the citizens became sufficiently aware and alarmed about threats to their privacy from personal data banks that they insisted Parliament pass a law to protect them.

The Federal Communications Commission *did not work* because, when the commission was set up, the citizens were unaware of the danger that, given the chance, commercial broadcasting companies, which the FCC was set up to referee, would grab the lion's

---

* A concern arises from the idea, however: What kinds of video games will be available to children?

Even games can be programmed, now, to reinforce a certain set of values in willing participants. To realize the implications of that, you have only to look at the concupiscent values reinforced by the entertaining commercials we watch on television. Already, war is being "promoted" by many electronic games sold in stores. In fact, war games are the best-sellers. After years of being enthralled and excited by hundreds of war games programmed into computer data banks for two-way distribution to the home, children may very well grow up thinking that war isn't really such a bad idea after all.

share of the airwaves without giving public-service organizations the opportunity to participate fully in broadcasting, as well. Until the 1960s there was no concerted citizen action to demand rules that would require the commercial radio and television stations to act in the public interest.

Law and regulations *can* effect social change. Because the nation arrived at a consensus that forbidding blacks the right to vote was morally wrong, the Voting Rights Act was passed in 1965, making it possible for blacks to register in places where they had been prevented from doing so before. This *changed* the situation of blacks in the South, and they were able to win races for mayor in large cities—Atlanta, and even heavily segregationist Birmingham—where they had a majority of the population.

In the new communications we *can* protect ourselves by law if we first become aware of what is at stake and then work out social policies that can be given the force of law. Ultimately only the common will acts to guard us from the dangers. If we don't *see* the problem, then the problem does not exist. (Certainly, there is no great problem, now, for the entrepreneurs and politicians who are intent on using the new communications to manipulate unsuspecting people to their wills.)

I hope the examples I have given in this book will help us see the problems—the research and reporting have helped me to clarify them in my own mind.

The temptation is to say, "If it's got all these problems, why not close it down—stop it from happening?" The trouble with that is, it has already *happened*. Billions of dollars have been invested to bring it about. And the people who have invested those billions—private corporations as well as taxpayers in the United States and the other industrialized countries—are not going to chuck it aside and forget about profits and other benefits that can be reaped from using the new technologies that they have developed. The best we can do is try to make the system work *for* us.

SOME CONCLUSIONS

In examining it from various perspectives, I have come to believe this about the new communications:

• Rather than standardization and conformity, the emerging system can lead to greater diversity of ideas and a wider variety of choices for viewers of entertainment, seekers of information, consumers of goods, and users of services.

• The technological developments can lead to a society that is better informed than the one we know today. An integrated media system can give us a truer picture of life in the community, nation, and world than could previous discrete systems. This in turn can provide a stronger basis on which we can make governmental and social decisions that affect our lives.

• The new technologies can lead to decentralization of decision-making, with greater local autonomy in government and corporations, rather than centralization of governmental and corporate control.

• A public that is well-informed via the system is less likely to be carried away on an emotional bandwagon driven by a demagogue.

• The new system can lead to greater humanization of society, not dehumanization.

• A coherent public policy aimed at developing the new communications along socially useful lines can help make us freer and happier than we have been before.

But:

• Improperly developed and employed, the new communications can lead to the antithesis of each of these things.

• Within the system lie serious threats to our privacy and our individual liberties. These will very likely materialize if we permit it to be guided primarily by market manipulations, military demands, and political power considerations.

And, most important:

None of the potential benefits of the new communications will come about unless we shape the technology to human ends and not let it shape us in a commercial or authoritarian mold.

CHAPTER NOTES

1 | THE NEW COMMUNICATIONS: PROMISE AND THREAT

1. *National Information Policy: Report to the President by the Domestic Council Committee on the Right of Privacy* (Washington, D.C.: National Commission on Libraries and Information Science, 1977).
2. See Harold Sackman, *Mass Information Utilities and Social Excellence* (New York: Van Nostrand Reinhold, 1970).
3. Arthur D. Little, Inc., *Telecommunications and Society, 1976–1991* (Springfield, Va.: National Technical Information Service, U.S. Department of Commerce, 1976).
4. Simon Nora and M. Alain Minc, "L'Informatisation de la Societé" (Paris: La Documentation Française, 1978).

2 | COLUMBUS DISCOVERS TWO-WAY CABLE

1. For a further discussion of this concept, see Monroe E. Price and John Wicklein, *Cable Television: A Guide for Citizen Action* (New York: Pilgrim Press, 1972).
2. *In Search,* Canadian Government Communication Quarterly, Winter 1979, p. 18.
3. Les Brown, "TV Set Views Viewer," *The New York Times,* 8 August 1978.
4. Jerrold Oppenheim, "Communications Include the Telephone: The Telephone May Soon Include All Communications," part of a report distributed by Telecommunications Consumer Coalition, New York, 1979.
5. Oppenheim, "Communications Include the Telephone."
6. *FCC* v. *Pacifica Foundation,* USSC No. 77–528.
7. George Orwell, *1984* (New York: Harcourt Brace & Co., Inc., 1949). Text is from Signet Books (New York) edition, 1950, p. 6, as follows:

Behind Winston's back the voice from the telescreen was still babbling away about pig iron and the overfulfillment of the Ninth Three-Year Plan. The telescreen received and transmitted simultaneously. Any sound that Winston made, above the level of a very low whisper, would be picked up by it; moreover, so long as he remained within the field of vision which the metal plaque commanded, he could be seen as well as heard. There was of course no way of knowing whether you were being watched at any given moment. How often, or on what system, the Thought Police plugged in on any individual wire was guesswork. It was even conceivable that they watched everybody all the time. But at any rate they could plug in your wire whenever they wanted to. You had to live—did live, from habit that became instinct—in the assumption that every sound you made was overheard, and, except in darkness, every movement scrutinized.

8. *The New York Times,* Sunday, 12 March 1978.

3 | IN VIDEOTEX, THE BRITISH CAME FIRST

1. Richard Hooper, "An IP's View: Six Propositions," *Intermedia,* Vol. 7, No. 3, May 1979.
2. John Short, "Evolving Information Systems—Some 'Personal' Suggestions," Long-Range Studies, Post Office Telecommunications, 88 Hills Road, Cambridge, England.
3. Bernard Marti, "France: A Total Approach to All Systems," *Intermedia,* Vol. 7, No. 3, May 1979.
4. Anthony Smith, "Will Consumerism Inhibit the New Media?" *Intermedia,* Vol. 7, No. 3, May 1979.
5. Tetsuro Tomita, "Japan: The Search for a Personal-Information Medium," *Intermedia,* Vol. 7, No. 3, May 1979.

4 | BIRTH OF THE ELECTRONIC NEWSPAPER

1. William Sharwell, AT&T vice-president for long-range planning; personal interview.
2. Jerrold Oppenheim, "Communications Includes the Telephone: The Telephone May Soon Include All Communications," a report distributed by the Telecommunications Consumer Coalition, 105 Madison Avenue, Suite 921, New York, N.Y. 10016.
3. N. R. Kleinfeld, *The New York Times,* 23 June 1978.
4. Les Brown, "Time Marching on with Video," *The New York Times,* 2 January 1980.
5. Nicholas Johnson, *How to Talk Back to Your Television Set* (Boston: Little, Brown & Co., 1970).
6. 47 U.S. Code, Para. 315a.

7. Everett C. Parker, address, "The Fairness Doctrine," Conference on Media Ethics, Boston University School of Public Communication, November 1977; published in *Television Quarterly*, Vol. XIV, No. 4, Winter 1978.

8. Anthony Oettinger, "Merging Media and the First Amendment"; address to the 1974 Nieman Assembly; published in *Nieman Reports*, Cambridge, Mass.; Winter 1974.

9. 44 FCC 2d 1027 (1973).

10. *NBC Inc.* v. *FCC* 516 F 2d 1101 (1974).

11. Bruce M. Owen, "The Role of Print in an Electronic Society," in *Communications for Tomorrow*, Glen Robinson, ed. (New York: Aspen Institute of Humanistic Studies in Association with Praeger Publishers, 1978).

12. Tadokoro Izumi, Chief, International Affairs Division, Japan Newspaper Publishers and Editors Association, "New Towns and an Advanced Cable System," *Studies in Broadcasting*, No. 14, March 1978 (Tokyo: Radio and TV Research Institute).

13. Hans Kimmel, "Germany: A Battle Between Broadcasters and the Press," *Intermedia*, Vol. 7, No. 3, May 1979.

14. 418 U.S. at 254.

15. William G. Bleyer, *Main Currents in the History of American Journalism* (Boston: Houghton Mifflin Co., 1927), p. 44.

16. Bruce M. Owen, "The Role of Print."

17. Carey Winfrey, "Type: How It Was, How It Is," *The New York Times*, 3 July 1978.

18. Michael Vastel, "Newspaper Technology: From Lead to Electronics," *In Search*, Department of Communication, Ottawa, Canada, Winter 1979.

19. Robert M. White III, editor and publisher of the *Mexico* (Missouri) *Ledger*, address at dedication of the Paul Miller Journalism & Broadcasting Building, Oklahoma State University, 18 March 1976; reported in *Editor & Publisher*, 27 March 1976, p. 46.

20. Bruce Owen, "The Role of Print."

21. Ben H. Bagdikian, *The Information Machines* (New York: Harper & Row Publishers, Inc., 1971), p. 206 et seq.

22. Anthony Oettinger, "Merging Media."

23. Bruce Owen, "The Role of Print."

24. Robert G. Marbut, president of Harte-Hanks Communications, Inc., San Antonio, Texas, "A Newspaper Executive Views the Future of the Newspaper Business," *ANPA Research Institute Bulletin*, No. 1293, 18 August 1978, p. 294.

5 | VIA SATELLITE FROM APPALACHIA

1. Education for All Handicapped Children Act of 1975, P.L. 94–142.

2. "Toward the Public Dividend," a report issued privately by the Public-Interest Satellite Association, New York, 1977.

3. Cees Hamelink, "Imperialism of Satellite Technology," *World Association of Christian Communication Journal,* London, Vol. XXVI, No. 1, 1979, p. 13.

4. William H. Read, "Communications Policy, An Agenda," Harvard University Program on Information Resources Policy, 1977, p. 12.

5. "What Happened at WARC?" a symposium held 17 January 1980, at the Massachusetts Institute of Technology, under the auspices of the MIT Research Program on Communications Policy, directed by Professor Ithiel de Sola Pool.

6. Arthur D. Little, Inc., *Telecommunications and Society, 1976–1991,* p. 119.

7. *Hermes/CTS: Its Performance and Limitations,* Vol. 3 (Royal Society of Canada, Ottawa, 1977), pp. 276–79.

8. Anna Casey-Stahmer, "The Era of Experimental Satellites—A Review of the Issues," *Journal of Communications,* Winter 1980.

9. Peter J. Shuyten, "Satellite System Shifts Gears," *The New York Times,* 27 February 1980.

10. See Vivienne Killingsworth, "Corporate Star Wars: AT&T vs. IBM," *The Atlantic Monthly,* May 1979.

11. Marc U. Porat, "Communications Policy in an Information Society," *Communications for Tomorrow,* p. 38

12. James Martin, *The Wired Society* (Englewood Cliffs, N.J.: Prentice-Hall, Inc., 1978), pp. 108, 109.

13. Cees Hamelink, "Imperialism of Satellite Technology," *WACC Journal,* Vol. XXVI, January 1979, p. 17.

14. "CIA Used Satellites in Spying on Antiwar Protesters in the U.S.," *The New York Times,* 17 July 1978.

15. Ivan Bekey and Harris Mayer, "1990–2000: Raising Our Sights for Advanced Space Systems," *Astronautics and Aeronautics,* 1 July/August 1976, p. 34 et seq.

6 | **PRIVACY: HOW SWEDEN PROTECTS ITS CITIZENS FROM THE COMPUTERS**

1. Robert Ellis Smith, *Privacy: How to Protect What's Left of It* (New York: Anchor Press/Doubleday, 1979).

2. Arthur R. Miller, *Assault on Privacy* (Ann Arbor: University of Michigan Press, 1971), p. 63.

3. John Curtis Raines, *Attack on Privacy* (Valley Forge, Pa.: Judson Press, 1974), p. 16.

4. Edward Bloustein, "Privacy as an Aspect of Human Dignity," *NYU Law Review,* 962, 968; 1964.

5. "The Dimensions of Privacy," study by Louis Harris and Associates Inc. for Sentry Insurance Co., Stevens Point, Wisconsin, 54481, 1979.

6. For an extensive discussion, see Alan F. Westin's excellent study, *Privacy*

and Freedom (New York: Atheneum, 1967). The issues he defines will never become dated.

7. Sir Norman Lindop, *Report of the Committee on Data Protection* (London: Her Majesty's Stationery Office, 1978).

8. *Report of the Privacy Protection Study Commission* (Washington, D.C.: U.S. Government Printing Office, July 1977).

9. *The Vulnerability of the Computerized Society*, A preliminary report by a Swedish Government Committee, Sarbarhetskommitten (SARK) (Stockholm: Ministry of Defense, 1978).

10. *Privacy and Computers*, a report by the Department of Communication/Department of Justice (Ottawa: Information Canada, 1972).

7 | BRAZIL DEVELOPS CONTROL BY MEDIA

1. *Folha da Tarde*, São Paulo, 28 March 1979, p. 6.
2 Para. 8, Ch. IV, Title II, 1969 Amendment to the Brazilian Constitution of 1967.
3. *Folha de São Paulo*, 5 March 1978, p. 12.

8 | CONCLUSION: TO GAIN THE PROMISE AND AVOID THE THREAT

1. Gene Youngblood, "The Mass Media and the Future of Desire," *CoEvolution Quarterly*, Sausalito, California, Winter 1978, p. 10.
2. *Report of the Privacy Protection Study Commission* (Washington, D.C.: U.S. Government Printing Office, July 1977).

INDEX